D1474210

The Role of Intelligence
in Soviet Military Strategy
in World War II

The Role of Intelligence in Soviet Military Strategy in World War II

David M. Glantz

PRESIDIO

Published by Presidio Press
31 Pamaron Way, Novato CA 94949

Library of Congress Cataloging-in-Publication Data
Glantz, David M.
    The role of intelligence in Soviet military strategy in World War II/David M. Glantz.
        p.   cm.
    Includes bibliographical references.
    ISBN 0-89141-380-4
    1. World War, 1939–1945—Military intelligence—Soviet Union.
2. Strategy.   3. World War, 1939–1945—Campaigns.   I. Title.
D810.S7G54   1990
940.54'8647—dc20   90–33390
                                                              CIP

Printed in the United States of America

To my wife Mary Ann, whose hard work and unstinting support made this volume possible

Contents

List of Maps

Introduction

This study investigates the role played by *razvedka* [intelligence and reconnaissance] in the military strategy of the Soviet Union during the Second World War. In the broadest sense, it focuses on two principal issues: first, the nature of Soviet wartime military strategy as reflected by Soviet conduct of strategic operations and, second, the role *razvedka* played in the formulation and implementation of Soviet strategic plans. As a vehicle for determining the link between *razvedka* and strategy, the study surveys Soviet strategic planning and relates how those plans developed to fruition in combat. Set against this backdrop, the study then assesses the role played by *razvedka* in determining the strategic course of the war.

In the broadest sense, *razvedka* encompasses Soviet intelligence collection and analysis, which sought to reveal the capabilities and intentions of enemy forces. No work exists, either within the Soviet Union or abroad, that approaches this question in comprehensive fashion. Some formerly classified Soviet studies published prior to July 1943 address the question directly or tangentially, and other Soviet unclassified studies written after war's end provide spotty coverage of the question. Works, primarily memoirs, written by Soviet officers who served in the General Staff or *front* commands address Soviet strategic planning in detail and often refer directly or indirectly to the intelligence basis of that planning. The memoirs of Soviet officers who served in lower command positions and the hundreds of campaign studies and unit histories published since the war refer to intelligence collection, but in tangential and often fragmentary fashion. Only by collating this mass of fragmentary material and by comparing it with Soviet classified studies does a meaningful pattern emerge.

German archival materials, primarily from the files of *Fremde Heere Ost* [Foreign Armies East], contain a thorough assessment of the Soviet intelligence system and an imposing assessment of its capabilities. These studies, however, fail to capture the ubiquitousness of that system and, I believe, understate its accomplishments.

Last, but not least, the best indicator of the effectiveness of Soviet intelligence was the flow of combat itself. Today, the student of Soviet operations can study the vast extent of Soviet operational accounts and verify or refute them by close study of the German archives. The student can observe the flow of combat and judge to what extent intelligence affected that flow. Very simply, patterns emerge over time—patterns that lead inexorably to judgments regarding the combat impact of *razvedka*. When viewed in concert with what Soviet and German archives reveal about Soviet intelligence operations, those judgments assume increased validity.

For the sake of brevity, this study draws heavily on research completed in the course of preparing several earlier studies: *Soviet Military Deception in the Second World War* (London: Frank Cass, Ltd., 1989); *Soviet Intelligence at War,* to be published by Frank Cass, Ltd. in 1990; and *Soviet Intelligence in the Kursk Operation (July 1943)* and *Soviet Intelligence in the Vistula-Oder Operation (January–February 1945),* both published by the Soviet Army Studies Office, Fort Leavenworth, Kansas, and due for commercial publication in 1990. Additional details concerning many of the issues addressed in this study are found in those works.

It is clear, however, that despite the voluminous material already available, definitive answers to many of the central questions regarding intelligence and strategy on the Eastern Front cannot be answered until full access is possible to Soviet archival materials. When that access is possible, I am convinced by virtue of my earlier research in this and associated areas, that this study will have understated the role played by intelligence in Soviet strategic decision making. Thus, this study simply represents a starting point and an initial view of what, in the last analysis, is one of the most important unanswered questions relating to the course of the Second World War.

1 Strategy and Intelligence: A Framework for Analysis

Military strategy [*voennaia strategiia*] occupies a dominant position in the intellectual framework the Soviets use to explain the nature and content of war. By definition, the Soviets consider military strategy to be the highest realm of military art [*voennaia iskusstva*], "encompassing the theory and practice of the preparation of the country and its armed forces for war and the planning and conduct of war and strategic operations."[1] As a system of scientific knowledge, the theory of military strategy investigates the patterns, mechanisms, and strategic character of war and the modes and methods of its conduct, and it works out the theoretical basis of the planning, preparation, and conduct of war and strategic operations. In a practical sense, military strategy:

Determines the strategic missions of the armed forces and the manpower and resources necessary to accomplish these missions

Formulates and implements measures to prepare the armed forces, theaters of military operations, national economy, and civilian population for war

Plans war and strategic operations

Organizes the deployment of the armed forces and their guidance during the conduct of strategic scale operations

Studies the capabilities of probable enemies to wage war and conduct strategic operations.[2]

Military strategy reflects the political aims and policies of the state as well as its economic and sociopolitical character. Conversely, military strategy in peacetime and wartime "exerts an inverse influence on policy."[3] As such, strategy reflects military doctrine, whose tenets guide strategy in the fulfillment of practical tasks, and is grounded upon the data of military science. Military strategy provides a framework for the other components of military art: operational art and tactics. It exploits the capabilities of operational art and tactics to convert operational and tactical successes into strategic success—the achievement of strategic aims.

Among the theoretical tasks of military strategy is organizing strategic intelligence collection and analysis [*razvedka*] prior to and during war. At the highest level during prewar periods, *razvedka* includes study of the potential enemy's strategic theories; the political aims of the enemy, based upon military and economic capabilities as well as morale; the enemy's military doctrine and strategic theories; and the enemy's likely method for initiating war. During wartime, *razvedka* must determine the enemy's intentions and capabilities for conducting war as well as strategic operations for offense and defense.

The Soviets translate *razvedka* as both intelligence and reconnaissance. They regard it as a process that produces hard intelligence. To them, *razvedka* is defined as

> the obtaining, collection, and study of data about military-political conditions in individual countries and in probable or actual enemy coalition nations; their armed forces and military-economic potential; the composition, dispositions, condition, nature of actions, and intentions of groups of forces; and also about the theater of operations.[4]

Razvedka is one of many functions the Soviets place under the rubric protective combat actions [*obespechenie boevykh deistvii*], which includes defense against weapons of massive destruction (ZOMP), *maskirovka* [deception], engineer protection, troop security, and rear area protection.[5] Collectively, these protective functions preserve the combat readiness of forces and facilitate their successful use in combat while reducing the effectiveness of enemy forces. Commanders and staffs at all levels are responsible for conducting *razvedka* at all times, in all situations, and under all circumstances. *Razvedka* can be strategic, operational, and tactical, depending on its scale and purpose. And, because activities at all three levels are closely interrelated, success at higher levels depends directly on the efficiency and effectiveness of like measures at lower levels.

At the highest level, strategic *razvedka* examines enemy planning and conduct of operations in a theater of operations or in war as a whole. It arises "simultaneously with armed struggle."[6] The means of conducting strategic *razvedka* have matured in consonance with advancing technology. Whereas, in the past, nations relied primarily on agents to obtain strategic information, today they rely heavily on aviation, communications, and cosmic *razvedka* (satellites, for example). The High Command and national political authorities organize and conduct continuous strategic *razvedka* to determine

> the composition, condition, and distribution of enemy armed forces in a theater of military operations; views on the nature and means of conducting war; enemy plans for preparing (conducting) war; military-economic potential; the condition and prospective development of arms and military equipment, especially weapons of mass destruction; measures for immediate preparation for unleashing war; and preparation of the theater of military operations.[7]

Today, the primary aim of strategic *razvedka* is determining the likelihood of nuclear war. It focuses on the timely disclosure of enemy concentrations of strategic nuclear weapons, determination of enemy preparedness to use those weapons, and judgments concerning the timing of those enemy preparations. All Soviet national *razvedka* assets concentrate on achieving that priority aim. The Soviets believe centralization of strategic *razvedka* assets is an absolute criterion for achieving effective results in a world potentially threatened by nuclear war. Strategic *razvedka* is also inexorably linked with the actions of operational and tactical *razvedka*.

Operational *razvedka* employs "an aggregate of measures for the gathering and study of information about actual or probable enemies in the region of military actions in the interests of preparing and successfully conducting operations."[8] Intelligence collection at the operational level (*front* and army) means seeking information concerning preparations for war; prospects for the use of nuclear weaponry; the grouping and capabilities of forces and weaponry; the probable nature of operations; the presence and location of enemy nuclear weapons, fire-support systems, radio-electronic means and control posts; the location and likely actions of aircraft, antiaircraft, and antirocket defenses; the system of rear area support; the political-morale condition of enemy forces; and other information required by the commander. In addition, operational *razvedka* must discern the physical nature of the area of operations, the availability of local resources, and the political sentiments of the local population.

Although strategic *razvedka* knows no geographical limits, the scope of operational *razvedka* varies with the size of the theater of military operations (TVD), the size and configuration of the force, and the nature of its assigned missions. Regardless of the dimensions of the TVD, *razvedka* is ubiquitous throughout its depth and breadth both before and during hostilities. At *front* and army level, as at all other levels, *razvedka* is a command function and responsibility.

Tactical *razvedka* relates to all measures undertaken to obtain and analyze information concerning the enemy in preparing for and conducting battle [*boi*]. It is organized at all levels below army and in all types of forces under direct supervision of the commander and the commander's staff. It is "conducted simultaneously on the land, in the air, and at sea by specially designated *razvedka* organs, by aircraft (helicopters), and by ships."[9]

Tactical *razvedka* organs are responsible for determining enemy strength, dispositions, combat readiness, manner of operations, and in-tentions; the presence and location of nuclear weaponry, fire-support systems (including high-precision weapons), radio-electronic means, and command and control posts; the location of air defense systems and the basing and operational methods of aviation; and new combat techniques and methods and means of conducting combat actions. In addition, tactical reconnaissance clarifies the physical nature of the area of operations by detecting the presence of obstacles and ground features that may affect operations; changes in terrain caused by use of nuclear weapons; the trafficability and presence of roads in the region; and enemy barrier systems, enemy engineer fortifications, and areas blocked by rubble. The depth of tactical *razvedka* varies with terrain, the size of the force, and its assigned missions. As is the case at higher command levels, the commander is responsible for conducting tactical *razvedka*.

The Soviets classify *razvedka* according to type and method of in-telligence collection. Distinct types of *razvedka* reflect the specific mis-sions to be accomplished, the force designated to conduct these missions, and how that force conducts its missions. Types of *razvedka* have mul-tiplied throughout the century and today include agent [*agenturnaia*]; air [*vozdushnaia*]; outer space–based, or cosmic [*kosmicheskaia*]; special [*spetsial'naia*]; radio [*radiorazvedka*]; radio technical [*radiotekhniches-*

kaia]; ship [*korabel'nia*]; troop [*voiskovaia*]; artillery [*artilleriiskaia*]; engineer [*inzhenernaia*]; radiological [*radiatsionnaia*]; chemical [*khimicheskaia*]; biological [*biologicheskaia*]; radio location [*radiolokatsionnaia*]; topographical [*topograficheskaia*]; mine [*minnaia*]; rear area [*tylovaia*]; and technical [*tekhnicheskaia*].[10] Although each type is separate and distinct, all types are centrally controlled and coordinated at whatever level of command they are employed. Agent, air, cosmic, special, and radio *razvedka* are especially suited to satisfy intelligence requirements at the strategic level.

The Soviets also classify *razvedka* functionally according to the method employed to collect intelligence information. These methods today include combat action of forces, observation [*nabliudenie*], eavesdropping [*podslushivanie*], photography [*fotografirovanie*], interception [*perekhvataia rabota*], direction finding [*pelengatsiia*], radio-electronic means [*radioelektronnye sredstva*], sweeps [*poisk*], raids [*nalet*], ambushes [*zasada*], reconnaissance in force [*razvedka boem*], interrogation of civilians [*opros*], interrogation of prisoners [*dopros*], and study of documents. Newer collection methods include thermal [*teplovaia*], magnetic-metrical [*magnitometricheskaia*], and radiothermal [*radioteplovaia*] techniques.[11] Although the Soviets catalogue a wide array of *razvedka* types and methods, often employing sophisticated technology, and emphasize the systematic and scientific planning and conduct of *razvedka,* they continually emphasize the human factor as the most critical element. They believe humans, using their judgment, are always more important than technology.

Regardless of type and method, the Soviets believe *razvedka* must be continuous, active, timely, authentic, and—above all—organized with a clear goal in mind. Its focus must correspond closely with the overall aim of any strategic, operational, or tactical plan to provide the unity of purpose necessary for all intelligence fragments to form a meaningful and useful mosaic of the enemy. The scope of that mosaic and the intelligence effort that produces it varies from operation to operation. The depth of *razvedka* and the amount of data required depend directly on the scale of the military operation, the complexity of combat missions, the nature of the terrain, and the strength and depth of enemy dispositions. Though *razvedka* at every level and on every scale must be centrally controlled and focused on a single set of aims, it must also be flexible enough to adjust to changing combat conditions. Otherwise, the best *razvedka* plan can become victim of what the Soviets call *shablon* [pattern or stereotype]. Stereotypical action defeats the purposes of *razvedka* by conditioning a force to be a victim of its own misperceptions.

Razvedka at every level is a command function performed by the commander through the commander's chief of staff and intelligence officer, who also serves as chief of reconnaissance. Today, as in the past, *razvedka* is controlled throughout the entire Soviet force structure from the top down by the head of the Chief Intelligence Directorate [*Glavnoe razvedyvatel'noe upravienie,* or GRU] of the General Staff. Intelligence work at lower levels is carried out by the intelligence directorate [*razvedyvatel'noe upravlenie,* or RU] at TVD and *front* level; by the intelligence department [*razvedyatel'nyi otdel',* or RO] of the army; and by the intelligence officer at divisional, regimental, and battalion levels. At each level, *razvedka* organs perform specific functions that have evolved over time but which, by virtue of centralized control, form a single unified effort. *Razvedka* is the first mechanism in the carefully orchestrated command and control cycle [*upravlencheskii tsikl*]. Effective *razvedka* assists the commander in reducing time spent gathering and collecting information on the enemy and, hence, creates conditions conducive for effective planning, smooth conduct of operations, and the achievement of battlefield victory.

Although the relationship between military strategy and *razvedka* is real and armies seek to harness *razvedka* to strategic ends, there is not always a direct correlation between strategic success or failure and the effectiveness of *razvedka*. Clearly, effective *razvedka* provides a sound basis for strategic planning and increases the chances for success in strategic operations. Conversely, poor *razvedka* deprives the strategic commander of one advantage over the foe. However, other factors, such as quantitative and qualitative force advantages, can negate the effect of *razvedka*. As Clausewitz has argued and operational experiences have proven, chance and the fog of war always have the potential for negating the effects of either effective or ineffective *razvedka*. In light of these realities, only examination of the circumstances surrounding each strategic operation can provide a basis for judging the impact of *razvedka* on the course and outcome of operations. That examination will be the focus of the remainder of this book.

2 The First Period of War

Context

The first period of war, by Soviet definition, encompassed the seventeen-month period from 22 June 1941, the day Operation Barbarossa began, to 19 November 1942, the day the Soviet Stalingrad counteroffensive commenced. Throughout this period the Germans maintained the strategic initiative—except from December 1941 to February 1942, when Soviet forces conducted the Moscow counteroffensive and temporarily forced the Germans to go on the defense. The first period of war was marked by the near destruction of the Soviet prewar army; severe alterations of the Soviet force structure to accommodate the demands of war; and serious testing of Soviet prewar operational concepts, which had proven difficult (if not impossible) to implement in wartime.

Marked weaknesses in Soviet force structure and doctrine, so apparent in combat late in the prewar years, were also strikingly evident in the initial period of war. The surprise German offensive accentuated these weaknesses, which wrought havoc on the Red Army and threatened its destruction. Throughout the summer of 1941 and into the fall of 1941, the Soviets sought, at huge cost, to slow and halt the German offensive. In late fall, assisted by deteriorating weather and the overextended state of German forces, they were able to do so successfully. In November and December, first on the flanks (Tikhvin and Rostov) and then in the center (Moscow), the Red Army launched counteroffensives that halted or threw back German forces. These hastily planned and conducted counteroffensives surprised the Germans, made limited gains on the flanks, and threw back German forces from the immediate environs of Moscow.

As fighting waned and the front stabilized, both contending High Commands planned for a resumption of combat in the spring. The Germans postured, pretending to restage the attack on Moscow. Actually, however, they prepared for a strategic offensive across southern Russia. The Soviets took the bait and prepared for a strategic defense in the Moscow region. To supplement that defense, the Soviet High Command planned offensives in the south, near Khar'kov and Kerch, to distract German attention and forces from the critical Moscow axis. In May 1942 German forces, secretly concentrated for the strategic drive in the south, thwarted these Soviet offensives.

After inflicting heavy losses on the Soviets in the Khar'kov and Kerch operations, German Army Group South commenced an offensive into the Donbas and toward the Don River. By mid-fall, after a series of unsuccessful Soviet counterattacks, German forces had plunged into the Stalingrad and Caucasus regions, while the Soviets strained to halt the advance and prepare a counterstroke of their own. During the summer and fall, Soviet forces to the north, in the Leningrad and Moscow regions, postured for or launched limited offensives to weaken the German southern thrust. By November 1942 the momentum of the German drive had ebbed, establishing favorable conditions for Soviet resumption of the offensive.

Prewar Intelligence and Operation Barbarossa

Soviet military strategy on the eve of Operation Barbarossa was clearly defensive, despite the fact that Soviet military theorists throughout the 1930s had been thoroughly imbued with the "spirit of the offensive." Military doctrine consistently emphasized the defense of socialism. Since the early 1930s, Soviet military theorists capitalized on the motorization and mechanization of the Red Army by espousing new theories of deep battle and deep operations. These theories posited reliance on offensive actions by mechanized and airborne forces to penetrate enemy tactical defenses and conduct operational maneuvers by exploitation into the depths. The Soviets paid special attention to the *razvedka* necessary to support such rapidly developing operations. The offensive spirit characterized by deep operations found full expression in the 1936 *Red Army Field Service Regulation* (USTAV). The USTAV embodied every aspect of Soviet military art, which the harsh realities of the late 1930s abruptly thwarted.[1]

The purge of the Soviet military from 1937 to the outbreak of European war stifled military thought and analysis. Furthermore, the experiences of Soviet military specialists and units in the Spanish Civil War, the invasion of Poland, and the Russo-Finnish War cast serious doubt on the feasibility of conducting deep operations in the manner envisioned in 1936. A brief period of retrenchment followed, during which the Soviets abolished their large armored formations and replaced them with smaller combined-arms formations. The retrenchment program was short-lived, however, in light of the German-Polish War and the 1940 War in the West. Soviet theorists could wink at German success in Poland and explain it as a product of Polish ineptitude; they could not dismiss the fall of France in so cavalier a fashion. Soviet theorists were shocked by the realization that Germany had successfully implemented the theories of deep operations, which the Soviets had developed and in part discarded.

Soviet military analysis published in the General Staff journal, *Voennaia mysl'* [Military Thought], and the Ministry of Defense journal, *Voenno-istoricheskii zhurnal* [Military-Historical Journal], accurately assessed what the Germans had done.[2] Moreover, it clearly articulated the implications of German success for the Red Army and the Soviet state in general. In fact, this analysis conveyed the message that a fate similar to that of France might befall the Soviet Union, and it provided a stimulus for subsequent Soviet defensive planning. Overnight, Soviet strategic plans began focusing on defensive measures, if only to permit the General Staff time to correct the recent errors and restore a deep operational capability to the Red Army.

Soviet strategic planning on the eve of Barbarossa reflected an understandable dichotomy between traditional adherence to offensive concepts (which were, in part, ideologically driven) and Soviet realization that only a well-founded defense could guarantee the near-term safety of the Soviet state. While the Soviet government embarked on a program to increase the size of the Red Army and restructure and reequip it to make it a formidable offensive tool (ostensibly by summer 1942), Soviet planners formulated defensive strategic plans to protect the Soviet state during the transition period.

The program to increase the strength of the Red Army proceeded apace.

In the course of two years—from 1939 to 1940—the quantity of divisions in the ground forces increased from 98 to 303. In 1940 command and control entities were brought up to strength: military districts, armies-7, corps-6; as well as rifle divisions-25, brigades-28, motorized regiments-14, and reserve regiments-42. At the same time, 9 mechanized corps, 20 tank divisions, 20 tank brigades, 18 automobile, and 18 motorcycle regiments were formed. The strength of the armed forces rose from 2 million men (September 1939) to 5.4 million (mid-June 1941).[3]

Drawing upon the experiences of the Soviet-Finnish War and the War in the West, the Soviets refined their views on contemporary war, reworked operational-strategic and mobilization plans, accelerated force training, created central control organs, and prepared command cadre. While formulating these plans, they began force regrouping, which culminated in a major strategic deployment of forces from May to June 1941. Despite extreme turbulence in the High Command (which employed three chiefs of the General Staff between August 1940 and July 1941), a strategic defensive plan emerged. Actual Soviet force deployments prior to Barbarossa evidenced the nature of that strategic defense, which provided the context for combat in the initial stages of Barbarossa.

In simple terms, Soviet strategic plans called for a defense conducted by rifle and mechanized forces echeloned in considerable depth (see map 1). The first echelon of rifle forces, arrayed in the immediate border regions, was itself composed of several echelons of rifle forces backed up by the most combat-ready mechanized corps. To their rear, a second echelon of rifle forces and mechanized corps formed at a depth of up to 150 kilometers. A third echelon of reserve armies and mechanized corps deployed prior to or shortly after the outbreak of hostilities along the line of the Dnepr River from Vitebsk in the north to west of Kiev. The first defending echelon had the task of slowing and wearing down enemy forces, the second with halting the enemy drive, and the third with counterattacking to expel the invader. Graphic prewar Soviet writings about battles of encirclement [boi v okruzhenie] indicated full Soviet realization of the perils that faced the forward defending echelons. Subsequent deployments also demonstrated a keen Soviet awareness of the challenges and perils they faced.[4]

Today, Soviet military theorists criticize Soviet defensive planning as being weak, primarily because of the purges and the negative influence of Stalin. V. N. Lobov has written

The deformation of military doctrine caused serious mistakes in working out a series of theoretical strategic positions and in conducting measures to prepare the armed forces for war. As a result, the problems of strategic defense, the escape of the mass of forces from under enemy blows, and going over to the counteroffensive were weakly worked out. General recognition of the importance of the initial period of war in circumstances of surprise were not in full measure confirmed by practical measures to increase the capabilities of forces to repel aggression. In particular, arising from the position of military doctrine, it was outlined that the first onslaught would be repelled by limited numbers of covering forces, while the main forces of the Soviet Army deployed for conducting a decisive offensive to carry combat actions to enemy territory. The variant of prolonged strategic

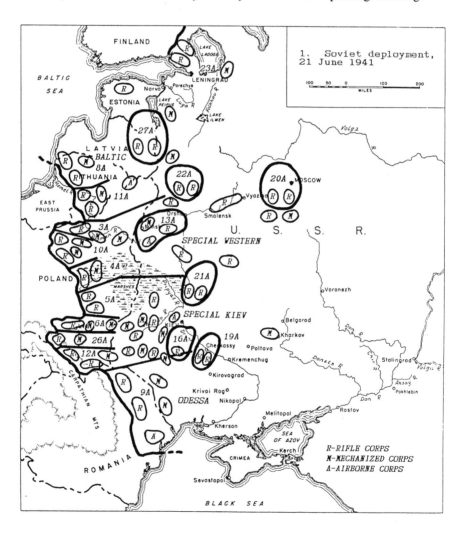

1. Soviet deployment, 21 June 1941

defense was not contemplated, and, in this connection, the creation of defensive groupings of the armed forces was not planned.

This was based on mistaken assumptions that the enemy would begin combat operations with only part of his forces, with subsequent strengthening of them during the course of war.[5]

This view has been echoed by numerous contemporary theorists as they catalogue the negative influence of Stalin on Soviet military preparedness and initial wartime strategy. These assessments, however, ignore the voluminous prewar writings that indicated the seriousness with which Soviet analysts approached the German threat. To a considerable degree, past and current de-Stalinization has colored the view of prewar Soviet planning and exaggerated the supposed neglect of defense.

The Soviet strategic defense plans were flawed because of faulty intelligence assessments, although the quality of prewar intelligence itself appears to have been fairly good. As they erected their defenses, Soviet planners ultimately concentrated on the Southwestern Direction (Kiev), where they assessed the main blow would fall. This judgment contradicted predictions of the General Staff.

Marshal B. M. Shaposhnikov, still during his tenure as Chief of the General Staff, on the basis of analysis of historical, geographical, and operational-strategic factors, reached the conclusion that, in the event of war with Germany, its command would strike the main blow on the Smolensk-Moscow direction. Stalin threw that conclusion "from the threshold." He declared that Germany needed bread to conduct war. Therefore, he said the main attack would be struck in the Ukraine. It is understandable that the opinion of Stalin became the directive for our military command.[6]

Consequently, Soviet forces formed their strongest strategic defense along the Southwestern Direction, where they erected three well-developed defensive echelons. Despite active General Staff planning, the actual defense plan was not submitted to the Commissariat of Defense until early May 1941. Military district staffs did not act on the plan until mid-June.[7]

Recent Soviet articles have elaborated on the intelligence collection effort. In the main, Soviet intelligence collection in support of the defensive strategy was effective. Soviet deployments themselves attest to the growing threat, as did the apparent existence of a Soviet prewar deception plan.

Soviet suspicions about German strategic intentions were sufficiently strong by April 1941 for the High Command (Stalin) to begin deploying strategic reserve armies forward into eastern Belorussia and the eastern Ukraine. In accordance with prewar planning assumptions, the bulk of these reserves were concentrated in the south. In fact, by 22 June four armies (16th, 19th, 21st, 22d) had deployed into position along the Dnepr River line from Velikie Luki southward to the Zhitomir and Cherkassy regions. Another army (20th) was assembling in the Moscow region. Within thirty days after hostilities had commenced, when the Soviets had correctly perceived the direction of the main German thrust, ten additional armies (24th, 28th, 29th, 30th, 31st, 32d, 33d, 34th, 43d,48th) formed two new strategic defense lines west of Moscow.[8]

Close investigation and comparison of actual Soviet force dispositions (along the border and in the depths) with German intelligence assessments reveal some interesting facts. Across the breadth of the front, German intelligence overassessed Soviet rifle forces deployed in proximity to the border by between 30 and 50 percent (see maps 2 and 3). Conversely, German intelligence failed to detect the presence of most Soviet mechanized corps along the border and, to a greater degree, in the depths of the border military districts.[9] Comparison of German intelligence data and actual Soviet dispositions strongly suggests the existence of a Soviet deception [maskirovka] plan. The plan seems to have had the dual objective of portraying greater defensive strength along the border (possibly to deter or force German commitment of more forces than otherwise required) and hiding the dispositions of the most critical offensive or counteroffensive force of the Red Army, the mechanized corps.[10]

It is clear that Soviet intelligence organizations had more than just minimal warning of the impending German assault, in particular at army level and below. Evidence of German preparation mounted across the breadth of the front in the days prior to the attack. General A. M. Vasilevsky, then serving on the General Staff, noted

In June 1941, the General Staff had been continuously receiving alarming reports from operations departments of western districts and armies. The Germans had completed the concentration of forces by our borders. In a number of places they had started dismantling their own wire entanglements and making passes in their minefields, clearly preparing ways of access to our positions. Large panzer groups had been brought up in the areas of departure, the roar of their engines distinct at night.[11]

Hundreds of Soviet memoirs and a few studies document the accuracy of Vasilevsky's statement. One recent view noted

> Documents and facts bear witness to the fact that the political and military leadership of the Soviet Union, even before the beginning of war, possessed information about preparations for the attack of Nazi Germany on the USSR. The General Staff had sufficiently full information about the strengthening of enemy forces along our western borders. The Soviet Command received from various sources information about the possible enemy attack and the period of his offensive. Border guards forces, as well as military councils of the border military districts, informed the government and People's Commissariat of Defense about the frequent occasions when enemy aircraft and agents violated the state borders.[12]

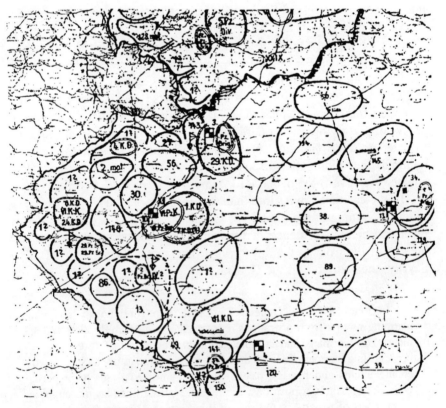

2. German intelligence assessment, June 1941.

Other recent articles detail the scope of German air and agent activity along the border from February 1940 on and include enemy strength assessments made by the border military district staffs in May and June.[13] The accuracy and gravity of these reports was amply attested to by a NKVD report of 2 June 1941.

From the Main Directorate of the Border Troops under the NKVD on 2 June 1941, it was learned that 80–88 infantry divisions, 13–15 motorized divisions and 7 panzer divisions, 65 artillery regiments and other units had

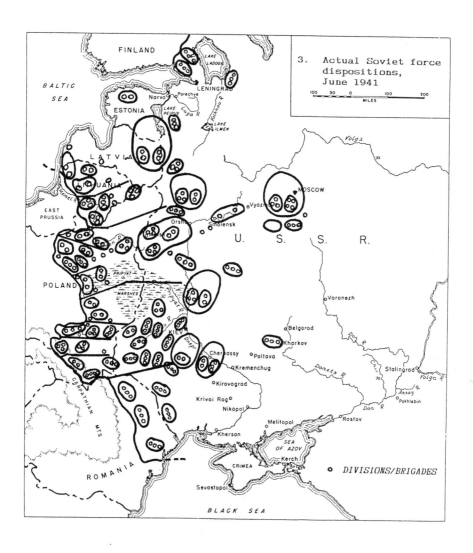

been concentrated close to our Western frontier (during April–May). On 5 June the command received information that almost daily 200 rail cars with ammunition, military supplies and food were arriving in the region of Iasi, Botosani and other areas. All the supplies were being concentrated along the railroad at temporary dumps under an awning. The infantry, artillery and tanks were being moved up to our frontiers predominantly at night. The entire zone in the immediate proximity of the frontier was reinforced by artillery and machine gun positions with "complete organization of telephone communications between the batteries, the command and observation posts." Subsequently, on 10 June, it was announced that "war should begin in the last days of June 1941" and "German tactics are based on a surprise attack and for this purpose they are presently concentrating their forces on the frontier with the Soviet Union." On the northern sector, in Finland, from 10 June there were outright mobilization and the moving of the units and formations to the Soviet frontier. At the same time, the civilian population was moved from the border areas into the interior of the territory.[14]

Other Soviet sources detail a steady stream of reports and warnings from NKVD and GRU agents abroad concerning impending hostilities. These include specific messages sent from Richard Sorge (code-named *Ramzaia*) in Japan.[15] The same source that outlined the vivid intelligence picture noted the readiness of the Soviet government but added an important qualification:

In response to the commenced deployment of the Wehrmacht, the NKO and the General Staff, upon instructions of the party Central Committee and the Soviet government, began to carry out a series of measures for the strategic deployment of the Soviet Armed Forces in the west of the nation. From mid-May, four armies began to move up there from the interior military districts and another three at the same time were preparing to move. These seven armies were to . . . [constitute] the second strategic echelon. The total volume of shipments from the interior military districts to the border ones was 939 trains.

Thus, the Communist Party and the Soviet government, in response to the aggressor's preparations for war, outlined and implemented a whole series of measures to boost the nation's military-economic potential as much as possible under those conditions, for strengthening combat might and carrying out strategic deployment of the Army and Navy. However, for a number of objective and subjective reasons, they could not or, more accurately, were unable to completely carry out all that had been planned.[16]

Among the objective reasons was uncertainty within the General Staff, probably prompted by the looming presence of Stalin. A recent critique noted

> Based on *razvedka* information, the General Staff considered that the German High Command would be forced to hold in the West and in occupied nations around half of its ground and air forces. In fact, up to the beginning of the attack on the Soviet Union, only around one third of his divisions remained there. For the Soviet highest military leadership, the concentration of such a mass of armored and mechanized forces and the creation of a compact grouping of enemy forces on main strategic directions turned out to be unexpected.[17]

Subsequently, however, political considerations clouded the picture, making it almost impossible for Stalin to accept the fact that an attack was imminent. Politics also precluded other Soviet commanders from reacting to that intelligence. Vasilevsky noted, "The political and state leaders in the country saw war coming and exerted maximum efforts to delay the Soviet Union's entry into it." In trying to deter the outbreak of war, Vasilevsky concluded that Stalin "overestimated the possibilities of diplomacy in resolving the issue." In essence, when faced with a decision of acting or not acting, "Stalin was unable to make that decision at the right time, and that remains his most serious political mistake."[18]

In his memoirs, General G. K. Zhukov, Chief of the General Staff, substantiated Vasilevsky's judgment and underscored the intelligence failure by citing a March 1941 assessment by General F. I. Golikov, chief of the Intelligence Division of the General Staff. Golikov's assessment correctly noted the possible variations and overall intent of a German offensive thrust. Golikov's conclusions, however, "nullified its importance and misled Stalin" by stating an offensive was not likely to occur before the fall of England and by attributing reports concerning the imminence of war in the East to English or German disinformation.[19] Vasilevsky criticized military intelligence assessments and national-level assessments, which he claimed were often not coordinated with those of their military counterparts:

> . . . The isolation of the intelligence agency from the General Staff apparently played a part here. The head of intelligence, being also the Deputy Defense Commissar, preferred to make his reports directly to Stalin without conferring with the Chief of the General Staff. If Zhukov had been

conversant with all the vital intelligence information . . . I am sure he could have made more precise conclusions from it and put them to Stalin in a more authoritative way. . . .[20]

Thus, despite numerous indicators and warnings, the German offensive achieved strategic, operational, and tactical surprise and benefited from the consequences. The complete motivation of the Soviet government (Stalin) in making the political decision to ignore indicators of the impending offensive remains unclear and controversial.

The Summer-Fall Campaign, June–December 1941

The strength and vigor of the initial German attack in June 1941 staggered and almost paralyzed Soviet forces as well as the Soviet High Command (see map 4). German operations during the first week of war dashed Soviet prewar expectations and led to an ever accumulating series of disasters, each seemingly worse than the last. It is clear that, initially, the High Command lost control of events. Subsequent inaction by Stalin only added to the calamity. Within days, the Soviet Southwestern and Northwestern Fronts lost all control of the situation. In the chaos that followed, defending forces were destroyed piecemeal. Mechanized corps and reserves conducted futile, uncoordinated, and often fatal counterattacks. Commanders were recalled to Moscow and shot, while new commanders were elevated to higher command and thrust into battle with orders to bring order out of chaos. Only in the south were Soviet forces able to slow the German advance and avert imminent force dissolution and ultimate disaster. While the Soviet government and Stalin groped for a suitable High Command arrangement, echelon after echelon of hastily mobilized armies, corps, and divisions were thrown into battle to stem the German advance.

Once some pattern had emerged from German actions and it had become apparent that the German priority thrust was toward Moscow and Smolensk, the newly organized *Stavka* [Headquarters of the High Command] hastily shifted two reserve armies (16th–19th) from the south northward to defend the Dnepr River line. At the same time it ordered other hastily assembled and incomplete armies to form multiple defensive lines along the Western direction as part of a reserve *front*. No sooner had these reserves assembled than they found themselves confronted by the rapid German advance.

In the face of this onslaught, the Soviets created a body to provide leadership, strategic guidance, and centralized command and control to the Red Army. On 23 June the *Stavka* of the Main Command was formed, chaired by Marshal S. K. Timoshenko but with Stalin as dominant member. This gave way on 10 July to the *Stavka* of the High Command, directly chaired by Stalin. Several weeks later, on 8 August, Stalin became

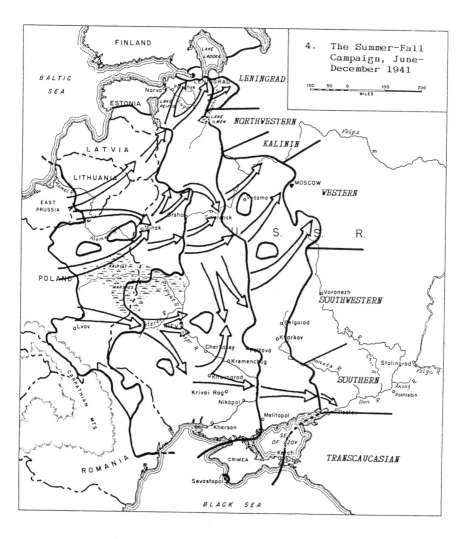

4.   The Summer-Fall Campaign, June–December 1941

Supreme Commander, a position he held throughout the war. The *Stavka,* together with the Politburo, the State Committee of Defense, and the General Staff made all strategic decisions related to the conduct of the war.

The *fronts,* by virtue of their initial performance, were obviously incapable of conducting strategic operations. To assist the *Stavka* and control operations of the *fronts,* three intermediate commands, called strategic directions [*strategicheskie napravlenii*], were formed. The commanders of the Northwestern, Western, and Southwestern Directions (initially, Marshals K. E. Voroshilov, G. K. Timoshenko, and S. M. Budenny, respectively) with their own military councils, but without planning staffs, were to coordinate strategic operations by *fronts* in their sectors. Similar centralized agencies were formed to direct mobilization and formation of forces and to coordinate logistical matters.[21] The principal task at all levels of command was to organize and conduct a strategic defense and restore stability to the front, without which counteroffensives were impossible.

With the initiative in German hands across the breadth of the front, the *Stavka* acted out of both desperation and necessity. While it strained to raise and field forces, the actual course of combat gave shape to Soviet strategy. Operating on the basis of the simple need to stem the German advance, the High Command fielded forces and erected defenses oriented to "the sound of the guns." This amounted to managing disaster by deploying forces to the most critical and dangerous sectors, based on the degree of threat and the importance of perceived German objectives. These criteria indicated that the Moscow approach remained the most critical, followed closely by the Kiev and Leningrad operations. The inability of the German High Command to establish firm priority objectives inevitably led to dissipation of the strength of the German advance. The Germans shifted their strategic focus and forces often, before ultimately deciding in October to thrust toward Moscow. The Soviets responded by concentrating their forces on the main (Moscow) axis and, although they suffered a disastrous loss at Kiev, they ultimately developed the capability of launching a counteroffensive of their own.

Thus the German advance ran its course, resisted at every step and in every sector by Soviet forces. Even major successes sapped German strength, which was natural for an army that had initially committed so much of its line strength to decisive combat. Time, distance, attrition,

and Soviet resistance inexorably shifted the correlation of forces away from the Germans and, by December 1941, provided favorable conditions for a Soviet counteroffensive.

Soviet strategy during the hectic first six months of war focused on one objective, the restoration of a stable front. Vasilevsky stated, ''In those days when Soviet forces had begun to retreat into the interior, all our thoughts were on a single objective: to hold on no matter what it took.''[22] This involved several critical Soviet decisions, such as to conduct the Smolensk counterattacks; to refuse to relinquish Kiev until disaster befell its defenders; and, subsequently, to defend decisively west of Moscow. Though none of these decisions succeeded initially, each took its toll on the German army's ability to fulfill its self-appointed mission.

The decision to defend from the west of Moscow proved to be the most critical strategic decision of the summer-fall campaign. There, from September to November, the *Stavka* concentrated virtually all of its strategic reserves and reinforcements from other directions. In fact, 50 percent of all Soviet reserves (150 rifle divisions and 44 rifle brigades) lent their weight to defense on the Western Direction.[23]

Participants in the strategic planning process in the summer and fall of 1941 have vividly described that process. Vasilevsky, in the General Staff, attested to the dominance of Stalin.

The Commander-in-Chief called in responsible people directly in charge of the problem under review (they could be members of the GHQ or not); they took the necessary decisions which were immediately issued as directives, orders or various instructions of the GHQ. One should not imagine the GHQ as a body permanently meeting in full under the Supreme Commander-in-Chief. After all, most of its members were carrying out responsible duties simultaneously, often finding themselves far from Moscow, mainly at the front. What was permanent about the GHQ was that each member kept in constant contact with the Commander-in-Chief. Stalin knew how important was the activity of GHQ members in their main jobs, so he never thought it necessary or possible to gather them together as a full body; periodically he would summon certain members, top commanders and members of front military councils so as to work out, review or confirm a particular decision concerning control of battle operations.

In all my more than 30-month work as Chief of General Staff and later also as GHQ member I do not recall it ever meeting in its full complement under the Commander-in-Chief.[24]

Regarding planning, Vasilevsky wrote

> As a rule, the preliminary draft of a strategic decision or plan for its implementation was drawn up by the Commander-in-Chief in a narrow circle of people. These were usually a few members of the Politburo and the State Defence Committee, as well as military men like the Deputy Commander-in-Chief, the Chief of General Staff and his first deputy. This work would often take several days. In the course of it the Commander-in-Chief would normally confer with commanders and members of military councils of the respective fronts, officials at the Defence Commissariat, and People's Commissars and especially heads of various branches of the war industry, receiving the necessary advice and information. Officials of the General Staff and the Defence Commissariat did an enormous amount of work in that period. As a result of comprehensive discussions, a decision would be taken and a plan would be ratified for implementing the decision; appropriate directives to the fronts would be worked out and dates confirmed for a meeting in the GHQ with commanders responsible for implementing the planned operations.
>
> At the meeting the plan was finally specified, operation dates fixed and the GHQ directive to be sent to the front signed. Then came the most important period; preparing the troops for carrying out the plan and providing them with all that was necessary within the set schedule.
>
> That was how the GHQ worked in preparing most big strategic operations of the fronts. Sometimes, however, depending on the situation, we deviated from this set procedure. Thus, on several occasions, the Commander-in-Chief and the General Staff, being extremely short of time, had to coordinate all issues with front commanders by telephone. These digressions did occur, yet we held one principle to be absolutely supreme: in working out strategic plans and in resolving vital economic problems, the Central Committee Politburo and army leadership always relied on collective decision-making. That is why the strategic decisions taken collectively and drawn up by the Supreme Command as a rule corresponded to the situation at the fronts, while the requirements made upon people were realistic because they were properly perceived and fulfilled by commanders and troops.[25]

Zhukov echoed Vasilevsky's view, stating, "Though usually calm and reasonable, . . . [Stalin] would at times become highly irritable. And when he was angry, he stopped being objective."[26] The extreme centralization of strategic decision making and planning and the dominance of Stalin, in part, contributed to strategic failure during the summer. This was evident in Stalin's early August decision to hold Kiev—a decision made against the advice of Zhukov and the General Staff.

Stalin outlined succinctly and pithily the general situation on the Soviet-German front, making a special emphasis on the Western and South-Western directions. He also gave us his brief evaluation of the enemy and what we might expect from him in the near future. He noted that the most likely course of action for the enemy was to continue his main efforts to take Moscow by making major thrusts with large panzer units on the flanks—from the north through Kalinin, and from the south through Bryansk and Oryol. For this purpose, the Nazis were holding the Guderian 2nd Panzer Group as their main strike force on the Bryansk direction. This direction was now in the greatest danger also because it was being covered by the Central Front which was weak and strung out over a large sector.[27]

Vasilevsky, Zhukov, and Shtemenko detailed the bitter arguments over this decision, which ultimately resulted in Zhukov's confrontation with Stalin and his subsequent reassignment to the Leningrad sector.[28] The disastrous destruction of the Soviet Southwestern Front at Kiev ensued.

Vasilevsky candidly admitted General Staff implication in the strategic failures in late September and early October at Viaz'ma and Briansk.

The setback in the Vyazma area was largely due both to the enemy's superiority in men and materiel and our lack of reserves, and to the GHQ's and General Staff's wrong gauging of the enemy's main thrust and, there-fore, the mistakes in the structure of defence. Instead of assigning particular defence sectors for the Western and Reserve Fronts with their complete responsibility for each sector both along the front and in depth, the 24th and 43rd Armies of the Reserve Front, by the time of the enemy offensive, were holding their defences in the first line between the left flank army of the Western and the right flank army of the Bryansk Fronts. The other three armies of the Reserve Front, strung out in a single line over a wide sector, were rather deep in the middle of the defence zone of the Western Front along the Ostashkov-Olenino-Yelnya line. The operational deploy-ment made it extremely difficult to control the troops and coordinate the actions of the fronts. Even with a well-planned and properly-organised defence in the direction of the main enemy attacks, neither the Western Front nor the troops on this direction generally had the upper hand.[29]

During the Moscow defense preliminary to the December counter-offensive, sounder strategic assessments by *Stavka* and the General Staff paved the way for German defeat. In this the staunch defense outside Moscow and the careful garnering of strategic reserves played a critical role.

The time that had been gained was used by Soviet commanders for further reinforcing the troops on the western direction and fortifying the lines of defence. One big measure was to complete the training of regular and irregular reserves formations. A new strategic reserve for the Red Army was set up at the [line] Vytegra—Rybinsk—Gorky—Saratov—Stalingrad—Astrakhan. Ten reserve armies were raised here following a decision taken by the State Defence Committee on 5 October. Their formation was one of the main and daily concerns of the Party Central Committee, the State Defence Committee and the GHQ throughout the battle of Moscow. We leaders of the General Staff in our daily reports to Stalin about the situation at the front lines also presented detailed accounts on the formation of these units. Without the slightest exaggeration I must say that the outcome of the battle of Moscow hinged decisively on the fact that the Party and the nation formed, armed, trained and deployed the new armies around the capital in time.[30]

Because of judicious commitment of reserves during the fall, by early December, "The Soviet Supreme Command had at its disposal large strategic reserves which the GHQ could use to strengthen its army in the field. The enemy's reserves on the Soviet-German front had largely been used up."[31] Adding to German discomfiture were smaller-scale Soviet offensives along the flanks near Leningrad and Rostov, whose success prevented full concentration of German forces at Moscow.

Throughout the summer-fall period, the role of Stalin proved crucial in both failure and success. As one recent critic noted, "The personal qualities of Stalin brought considerable detriment to the organization of command and control in operating fronts in 1941, often manifested in irritability and even hysteria."[32] One natural by-product of the personal involvement of Stalin and the dominance of Stalin's personality in strategic decision making was that his "intuition" often interfered with objective judgment in all realms, including intelligence.

In fact, to a major degree, the state of Soviet *razvedka* during the summer and fall made the formulation of strategic decisions particularly difficult. Once the German offensive had materialized, the Soviet intelligence system at all levels collapsed under the weight of combat realities. A rapidly collapsing front, exacerbated by the almost total disruption of communications and the destruction of the Red Army air force on the ground, made systematic intelligence collection impossible. Zhukov noted the information vacuum within the General Staff: "[Early on 22 June, the] General Staff was unable to obtain credible information from district headquarters and field commands, and this, naturally, placed the High Command and the General Staff in a very awkward situation."[33] The situation did not appreciably improve by day's end. "By the end of June 22, despite vigorous measures, the General Staff had failed to receive accurate information about our forces and the enemy from *front,* army, and air force headquarters. The information on the depth of enemy penetrations was contradictory."[34] What information did arrive concerning the enemy was derived from scattered unit contact reports (where communications existed) and from those few air reconnaissance units that had escaped destruction in the early fighting. In the absence of any other reports from *fronts,* armies, or separate corps, these fragmentary bits of information and intuition itself governed General Staff planning.

The almost total lack of precise intelligence data continued throughout the first several weeks of war. In retrospect, Zhukov noted

> In those days neither the Front commands, nor the High Command, nor the General Staff had complete enough information about the enemy forces deployed against our Fronts. The General Staff was receiving plainly exaggerated intelligence from the Fronts about the enemy panzers, air, and motorized units.[35]

The intelligence picture, of course, varied from *front* to *front.* Understandably, where German forward progress was more rapid, intelligence was the weakest. In the Soviet Northwestern Front sector, German Army Group North advanced rapidly into the Baltic States. "In all this time, the General Staff had received no clear and exhaustive dispatches from the staff of the North-western Front as to the position of its troops, the deployment of the enemy, or the location of its panzer and motorized forces." Hence, the General Staff "had to judge the developments by conjecture—a method that is no guarantee against mistakes."[36]

The intelligence situation was no better in the critical Western Front sector covering the important Bialystok-Minsk-Smolensk axis. There the rapid German advance and enemy diversionary activity severed *front* communications with the High Command and its subordinate armies. Consequently:

> The decisions of the *front* commander, made in those days, emanated from such assessments [false] of the situation. Because of an absence of data, he could not see the threat hanging over the forces on his left wing. All

measures were directed basically at localizing the enemy penetration on the right wing of the *front*.[37]

In the south, where the Southwestern Front prepared to deal with what the High Command assessed to be the major German effort, the higher density of Soviet forces somewhat alleviated intelligence problems—but not entirely. The *front* chief of staff, General I. Kh. Bagramian, commenting on the effects of the German attack on the critical 5th and 6th Army sectors between Vladimir-Volynsk and L'vov, stated

It was natural that, in these conditions, neither the chief of intelligence nor I could present the commander such information that could have satisfied him. . . . Our reconnaissance forces did not possess any concrete information about the quantity and make-up of enemy forces invading our land and about the direction of his main blow.[38]

In effect, the combat situation in the Southwestern Front sector, as was the case elsewhere, became clearer only as combat operations unfolded. As unit contact reports came in to higher headquarters, a picture of the operational situation slowly emerged, only too late for Soviet commanders to remedy the numerous looming disasters. Across the entire front, the Soviet High Command was condemned to a reactive stance that persisted well into July. Since, at least initially, the Soviet High Command was not able to anticipate German actions, German armored columns across the breadth of the Eastern Front advanced rapidly and penetrated deeply to produce numerous encirclements of Soviet forces, some of strategic proportions.

During this initial period of war, spanning late June and July, most Soviet intelligence data came from unit contact reports and visual ground observation of German forces as they advanced. By early July this information was supplemented by some information obtained from visual air reconnaissance units, which could detect enemy concentrations and movements but could not precisely identify enemy units. In time, the mosaic of German intentions emerged, primarily as a result of ongoing German operations. The blue arrows spreading across Soviet operational maps provided a crude basis upon which Soviet commanders could begin to adopt sounder countermeasures. It would be months, however, before intelligence would be able to provide a more refined view of what was actually occurring.

Weak Soviet strategic intelligence regarding German intentions and Soviet deployment of reserves across a wide front produced crises in August 1941, when the Germans shifted the focus of Army Group Center southward, to encircle Soviet forces in the Kiev region, and in October 1941 when the Germans finally resumed their drive on Moscow. The August 1941 crisis resulted from the German High Command decision to halt its drive on Moscow, and instead turn Guderian's Second Panzer Group southward into the region east of Kiev. Stalin, firm in his belief that the German thrust toward Moscow would continue, deployed his force accordingly. Meanwhile Zhukov, Vasilevsky, and others in the General Staff warned of a possible German advance southward into the rear of the Soviet Southwestern Front defending Kiev. They urged Stalin to withdraw that *front*'s forces eastward across the Dnepr River. Stalin, however, resisted the advice.

Zhukov noted

In the second half of August, having analyzed the strategic situation and the nature of enemy action on the Western direction again and again, I became even more convinced that my forecast of possible actions by the Nazi Command in the nearest future set forth in the report to Stalin on July 29 was correct. . . . My certainty was strengthened by information obtained from prisoners-of-war captured on our front that Army Group Center was passing over to a temporary defensive on the Moscow sector.[39]

He reiterated his views in a 19 August telegraph to Stalin.

The enemy has temporarily abandoned the idea of an assault on Moscow and, passing over to an active defense against the Western and Reserve Fronts, has thrown all his mobile and panzer shock units against the Central, Southwestern, and Southern Fronts. The possible enemy plan: to crush the Central Front and, reaching the Chernigov-Konotop-Priluki area, to smash the armies of the Southwestern Front with a strike from the rear.[40]

Vasilevsky echoed Zhukov's view, writing

Right up to 17 September, he [Stalin] refused even seriously to consider, let alone accept, the proposals he was receiving from the commander-in-chief of this direction, GHQ member Zhukov, the South-Western Front military council and the leadership of the General Staff. This is explained, in my view, by the fact that he underestimated the threat of encirclement

of the Front's main forces, he overestimated the Front's potential in elim-
inating the threat on its own and even more he overestimated the offensive
undertaken by the Western, Reserve, and Briansk Fronts toward the flank
and rear of the enemy's powerful grouping, which was engaged in striking
along the northern flank of our South-Western Front.[41]

Stalin responded by prohibiting the abandonment of Kiev. For his resistance to Stalin's view, Zhukov was removed from his post and transferred
to Leningrad.

A. I. Eremenko, Briansk Front commander, also noted the tenuous
intelligence data upon which these fundamental decisions were based. He
stated, "Up to 16 August the grouping of enemy, expected in this sector
of front, had still not been established." Consequently, when the groupings did not materialize in the expected manner, "All commanders and
staffs were ordered to conduct *razvedka* to establish the enemy grouping
of forces." On 23 August a German prisoner revealed that his division
(3d Panzer) and 4th Panzer Division had orders to advance south. Two
days later *front* aviation units confirmed the POW report when it observed,
"A motor-mechanized column of the enemy (more than 500 vehicles)
moving along the road Unecha-Starodub and further south."[42] Eremenko
forwarded this information to the General Staff the following day. Shortly
thereafter, heavy German attacks on Eremenko's left flank confirmed the
validity of the intelligence information.

At first Eremenko and the General Staff believed the Germans were
pressing to seize Briansk. "The *Stavka* of the High Command, failing
to discover this strategic maneuver of the enemy, oriented us on the fact
that the main group of Guderian was aimed at the right (northern) wing
of the Briansk Front." Eremenko concluded from these and other ex-
changes with the *Stavka* that the "*Stavka* did not know about conditions
in the *front*s and accepted the dissolution of the Central Front, defending
that sector, upon which the enemy was striking his main blow." Neither
Eremenko nor the *Stavka* "knew about the fundamental changes in enemy
intentions."[43] Weak *razvedka* was, in Eremenko's view, a chief reason
for the intelligence failure.

Although the High Command had *razvedka* assets and information
available upon which to base a judgment regarding German intentions,
they misjudged the information received. Lieutenant General K. S. Moskalenko, 40th Army Commander, noted

On the night of 11 September the Chief of the General Staff declared that, according to his information, "Aviation reconnaissance discovered at 1325 and 1425 [10 September] the approach of two columns of vehicles with tanks and a gathering of tanks and vehicles at the village of Zhitnoe, north of Romny. . . . [Judging] by the length of the columns, there were small units here, of no more than 30–40 tanks. . . ." From this the Chief of the General Staff concluded, "All this information does not provide a basis for accepting that fundamental decision, about which you request, namely—about withdrawal of the *front* to the east."[44]

Moskalenko wryly added, "But those enemy units which the Chief of the General Staff considered 'oozing' into the Romny region in reality represented the advanced force of 2d Panzer Group." In Moskalenko's view, Stalin "clearly underestimated the danger hanging over the forces of the South-Western Front."[45]

By the end of September, the Germans had completed the destruction of Soviet forces in the Kiev region and were ready to resume the advance on Moscow. Soviet intelligence was able to discern overall German intentions from the general situation but did not possess intelligence refined enough to act to prevent another series of initial disasters similar to those experienced at Kiev in September. To prepare defenses along the Moscow axis, the High Command deployed three *fronts* (Western, Reserve, and Briansk) along the western approaches to the capital. "Having revealed by means of agents and air reconnaissance preparations of enemy forces for an offensive on Moscow, the *Stavka* on 27 September ordered forces of these *fronts* to undertake a rigorous and stubborn defense along the entire front."[46] Simultaneously, the *Stavka* ordered its remaining strategic reserves to deploy throughout the depths of the defense.

Although correctly assessing the German strategic intention to move on Moscow, the *Stavka* and *fronts* had less success in determining precise German operational and tactical intentions. Eremenko faulted the Briansk Front's reconnaissance effort, which failed to reveal German intentions and attack locations. The Chief of Staff of Soviet 4th Army, Colonel L. M. Sandalov, described a meeting of the Briansk Front military council on 28 September. Eremenko asked his chief of intelligence whether enemy attack indicators were apparent. The chief of intelligence responded

Judging from prisoners taken in the last two days and by documents taken from dead Germans, two new infantry divisions of Second Army have appeared on the approaches to Briansk. The enemy has filled out his forces in front of the left flank of 13th Army, where radio *razvedka* had noted the staff of a new army corps.

—Today, in the second half of the day, aviation reconnaissance revealed intensive movement of auto-transport from the southwest on Glukhov and Shostka, —received new information about the enemy from General Polynin. —Our aircraft bombed one column of up to 300 vehicles.[47]

Despite these indicators, the Briansk Front failed to detect the presence of German XXXXVII Motorized Corps and did not appreciate that the Glukhov-Shostka area was the best route for an advance on Orel' and Tula. According to Sandalov, "However, the commander and staff of the Bryansk Front could not decipher that easy code. They underestimated the concentrated force of the enemy and overestimated the forces of Ermakov [defending Briansk]."[48] Consequently, within two days after the beginning of his assault, Guderian's forces had cut a 60-kilometer swath through Eremenko's defenses to a depth of 100 kilometers into the Soviet rear.

This Soviet intelligence failure of October 1941 was followed by the two-phase German offensive which, by early December, propelled German forces to the very gates of Moscow. Once the German offensive had fully developed, Soviet intelligence kept better track of German progress and was able to discern where the German armored spearheads were aimed. Zhukov, restored to Western Front command after his relief and transfer to Leningrad in late August, stated, "The important thing is that at the beginning of November the concentrations of the enemy striking forces on our *front*'s flanks had been detected in good time, which allowed us to anticipate correctly the directions of the enemy's main effort."[49]

Throughout the summer and fall of 1941, the Soviets had experienced severe problems with both operational and tactical *razvedka*. These problems had serious implications for Soviet prospects of halting the German thrust. Soviet *razvedka* procedures were uneven, and reconnaissance forces either did not exist or were used with mixed effectiveness. Consequently, Soviet *front* and army commanders often operated blindly. They compensated for their blindness by deploying their forces on wide frontages, to counter any contingency. In addition, they launched broad-front counterattacks, without paying sufficient attention to either reconnaissance or concentration. Although Soviet tactical and operational *razvedka* procedures and forces had improved somewhat by late 1941, serious deficiencies with *razvedka* at all levels persisted well into 1942. Only then, after the Soviets devoted greater attention to the problems, did *razvedka* begin to improve.

One circumstance, unfortunate in the main, did contribute to improvements in *razvedka*—at the strategic level in particular. In 1941 German forces encircled and bypassed several million Soviet troops. A sizable minority of the Soviet forces escaped destruction and ended up surviving behind German lines. These forces joined with elements of the local population to form partisan units. After a time, these units were organized into a military hierarchy and slowly integrated into the *Stavka* command structure. Ultimately, this partisan structure served the needs of the High Command by conducting *razvedka* and diversionary operations in the German rear, increasingly on a planned basis.

By late summer the High Command began dispatching intelligence and saboteur teams, which had been specially trained by the GRU, into the German rear. These teams often cooperated with partisan units. Zhukov referred to one such team:

> In early July, when the enemy had occupied Minsk and enemy troops were streaming toward the Berezina River, an intelligence and saboteur group was to be sent behind the enemy lines in the Minsk area. It was made up of two girls and two boys, all of them members of the Komsomol who had a good command of the German language. If my memory serves me well, the girls had been students of the Institute of Foreign Languages.[50]

Throughout the summer, German operational situation maps attested to Soviet reconnaissance and diversionary activities in the German rear area by displaying numerous small parachute symbols. Each parachute indicated the supposed location of a Soviet airborne insertion. The Soviets also employed a portion of their regular airborne force in a reconnaissance-diversionary role. For example, the 214th Airborne Brigade spent most of three months (July through September) playing such a role around Minsk. During July, the 204th Airborne Brigade of 1st Airborne Corps also conducted more than ten airdrops of teams in the Ukraine to conduct diversionary and intelligence operations.[51]

Soviet use of agents, partisans, and airborne forces to conduct intelligence and diversionary operations in the German rear was haphazard and random. Consequently, the operations had only minimal effect on *razvedka* efforts during the summer. After August 1941, when the High

Command formed more highly specialized intelligence and diversionary forces and when partisan organizations became more structured, this dimension of *razvedka* grew. By 1943, agents, partisans, and airborne forces became one of the most important means of strategic and operational intelligence.

The Winter Campaign, December 1941–April 1942

By late November, with German forces worn down in incessant and ever more bitter fighting, Stalin and the *Stavka* began planning for a counter-offensive spearheaded by several new armies deployed forward from the strategic reserve (see map 5). This offensive, launched on 5 December, ended a long string of difficult Soviet defensive operations extending back almost to the beginning of the war. Soviet planners of the Moscow operation were driven as much by desperation and circumstances as by a conscious well-planned effort to deceive and defeat German forces. They were unwittingly assisted by the German command, which maintained an optimistic outlook and continually depreciated the Soviet ability to generate and employ fresh forces.

Vasilevsky described the genesis of the Moscow operation:

> The idea of a counter-offensive around Moscow arose in the GHQ back in early November, immediately after the first enemy attempt to break through to the capital had been foiled. But it had then had to be abandoned because of the new fascist assault which necessitated committing our reserves to repulse the enemy. Only in late November, when the enemy had exhausted his offensive capabilities and his assault groups were stretched out over a wide front and he had no time to dig in on the new defence lines, did the GHQ return to the idea of a counter-offensive.[52]

The Soviet counteroffensive, ordered by Stalin and planned by Zhukov, again commander of the Western Front, envisioned use of three new reserve armies as shock groups to spearhead the new offensive. Vasilevsky described the plan:

> The idea of the counter-offensive on the Central direction was to strike with troops of the right and left flanks of the Western Front in concert with the Kalinin and South-Western Fronts so as to smash the enemy assault groupings trying to pincer Moscow from the north and south. The GHQ

had issued general instructions to the commanders of the Western and South-Western Fronts beforehand and asked for their specific proposals. The Western Front was to play and actually did play the main part in this historic counter-offensive. On 30 November, the front commander, Zhukov, sent the General Staff a plan of the Western Front's counter-offensive and asked me urgently to convey it to People's Defence Commissar Stalin and issue a directive for the operation's commencement, so as not to be late with preparations. . . .

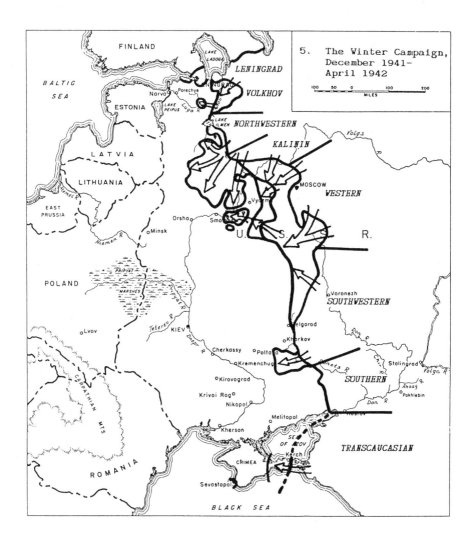

5.   The Winter Campaign, December 1941–April 1942

In essence, the plan envisaged defeating the enemy's flanking groups on the Moscow approaches: north of the capital by the 30th, the 1st Shock, the 20th and 16th Armies . . . south of the capital by the 50th and the 10th Armies. . . .

Neighboring armies were to give active support to the Western Front. The Kalinin Front to the right of the Western Front was to make a thrust with the 31st Army . . . while to the left of the Western Front the South-Western Front was to go into action with the 3rd and 13th Armies. . . .[53]

Deployment of the new armies into the forward area began on 24 November and continued until early December, in time for the designated attack date of 5 December. The Soviets employed deceptive measures to conceal the movement of the three armies, but these measures were neither systematically planned nor part of any well-organized strategic deception plan. Yet specific aspects of planning and deployment did have seemingly positive results—in particular, the improved Soviet ability to cover large troop movements. Because of this and poor German intelligence, the Moscow counteroffensive surprised German Army Group Center and the German High Command.

Soviet planning for the Moscow counteroffensive was completed within six days in the utmost secrecy. Only select individuals within the *Stavka* and Western Front headquarters knew of the plan, and even army commanders knew only their portion of it. In this the Soviets resorted to sequential planning—that is, to going step by step through various levels of command—and it was a method they would use again in the future. This type of planning improved secrecy but limited the time subordinate headquarters had to prepare for operations. In the Moscow operation, however, sequential planning prevented disclosure of the plans to German intelligence. The pressure of the ensuing Soviet attack collapsed the German front in several sectors. For the first time in the war, German generals experienced the frightening prospect of losing control of the situation.

In the end, the harsh winter conditions that had weakened German offensive capabilities also took a toll on the advancing Soviets. Ill-equipped for mobile operations and lacking a supply system adequate to support such a major effort, the Soviet advance ground to a halt in late December. By then Army Group Center found itself deployed in a huge salient jutting eastward toward Moscow from Kalinin in the north to Kirov in the south. All along this strategic sector, German units clung for dear life to their defenses, waiting for the Soviet offensive impulse to expire.

In ordinary circumstances it would certainly have been time for the Soviets to halt their forces, replenish and reequip them, and consolidate their gains. But these were not ordinary times. The *Stavka* and Stalin sensed imminent victory. Having invested major reserves in heavy and costly combat, the *Stavka* felt it was now time to reap the ultimate reward: the destruction of Army Group Center. It appeared that only a final blow needed to be struck to accomplish that goal.

Consequently, in early January the *Stavka* ordered the Northwestern, Kalinin, and Western Fronts to mount new offensives fueled by the commitment of fresh *Stavka* reserves. Deep thrusts would cut into both flanks of Army Group Center, unite at Viaz'ma, and entrap the Germans. Simultaneously, other forces would strike hammer blows directly at German positions west of Moscow. An additional deep strike from the north would penetrate the forests near Toropets and cut German communications lines west of Smolensk.

Such was the Soviet grand design. Fueled by unbridled optimism and remnants of that earlier desperation, in most instances the Soviets bothered little to conceal their intent, since German intelligence had an easy time keeping track of the Soviet forces that had been engaging them since early December. However, the Soviets had learned from their December operations that in sectors where combat was heaviest or where the Germans were weakest, concealed offensive preparations were indeed possible. They were also possible in regions that the Germans considered unsuited for combat operations. The Soviets had also learned that it was possible to conceal the regrouping of forces within portions of the front.

Armed with their experiences of December and early January, the Soviets launched their new wave of offensive operations. A series of dramatic successes pushed German forces westward from Moscow and threatened the very survival of German Army Group Center. By late February, however, the Soviet offensive expired. Soviet forces had seized much of the countryside in the German rear, but they had failed to break the main German line of resistance east of Viaz'ma or seize the key roads and population points that were the backbone of Army Group Center's defenses. Despite Soviet attempts to break the stalemate in March and April, exhaustion on both sides brought fighting to a halt. In effect, while reducing the German threat to Moscow, the Soviet High Command had attempted to do too much. Its strategic vision and goals far exceeded the capabilities of its forces. By April, that fact was evident to all.

One recent Soviet assessment noted, "The fronts certainly went over to the offense, but nowhere did they succeed in achieving any decisive results." G. K. Zhukov noted that Stalin had demanded an attack.

> He said, "If you have no results today, then there will be [results] tomorrow; moreover, you will contain the enemy, and at this time there will be results on other sectors." Of course, these arguments are infantile. . . . As a result there were many sacrifices, materiel expenditures were great, and there was no overall strategic result. But if the forces and means which we had at that time had been used on the western direction, then the result would have been different.[54]

Although the ultimate aims of the two-phased Moscow counteroffensive were not achieved, the Germans had been dealt a major strategic defeat—in fact, the first ever experienced by the Wehrmacht. This Soviet achievement, at least in part, could be attributed to improved intelligence collection and analysis.

By the time of the Moscow counteroffensive of 5 December 1941, the Soviet High Command and subordinate headquarters had taken some steps to implement sound *razvedka* procedures in accordance with prewar regulations. Based on war experience, on 18 September 1941, the People's Commissariat of Defense issued Order Number 308 pertaining to conduct of operational and tactical *razvedka*.[55] Soon this was expanded upon by General Staff directives. The order required all units to conduct systematic *razvedka* before beginning an offensive. Among its specific recommendations, it required commanders to perform personal visual reconnaissance of the enemy and terrain over which his unit would operate. Despite the order, few units employed reconnaissance in force or troop reconnaissance to the extent required. Armed with considerable experience (much of it unpleasant) and new orders regarding *razvedka*, the Soviet High Command conducted the Moscow counteroffensive.

Soviet attack dispositions in the initial phases of the operation reflected uncertainty over exact German force dispositions. Soviet armies attacked in timed sequence and in almost uniform sectors along a broad front extending from Kalinin in the north to Elets in the south. Ultimately, the attack encompassed virtually every possible offensive axis. All available aviation assets supported the effort. At the height of the offensive, the

Soviets dropped numerous reconnaissance-diversionary teams in the German rear to monitor troop movements; detect German force dispositions; and disrupt command, control, and logistics networks. By February, the lack of focus and the fragility of Soviet forces had created a crazy quilt of overlapping German and Soviet positions. Several large Soviet troop concentrations had been isolated in the German rear. Several penetrating Soviet forces (i.e. 33d Army) were cut off and destroyed by counterattacking German reserves.

At least part of the explanation of why the Soviets failed to achieve their full offensive aim (the destruction of German Army Group Center) rests in the spotty nature of Soviet intelligence at this stage of the war. A few examples drawn from the Moscow operation and from supporting sectors will suffice. On 8 January 1942, the second phase of the Moscow counteroffensive began as the Northwestern, Kalinin and Western Fronts sought to envelop Army Group Center by an attack toward Smolensk. On the left flank of the Northwestern Front, Eremenko's newly formed 4th Shock Army had the mission of attacking from the north via Toropets through the forests toward Smolensk. This was one of the first occasions when the Soviets used deception successfully and achieved surprise, for the Germans failed to detect the Soviet force concentration before Soviet forces were well into their rear area.

The Soviets did not fully realize how well their plan had succeeded. The 249th Rifle Division, whose mission was to cover the secret forward deployment of 4th Shock Army, performed well because it was composed of former border guard forces who knew how to conduct reconnaissance. Therefore, the Soviets had a fair picture of the German forward defensive positions. The same, however, was initially not true regarding deeper reconnaissance. According to Eremenko:

> Information about the enemy, which I received in the *front* headquarters, unfortunately did not at all correspond with reality. Thus, for example, the second defensive belt which, according to the information of the *front* staff, was supposedly created along Lakes Sterzh and Vselug and had a system of strongpoints, pillboxes, and barbed wire entanglements, did not turn out to be. In the *front* staff I received information that an enemy tank division was concentrated in the Selzhanov region. That was also not confirmed. The *front* staff affirmed that the axis Ostashkov-Andreapol' was unfavorable for the offensive. However, I treated them critically, since, in the course of two months, the *front* staff had not had one prisoner in that sector.[56]

Consequently, Eremenko ordered the 249th Rifle Division to seize prisoners on all critical axes and conduct deeper reconnaissance. Within five days 4th Shock Army possessed a complete picture of German dispositions and finally determined there was no second defensive line from 15 to 20 kilometers behind the forward defenses. To collect intelligence during 4th Shock Army's successful operation, the Soviets relied heavily on agents, small intelligence groups dropped from aircraft in the enemy rear, and long-range ski patrols. The use of ski units proved especially useful and was highlighted in subsequent Soviet critiques of *razvedka* during the winter campaign.

Farther south, in the Elets sector, where 13th and 38th Armies conducted an offensive operation in December, enemy documents captured by reconnaissance units materially contributed to Soviet success. According to Moskalenko of 38th Army:

> On the day that General Kostenko's [mobile] group began its offensive, prisoners were taken at the village of Zamaraika, among which was an officer from the 95th Infantry Division staff. A combat order of 5 December 1941 turned up on him. From this document it was apparent that even the division commander, General Arnim, did not suspect the concentration of the *front* cavalry-mechanized group against his units. Conversely he wrote in his order, "The enemy in front of the 95th Infantry Division have weak covering detachments only in separate places, which in the event of energetic attacks, will withdraw to the east and not accept battle."
>
> Thus, the command of the German-fascist group, being persuaded that there were no Soviet forces on the right flank, threw large forces to the north of Yelets where they were pinned down by our cavalry-mechanized group. So we were better able to strike a flank attack with our *front* group against the unsuspecting enemy.[57]

Later in January in the Donets Basin, the Southwestern and Southern Fronts launched an offensive across the Northern Donets River against German Army Group South. Before the attack the Soviets collected intelligence from the *Stavka,* from agents operating with partisans, and from combat units. The intelligence formed an accurate picture of German dispositions. Southwestern Front Chief of Staff Bagramian noted

> To everyone it was clear that the precious information about the grouping of enemy forces was not simple to obtain. Besides troop and aviation *razvedka,* it was obtained by hundreds of people, risking their lives in the enemy rear.[58]

The *front* chief of intelligence, Colonel I. V. Vinogradov, helped prepare a plan to take advantage of the intelligence picture. In the subsequent Lozovaia-Barvenkovo operation, the Soviets took advantage of accurate intelligence to conduct a surprise offensive and seize a sizable bridgehead on the south bank of the Northern Donets River.

During the same time frame, Soviet intelligence used different methods to assess the nature of German positions in the Demiansk region, where German forces had been isolated in a pocket during the Soviet offensive in January. There the German Sixteenth Army had established a strong defense based on extensive dug-in fortifications. It was the Northwestern Front's task to first analyze and then overcome the defense. Here, for the first time, the Soviets attempted to use aerial photography to decipher the defense. Reconnaissance by units of the 6th Air Army used aerial photography to conduct a survey of German positions. The photographs were deciphered by the 21st Motorized Topographical Detachment of the *front*'s topographic section. The results were recorded on maps of 1:25,000 and 1:50,000 scale and analyzed by *front* cartographers. Later, the results were verified by ground reconnaissance. The accuracy of the photographic plots ranged from 80 to 100 percent for firing points, trenches, and pillboxes; 75 percent for artillery fire positions; and from 30 to 50 percent for individual machine guns, mortars, and antiaircraft gun positions. A Soviet after-action report concluded, "Aerial photography is a most effective means for revealing the actual outline of enemy defenses. The results of deciphering, assisted by ground reconnaissance, provides, in the final analysis, exhaustive information about the enemy's defense."[59]

A negative example of *razvedka* occurred during preparations for the Soviet amphibious assault at Kerch in the Crimea in late December 1941. Although the Soviets successfully seized a foothold in the Crimea, Soviet critiques of the operations faulted the intelligence effort.

> Cooperation of fleet, army, and air force *razvedka* forces and means was weak. *Razvedka* work was passive: there was no systematic reconnaisance of the forward area or depth of the enemy defense in places and regions of assault landings and an absence of study of tactical positions and technical means of the enemy. As a rule, with a few exceptions, there was no *razvedka* of the landing areas by special groups from submarines, cutters, and aircraft; or by means of seizing prisoners, interrogation of the local population, aerial photography, demonstrative reconnaissance actions, disinformation, use of radio, light, and sound *razvedka*.[60]

Consequently, the forces landed blindly, without knowing much about potential enemy opposition. Although these deficiencies did not abort the Kerch effort, the report noted that similar problems had produced earlier failures (such as Shlissel'berg near Leningrad in September 1941).

It was clear that intelligence collection and analysis had improved over the summer months. Most of these improvements, however, occurred in the tactical and shorter-range operational realm. Strategic collection remained weak and was a slender reed upon which to base the formulation of military strategy and to conduct strategic operations. Moreover, the continued dominance of Stalin over planning ensured that subjective factors such as perception and intuition would continue to play a significant role and often outweigh or pervert objective assessment.

The Summer-Fall Campaign, May–October 1942

As spring approached on the Eastern Front, both sides sought to seize the initiative and achieve strategic goals unrealized in 1941 (see map 6). The Germans intensely examined strategic questions and argued about what strategic military goals Germany should strive to realize in 1942. Simultaneously, the Soviet High Command sought to divine German strategic intentions and resume active operations to maintain the initiative, which had passed into their hands in December 1941.

Ultimately, Hitler defined German strategic intentions but not without vociferous arguments from elements of the German High Command. Hitler decided that Germany would resume the strategic offensive in early summer. But, unlike the offensive of 1941, which had unfolded in three axes, that of 1942 would thrust across southern Russia into the economically valuable Caucasus region. Thereafter, with Soviet defensive strength weakened and her economic base undermined, German armies would loosen the Soviet grip on Leningrad. This was basically the concept of ''Operation Blau,'' the strategic drive that would end in disaster at Stalingrad. Within a few months, the Germans would begin a major strategic deception of their own, designed to reinforce the impression that the focus of German strategic efforts would occur on the Moscow axis.[61]

The Soviet High Command and Stalin were transfixed by the traumatic ebb and flow of combat in the Moscow area in late 1941 and early 1942. They allowed the Moscow axis to dominate their attention and plans for the summer of 1942. Zhukov recalled

The Supreme Commander assumed that in the summer of 1942 the Germans would be capable of waging major offensive operations simultaneously in two strategic directions, most likely the Moscow and the southern. In the north and north-west, he maintained, the enemy's activity would be of little significance. At most he might try to cut off salients in our defence line and improve the deployment of his troops.

Of the two sectors in which Stalin expected strategic offensive operations, he was most concerned about the Moscow sector, where the Germans had assembled more than 70 divisions.[62]

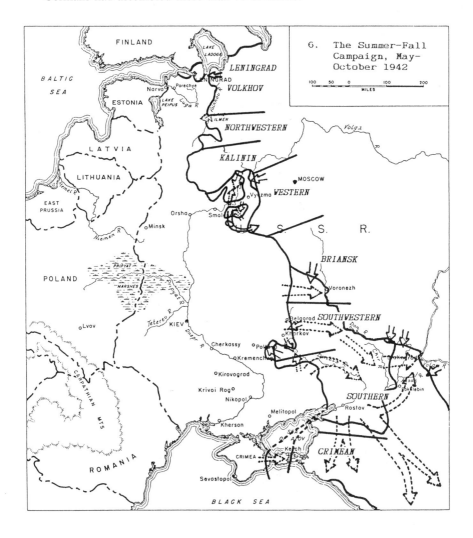

6.   The Summer–Fall Campaign, May–October 1942

While Chief of the General Staff Shaposhnikov argued for the cautious conduct of a strategic defense, Stalin demanded active limited offensive activity to preempt German action or distract them from their principal aim. Stalin stated, "We cannot sit on the defense with our arms folded and wait until the Germans strike the first blow. We must ourselves strike a series of forestalling blows on a broad front and feel out the readiness of the enemy."[63] Meanwhile, Stalin concentrated the bulk of Soviet strategic reserves in the Orel'-Kursk sector to defend the southwestern approaches to Moscow. Vasilevsky, then chief of the Operations Department of the General Staff, recalled

> The biggest enemy grouping (over 70 divisions) was located on the Moscow approaches. This gave the GHQ and General Staff grounds for believing that the enemy would try to make a decisive attack on the Central direction with the start of the summer season. This opinion, as I know very well, was shared by the command on most fronts.[64]

By 15 March the *Stavka* concept for 1942 operations was complete. It envisioned the conduct of an active strategic defense, a buildup of reserves, and then a resumption of the decisive offensive on the Moscow-Smolensk "direction [axis]." The *Stavka*, over Zhukov's objections, planned supporting offensives in the north, near Leningrad, and at Khar'kov and the Crimea in the south to distract German attention from the Moscow area. According to Vasilevsky, "Stalin gave his permission [for the Khar'kov offensive] and ordered the General Staff to consider the operation the internal affair of the sector and not interfere in any matters concerned with it."[65] The chief of staff of the Southwestern Direction, Bagramian, later recalled

> From the point of view of strategy and operational art the intention of our High Command to undertake the Khar'kov operation in May 1942 was correct since it was based on the firmly held *Stavka* view, that with the beginning of the summer campaign, Hitler's High Command would strike the main blow on the Moscow direction, with the aim of capturing the capital of our country—and against the forces of the Southwestern Direction simultaneously as a secondary attack by limited forces. . . . Personally I also firmly held that opinion, which turned out to be mistaken.[66]

Bagramian noted that the Khar'kov operation, in addition to securing that important city, would also divert German forces from the critical assault on Moscow. Thus, while the German High Command prepared to initiate a major strategic offensive in southern Russia, the *Stavka* implemented a strategic defensive with supporting operational thrusts, also in the south. Both sides implemented effective deception plans to support their offensive intentions; however, the Soviet plan was irrelevant.

The Soviet offensives developed as ordered in Karelia, the Leningrad and Khar'kov regions, and on the Kerch peninsula of Crimea. All met with almost instant failure.

> The majority of them [these operations] were poorly prepared in a materiel sense and did not achieve their designed ends. Moreover, the operations on the Khar'kov direction and in Crimea turned out catastrophic for us and offered up the beginning of new defeats. As a result of these failures, as well as the failure of our forces around Voronezh, the enemy secured the strategic initiative and conducted a decisive offensive to the Volga and the Caucasus.[67]

The disasters at Khar'kov and Kerch represented an inauspicious beginning for Soviet operations in 1942 and paved the way for future defeats. After the Khar'kov debacle, the initiative fell firmly into German hands, and the Soviets could only react to forestall even greater disaster. The new strategic duel began in late June, when German forces commenced Operation Blau with attacks across a broad front from Kursk to the Northern Donets River. These attacks caught Soviet forces unprepared and forced their precipitous withdrawal.

The German offensive across southern Russia initially carried German forces to the Don River near Voronezh and then southeastward along the southern bank of the Don River toward Millerovo. As German forces in the Donbas joined the attack, the entire mass of German Army Group South pressed Soviet forces back toward Stalingrad. From July to November 1942, combat took on a dual nature within the context of the German strategic offensive. First, the Soviets sought to stabilize the front in the south both by launching counterattacks to slow and channelize the progress of German forces and by conducting defensive operations to halt the Germans and create conditions suitable for a counteroffensive. Second, in other sectors of the front but primarily in the central sector, the Soviets mounted limited objective offensives to distract German attention and forces from the south.

In bitter, often confused, fighting from late July to late September,

Soviet forces used delaying tactics, occasional counterattacks, and terrain to shape and ultimately limit the German advance in southern Russia. By the end of the period, the Don and Volga rivers and the Caucasus Mountains delineated the extremities of the German advance. Late in the period, as German forces became transfixed by the battle for Stalingrad itself, by means of counterattacks and localized combat the Soviets jockeyed for suitable positions from which they could launch a counteroffensive. All the while, in actions analogous to those it undertook in 1941, the *Stavka* marshaled reserves with which it could, at some point, conduct a counteroffensive.

Initially, in the spring of 1942, Soviet strategic *razvedka* suffered a major setback when Timoshenko's Southwestern Direction fell victim to German strategic deception. By 10 April 1942 Timoshenko had formulated a plan for the Khar'kov operation. The plan included a major deception to conceal Soviet force concentrations and offensive intent. While the deception worked to a certain extent, poor Soviet intelligence work ultimately spelled doom for the operation. Success in the Khar'kov operation was based on the premise that German forces were concentrating near Moscow. Timoshenko thought Soviet forces could attack from bridgeheads across the Northern Donets River, north and south of Khar'kov, and subsequently exploit and encircle German Sixth Army in the Khar'kov region *without* interference from German reserves. Thus, it was essential for the Soviets both to determine accurately German strength in the Moscow and Khar'kov areas and to ensure that no German forces could threaten the operation from the south.

Timoshenko's chief of staff, Bagramian, noted it was particularly difficult to determine what additional forces German Army Group South had received from other sectors.

> To elucidate this question we did not have much important information. We did not know even the most general outline such as the human and materiel-technical resources at the disposal in the rear of Fascist Germany and her allies to create new troop formations . . . and the degree to which they had succeeded in filling the combat losses in personnel and weapons, lost during the winter campaign.[68]

To answer those questions, the Southwestern Direction command used all available intelligence, including reports from neighboring *fronts*. However, Bagramian admitted, "Our progress was based more on conjecture than on real information,'' although he claimed there was ''rather convincing information'' that the main attack would be along the Moscow axis. ''According to information from agents and testimony of prisoners, the enemy was concentrating large reserves with a considerable quantity of tanks east of Gomel' and in the Kremenchug-Kirovograd and Dnepropetrovsk regions—evidently with the aim of crossing over to decisive action in the spring.''[69] Bagramian admitted it was impossible to tell for sure where they would be employed. For his part, he believed the main offensive would be toward Moscow, with a secondary thrust between the Northern Donets River and Taganrog. The offensives, he thought, would begin after the middle of May. He added, ''Our *razvedka* took some pains to reveal conditions on the enemy side. Furthermore, our actions during the Barvenkovo operation [January 1942] brought us, as well, fully trustworthy and extensive information about the state of German defenses.''[70] This, however, applied primarily to its tactical depths. Bagramian later admitted, ''Personally, I also firmly supported that [the *Stavka*'s] opinion, which turned out mistaken.''[71]

The Soviet offensive commenced on 12 May and continued through 16 May. During this period, according to Bagramian:

> Our *razvedka* opportunely revealed the whereabouts of enemy tactical reserves. The matter of exposing operational reserves developed poorly. Nevertheless, aviation detected the accumulation of enemy forces on the left flank of the [northern] shock group. True, they reported only about two tank divisions. The arrival there of three infantry regiments was reported later.[72]

These reports affirmed the earlier Soviet assumption that the principal German concern was to defend Khar'kov, in particular against the northern Soviet shock group. On 14 May another serious indicator appeared in the form of German seizure of air superiority over the region. Such a seizure should have indicated the concentration of a larger German force in the area than was originally thought to exist. Later the Soviets realized it was the German Fourth Air Fleet. At the same time, Soviet air reconnaissance focused on new German troop movements from the Belgorod region in the north. These troops threatened the northern shock group. On 16 May, when Bagramian questioned the Southern Front about conditions in its area, he received the response, ''Kleist [First Panzer Army] is motionless.'' In fact, according to Bagramian, ''In these days the command and staff of the Southern Front, in their reports and dispatches, provided no kind of alarming news, which would provide a basis to assume the possibility of the enemy going over to an offensive against its right flank armies.''[73]

The major German counteroffensive materialized on 17 May, and within six days German Army Group South encircled and destroyed virtually the entire Soviet southern attack force. Soviet authors have since asked, ''How could that have happened?'' Bagramian cryptically explained that the Southern Front made some mistakes, the most serious of which related to lack of intelligence on German forces or intentions. Simply stated, ''The Southern Front staff did not devote required attention to *razvedka* and could not correctly evaluate the enemy groupings and his intentions.''[74]

By the night of 17 May, indicators had clearly evidenced a strongly developing German counterstroke. However, it then became a matter of convincing Timoshenko and Stalin to call off the offensive in order to deal with the new threat. That took another three days, by which time the fate of the Soviet offensive and its attacking forces had been sealed. Zhukov, from his vantage point in Moscow, confirmed Bagramian's explanation, adding

> If one analyzes the course of the Khar'kov operation, it is not difficult to see that the main reason for our defeat lay in the underestimation of the serious threat posed by the South-Western strategic direction, where the necessary Supreme Command reserves had not been concentrated.[75]

Vasilevsky placed even greater blame on the General Staff, stating, ''The preconceived, mistaken opinion that in the summer the main enemy blow would be delivered along the central direction prevailed within the High Command right up to July.''[76]

Soviet intelligence failures at Khar'kov extended from the strategic-operational areas into the tactical realm as well. Uncertainty over German tactical dispositions led Timoshenko to procrastinate and fail to commit his powerful mobile reserves until it was too late for them to be of any use. One major legacy of the Khar'kov operation, which would be reinforced by events in the late winter of 1942, was a growing tendency on the part of the *Stavka* to take a more prudent view of enemy intentions—that is, to be sure to cover all eventualities in the event assessments, in particular strategic ones, turned out to be erroneous.

As had been the case in 1941, however, the single German thrust across southern Russia ultimately eased the job of Soviet intelligence. Unlike 1941, in 1942 Soviet armies more nimbly dodged the German thrusts and avoided wholesale encirclement. By early July any doubts within the *Stavka* over the direction of the German thrust had been dispelled. From that point until mid-fall, the Soviets simultaneously sought to slow or stop the German offensive in the south, mount offensives elsewhere along the front to distract the Germans, and marshal new reserves with which to mount a new strategic counterstroke. As had been the case in May, in June *Stavka* assessments that a Moscow thrust was imminent clouded Soviet judgments regarding German intentions; again the Soviets fell victim to an intelligence failure. Soviet misjudgments, in part, can be attributed to a major German deception plan called Operation Kreml, which portrayed false German intent to strike along the Moscow axis.[77]

While the *Stavka* operated on the mistaken assumption that the Germans would attack toward Moscow, the Southwestern Direction also wrongly assessed where the main German blow would occur. In late May air reconnaissance and prisoner interrogations detected a major German buildup in the Chuguev bridgehead opposite 38th Army.[78] This area, which the Germans had held to tightly during the May battles, was a natural launching pad for new German attacks in the south. Based on this intelligence, improved German air capability, and reports of new German units arriving from the west, the Southwestern Front staff believed the Germans would attack from the Chuguev area toward Kupiansk.

On 29 May the Southwestern Direction used this and other intelligence information to formulate a new estimate of German dispositions and intentions. This estimate was based on the assessment of German strength that follows.[79]

Sector	Strength
Oboian-Khar'kov	7 infantry divisions
Pechenegi-Izium	14 infantry divisions
(Chuguev)	6 panzer divisions
	1–2 motorized divisions
Izium-Lisichansk	7 infantry divisions
Lisichansk-Taganrog	16 infantry divisions
Enroute from Crimea	5–6 infantry divisions
	2 panzer divisions

The correlation of forces was favorable for defense in three of the sectors; in the fourth, Chuguev, it was markedly unfavorable. Consequently, the Southwestern Direction assessed a high likelihood of a German advance in that sector toward Kupiansk during the five to ten days after 29 May and a secondary thrust occurring from Izium toward Starobel'sk.[80] Repeated attempts by the Southwestern Direction to wring new reserves from the *Stavka* failed in light of the perceived threat to Moscow. Even the Southwestern Direction misjudged the Germans, however. Planners considered the probable thrust a short-term danger and believed the main attack would occur at Moscow. In short, they believed the German concentration in the south was for a secondary attack.

Midst the confusion of conflicting estimates, a fortuitous event occurred which, if interpreted properly, could have resolved the entire matter. In Moskalenko's words:

> On 19 June 1942 soldiers of one of the subunits of 21st Army's 76th Rifle Division shot down a fascist "Frisher Storch" aircraft near the village of Belianka. On one of the dead crew-members, who turned out to have been chief of the operations department of 23d Panzer Division, Major Reichel, documents were taken relating to operation "Blau." From these, the Soviet High Command learned of the preparation, concept, and operational aims of the German-Fascist command. It was revealed that one of the blows would be conducted in the 21st Army sector by the forces of Sixth Army and XXXX Panzer Corps, and another—to the north, in the 40th Army's sector of the Briansk Front by the forces of Fourth Panzer Army. The aim of the offensive was the encirclement of Soviet forces west of Staryi Oskol.[81]

A dilemma now arose for the Soviets concerning whether the documents were accurate or merely a case of disinformation. Moskalenko stated that the

> trustworthiness of the documents was subjected to aviation and radio *razvedka*. Although the date of the beginning of the enemy operation remained unknown, it was clear that it could be expected in the near future. The staffs of our forces were then warned about this.[82]

Shtemenko noted receipt of these documents by the General Staff, stating, "This caused much excitement . . . for such things rarely happened. . . . We now had in our possession a map with the objectives of the 40th Panzer Corps and the 4th Panzer Army and many other documents, including some in code. These did not take long to decipher.''[83] Timoshenko reportedly believed the documents and passed them to Vasilevsky who, in turn, brought them to Stalin. Clinging to his earlier estimates, ''Stalin suspected that they might have been fed to us deliberately in order to throw a veil over the true intentions of the German command.'' Consequently, ''Stalin demanded that everything about the plans of the German command should be kept secret,'' while assuaging Timoshenko's concern by promising to pay closer attention to all threatened sectors.[84] The following day, 21 June, the *Stavka* abolished the Southwestern Direction command and assigned Timoshenko to command only the Southwestern Front.

On 28 June the German offensive began when Army Detachment Weichs struck the joined flanks of the Briansk Front's 13th and 40th Armies east of Kursk. Two days later German Sixth Army and XXXX Panzer Corps launched their attack (as indicated in the captured orders) against the Southwestern Front's 21st and 28th Armies. The two German thrusts penetrated deeply toward Voronezh and Ostrogozhsk and threatened to encircle Soviet 21st and 40th Armies.

In essence, the German assaults capitalized on confusion in Soviet intelligence circles. Vasilevsky answered these charges from the perspective of the General Staff, stating

> An opinion is now voiced sometimes that the main reason for the defeat of our troops on the Bryansk Front in July 1942 was that the GHQ and the General Staff had underestimated the Kursk-Voronezh direction. I do not share that opinion. Nor is it true that the GHQ and the General Staff had not expected the attack.[85]

Vasilevsky admitted that the General Staff expected the German attack to occur in the central sector rather than the south. But in planning for the defense of Moscow, he claimed the *Stavka* had reinforced the Briansk Front with a considerable number of reserves, including the newly formed 5th Tank Army. Vasilevsky attributed Briansk Front problems to a failure on the part of the *front* to organize its defense properly and mount a coordinated counterattack with its sizable reserves.

Despite the *ex post facto* arguments, two facts were clear by early July. The Soviet High Command had seriously misjudged German force dispositions and intentions; and, because of this misjudgment, German forces had crushed Soviet defenses and had begun a major advance across southern Russia toward the Don River. Intelligence and *razvedka* failures had contributed in a major way to the military disaster. If further disaster was to be averted, Soviet intelligence would have to do better in the future.

Throughout the three-month German advance, which commenced on 28 June, the Soviets mobilized all intelligence means at their disposal to understand better the focus of the German offensive effort. The fluidity of the combat situation at first hindered this effort. Despite this confusion, it was relatively easy to discern German strategic intent, just as German intent had become very apparent the year before. Moreover, by July, the German plan captured on 19 June (which contained the outline of actual German strategic aims) became more credible. The truth of the document dawned slowly on the Soviets throughout late June and early July. Shtemenko noted that even after German forces reached the Don River near Voronezh, "Stalin then concentrated his attention on the Voronezh area. Possibly he assumed that, if the German forces broke through there, they would force the Don and begin an encircling movement in the rear of Moscow."[86] Consequently, Stalin dispatched three reserve armies (renamed 60th, 6th, and 63d) to the threatened sector and ordered newly formed 5th Tank Army to conduct a counterstroke. Due to the army's complex makeup (infantry, tank, and cavalry units), inexperienced command leadership, and poor intelligence, 5th Tank Army's July counterattack aborted almost from the start.

Operationally and tactically, the Soviets had difficulty pinning down German intent and dispositions. Despite this, Soviet forces displayed an agility absent in 1941, and most forces parried the German thrusts and were able to withdraw without significant encirclements and losses. Symptomatic of the cloudy intelligence picture was one instance during the early stages of the Soviet withdrawal, which Shtemenko described.

> At the crucial moment of withdrawal [early July], the General Staff stopped receiving reports on the situation from the Southwestern Front. There was nothing for 24 hours. And by this time the enemy was attacking near Rossosh, where our forces were trying to organize the defense along the southern bank of the River Chernaya Kalitva. The General Staff operations officers were at their wits' end and trying to discover whether the enemy had been halted. . . . Naturally, the uncertainty was extremely worrying to those in charge of strategy.[87]

Other Soviet forces, like the hastily assembled 1st and 4th Tank Armies, went into combat on the approaches to Stalingrad with an obviously unclear understanding of where German units were and what they intended to do. In reality, however, the results would probably have been no better had they possessed accurate intelligence data.

In spite of the problems, the failed counterattacks exacted a toll on the advancing Germans, slowed the German advance, and led to the stalemate that would ultimately result in the Stalingrad area. Through judicious use of troop and air *razvedka,* the Soviets finally grasped German intentions. By mid-July

> It became clear that the enemy's main efforts were aimed at piercing the junction between our South-western and Southern Fronts and also out-flanking from the north the densely populated industrial areas of the Donets Basin. . . . Now the concept of the Nazi command had revealed itself to the full.[88]

This impression soon evolved into a firm Soviet belief that the Germans would focus their attention on the Stalingrad area, a view confirmed as operations on the close approaches to Stalingrad unfolded.

> With relative accuracy the Soviet General Staff had foreseen how, where, and why Paulus's army would advance. Analysis of the engagement fought by the German forward detachments [on the distant approaches to Stalingrad] and their subsequent combat operations had shown that the enemy intended to break through to the Volga.[89]

Throughout the period of the German advance toward Stalingrad and the Caucasus, Soviet participants in the operations repeatedly stressed the positive role of air *razvedka* in determining the operational dispositions and direction of advance. This was particularly true during the defensive fighting and Soviet counterattacks of August and September 1942 near Stalingrad and farther north. Although air *razvedka* functioned well, the Soviets experienced continuous and persistent problems with tactical *razvedka.* This inability to detect the precise composition, identification, and tactical disposition of German forces limited the effectiveness of Soviet counterattacks and persisted even into November, when the Soviets launched their major counteroffensive.

Summary

Soviet military strategy in the first eighteen months of war evidenced an unevenness and uncertainty reflecting the nature of the initial period of war, the subsequent course of combat, inexperience within the Soviet High Command, and the role of personality (namely, Stalin) on the workings of the *Stavka*. The latter factor operated throughout to pervert the nature of prewar assessments and shaped military strategy once war had commenced.

The catastrophic course of combat in June and July 1941, produced in part by erroneous prewar assessments, stripped the initiative from Soviet strategic planners. As a result, the newly emergent *Stavka* was limited to reactive planning based on the single imperative of restoring stability to the front. Virtually all strategic decisions throughout the summer and fall reflected that reality. Throughout the period, the single most redeeming factor was the single-minded effort by the *Stavka* to amass strategic reserves and apply them at the point of most acute danger. This process capitalized on the innate strength of the Soviet state—her large population—and exploited the most obvious German weaknesses—a limited supply of manpower and an inability to establish strategic priorities. By playing that strength against German weakness, the Soviets were able to maintain a reasonable correlation of forces and, ultimately, achieve their preeminent strategic aim of conducting a viable strategic defense and halting the German drive, albeit just short of its initial strategic objectives. Exploitation of this strength enabled the Soviets to survive several strategic defeats and compensated for a host of obvious Soviet weaknesses, one of which was poor intelligence. All the while, Soviet military leaders amassed experience, often on the premise that failure educates those who survive.

Throughout this period Stalin dominated. Although he personally unified the Soviet strategic effort, the power of his personality and his threatening demeanor, as illustrated by prewar purges and his actions during the initial period of war, intimidated the General Staff and high-level military leaders. Often operating on the basis of whim and prejudice, his subjective judgments frequently overcame objective reality. His single-minded insistence upon marshaling reserves and his ruthless allocation of those reserves strengthened the Red Army strategy, but his meddling in strategic decision making often produced disaster. At Moscow his strength of will was, in part, reflected by the energy and determination of the counterattacking Red Army. Strategic blunders notwithstanding, the threadbare Red Army of December 1941 fought with a ferocity and desperation mirroring the determination of its leader.

Again in 1942, Stalin's misjudgments, forcibly imposed on the High Command, produced disaster after disaster until, in November 1942, Stalin replicated his performance of December 1941. By fall 1942, however, there was evidence that Stalin was, to a greater degree, listening to the counsel of his, by now, tested and more trusted key military advisors. According to one recent Soviet critic:

> The defeat of the Red Army on the southern wing of the Soviet-German front could not be explained by the peculiarity of conditions, since it served in some measure to justify our defeat in the summer of 1941. The chief reason for the failure of the summer's campaign of 1942 was the mistaken decision of the High Command "to affix" to the strategic defensive operation numerous individual offensive operations on all fronts. This resulted in a dispersal of strength and a premature expenditure of strategic reserves that certainly doomed the Stalin plan to failure.[90]

The critic blamed the disaster directly on Stalin.

Soviet intelligence failures of 1941, which contributed to the numerous Soviet defeats, served the purpose of elevating that subject to the scrutiny of the General Staff. By early 1942 individual *fronts*, and later the General Staff, systematically studied all aspects of *razvedka* and recommended solutions to the problem. Soviet analysis of *razvedka* in 1941 and early 1942 demonstrated what could be achieved in all aspects of air and ground reconnaissance, even in the more technologically sophisticated realms. As a result of this analysis, orders went to all commands to capitalize on these experiences. Meanwhile, the General Staff worked on orders and instructions that specifically addressed *razvedka* issues. One such order, issued on 5 April 1942 and entitled *Instruction on the Reconnoitering of Field Reference Positions,* laid out specific requirements for on-site personal reconnaissance by all commanders and staffs.[91] *Front* and General Staff analysis in the winter and spring of 1942 was designed to provide a sound basis for Red Army performance in the critical operations planned for the spring and summer of 1942. Despite the strategic intelligence failures in the spring of 1942, the Soviet High Command continued to improve its *razvedka* procedures while combat experience contributed to officer education by vividly revealing what was possible and what was necessary.

Combat in 1942 indicated in gross terms the strengths and weaknesses of Red Army *razvedka*. Soviet strategic intelligence was still frail, the victim of the limited range and fragile nature of long-range collection means. Air *razvedka,* although more effective than it had been in 1941, still suffered from German dominance of the skies. Although it could detect heightened German activity and major troop concentrations, it could not identify precise units or keep track of them for more than short periods. Fledgling agent, partisan, and reconnaissance-diversionary *razvedka* became more important in 1942, fueled by the infusion of new Soviet units in the German rear and by the emergence of a partisan network linked to field commands of the Red Army. Supplementing air and agent *razvedka* were early attempts at radio interception organized at *front* level and within the air warning system (VNOS) of air defense forces. All three of these means of strategic *razvedka* were still in their infancy and formed a shaky foundation upon which to base strategic assessments. In the last analysis, Soviet planners were forced to rely on their understanding of the flow of combat and their perceptions of German future intent. This "intangible" system worked poorly at the onset of operations, particularly when the Germans employed active deception in the early summer of 1942. It fared better after offensives had unfolded and after time and distance had taken their toll on German maneuver capabilities.

Operationally, Soviet intelligence slowly improved because of greater stability along major front sectors and the improved quantity, range, and coordination of Soviet *razvedka* means. Often, however, misperceptions overruled objective strategic judgments. Intelligence was best in stable situations, when the Soviets were planning offensives or while German offensive drives were grinding to a halt. Tactically, effective short-range aviation and radio *razvedka*; systematic observation; and more refined search, ambush, and patrol techniques permitted identification of opposing German units, particularly in sectors where these units were on the defensive. It was less effective in fluid periods, when rapidly changing conditions challenged Soviet collection means and overburdened evolving Soviet communications systems and staffs. Active and passive German concealment and deception still confounded Soviet *razvedka,* and Soviet study of the terrain was weak. Soviet units on the move, particularly mobile forces being committed to combat, were unable to gather enough intelligence to react effectively to changing conditions.

Detailed Soviet classified operational critiques underscored these problems.[92] These critiques provided the basis for the *Red Army Field*

Service Regulation of 1942, published late in the year. In an expanded *razvedka* section, the regulation stated

> One of the main duties of headquarters is to organize *razvedka* and compile all that data it provides. The Commander will tell the Chief of Staff what data he requires, when he requires it, and what forces and means may be used to conduct *razvedka*. In the absence of such instructions from the Commander, the Chief of Staff himself must organize *razvedka* at the proper time.[93]

The chief of staff personally supervised the *razvedka* process and ensured that it was coordinated with the efforts and needs of higher headquarters. Thus, *razvedka* was to form a focused continuum throughout the entire chain of command. The regulation insisted that commanders allocate adequate resources to *razvedka,* detailed the purposes and contents of *razvedka* plans, and established strict security requirements for planning.

Razvedka plans were to incorporate air, artillery, and ground *razvedka.* Redundant air *razvedka,* under army or *front* control, was to clarify the ground situation by visual and photographic techniques and verify the findings of ground *razvedka.* Air and artillery *razvedka* were centrally coordinated by *front* and army to ensure unity of effort and analysis. The regulation stressed the importance of capturing and interrogating prisoners to verify intelligence data and provided detailed interrogation instructions. Analysis of agent, deserter, or interrogation reports also provided an important basis for planning subsequent *razvedka.* Information regarding the presence of new enemy units was particularly sensitive. Thus, when

> a new enemy unit appears on the front, the Intelligence Branch organizes a systematic study of its condition. Corps headquarters, and sometimes also divisional headquarters, maintain a "field chart of enemy forces" on which all information on the battle composition of enemy troops is entered. . . .

In addition, intelligence organs at all levels were to prepare working maps and periodic charts about the enemy.[94] To close the gap between intelligence and operations organs:

> All information about the enemy is to be sent immediately by Intelligence to operations; similarly, all such information received from the troops by operations and other branches of headquarters is immediately communi-

cated to Intelligence. A periodic exchange of fresh data between the Chiefs of Operations and Intelligence Branches is necessary to keep both parties well-informed.[95]

Finally, the regulation provided detailed instructions regarding the integration of all types of observation posts into the intelligence collection system to foster closer links between troop units and intelligence. Accordingly, "observation journals" at the tactical level became intelligence documents.

By November 1942, sound principles for intelligence collection, processing, and analysis had emerged; the Soviets had begun organizing a logical system at all command levels for efficient conduct of *razvedka*. Success, however, depended in large part on the efficiency of each collection means, on the reliability of communications, and on the emergence of staff procedures necessary to convert raw data into meaningful estimates that could then be acted upon. During the first two years of war, intelligence collection and processing problems often caused the Soviets to fall short of these goals. What was abundantly clear was that sound intelligence was fundamental to the success of strategic plans. Moreover, intelligence analysis had to prevail over personal whim and preconception if *razvedka* and strategy were to emerge as an effective combat combination.

3 The Second Period of War

Context

In November 1942 the *Stavka*—using several of its reserve armies, one tank army, and the majority of its new tank and mechanized corps—launched a surprise counterattack against overextended German, Rumanian, Hungarian, and Italian forces in the Stalingrad area. The success of the ensuing operation exceeded Soviet expectations. The Soviets encircled German Sixth Army and a major portion of the Fourth Panzer Army at Stalingrad. This first successful Soviet encirclement operation wrested the strategic initiative from German hands. Thereafter, the *Stavka* attempted simultaneously to reduce surrounded German forces at Stalingrad, defeat German relief attempts, and expand the Soviet offensive to encompass the entire southern wing of the Eastern Front and, thereby, destroy German Army Group Don. As had been the case in the winter campaign of 1941 and 1942, Stalin was overoptimistic and tried to achieve too much, too soon, with too little. The Soviet forces reduced the Stalingrad "Cauldron," forced the upper and middle reaches of the Don River, cleared the Caucasus region, and pressed westward through Khar'kov and into the Donets Basin (Donbas). Threadbare Soviet armies, led by weakened tank corps at the end of tenuous supply lines, advanced too far. A brilliant counterstroke delivered by Field Marshal Erich von Manstein's Army Group South struck the overextended Soviet force and drove it back across the Northern Donets River, liberating Khar'kov and forming the inviting yet ominous Soviet salient around Kursk. It was on that salient that the Germans next focused their attention.

Hitler and the German High Command selected the relatively narrow Kursk sector for their next major offensive, an offensive finally launched in July 1943 in an attempt to crush Soviet operational and strategic reserves, restore equilibrium to the Eastern Front and, if possible, restore to Germany the strategic initiative. For the first time in the war, at Kursk the Soviets eschewed a preemptive offensive and instead initially prepared an imposing strategic defense, unparalleled in its size and complexity, in order to crush the advancing Germans. Once the German offense had stalled, Soviet forces planned to go over to the offensive at Kursk and in other sectors. The script played as the Soviets wrote it. The titanic German effort at Kursk failed at huge cost, and a wave of Soviet counteroffensives rippled along the Eastern Front, ultimately driving German forces through Smolensk and Khar'kov back to the line of the Dnepr River. There, in a brilliantly conceived operation during the late fall, Soviet forces suddenly forded the Dnepr River north of Kiev, liberated the city, and created an extensive bridgehead on the right bank of the river. The struggles of mid-1943 marked the beginning of the end for the Germans. Never again would they launch a major offensive. Stripped of a significant portion of their allied forces, increasingly bereft of operational reserves, the Germans could only defend and delay, relying on scorched earth and strained Soviet logistics to impede the Soviet advance and a tenuous defense to further erode Soviet combat capability. Increasingly, the Germans hoped Soviet exhaustion and depleted manpower would produce stalemate or Soviet collapse in the east.

Stalingrad and the Winter Campaign, November 1942–March 1943

After experiencing eighteen months of often unsuccessful combat, in late fall 1942 the Red Army prepared its second strategic counteroffensive designed to wrest again the strategic initiative from the Germans (see map 7). Unlike 1941, in late 1942 the Soviets retained the planning initiative and avoided the hasty, reactive type of planning so prevalent during the Moscow operation. By October 1942 German forces were locked in a bitter and costly struggle for the city of Stalingrad, a struggle that consumed critical German operational reserves. The German decision to conduct simultaneous offensive operations at Stalingrad and deep into the Caucasus region strained German resources to the breaking point and forced the German High Command to deploy extensive but poorly equipped allied forces along the overextended flanks of the main German shock groups. Those long flanks became a focal point of Soviet planning.

As in 1941, in the summer and fall of 1942 the *Stavka* carefully marshaled strategic reserves. It formed ten reserve armies and new tank armies and mechanized corps under *Stavka* control and judiciously used some of these reserves to halt the German drive. Although three of the four new Soviet tank armies created in June 1942 were consumed in defensive fighting on the approaches to Voronezh and Stalingrad, one of the original four remained intact; a new fifth tank army formed to increase Soviet mobile reserves substantially. The High Command also made a concerted effort to capitalize on its war experiences through systematic

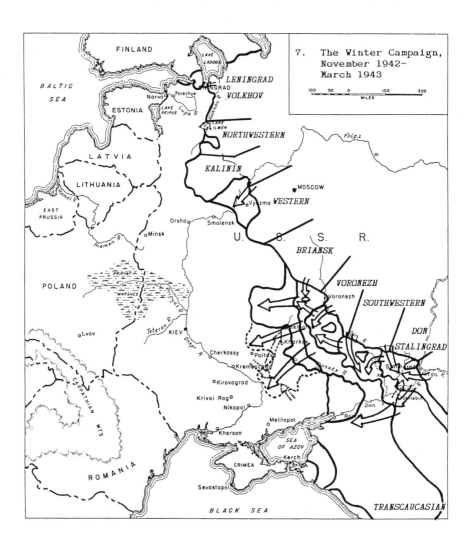

7. The Winter Campaign, November 1942– March 1943

collection and analysis and, on the basis of this analysis, issued orders and directives to correct improper practices in virtually every aspect of military operations.

In early September 1942, the Soviet High Command began planning a major counteroffensive to expel German forces from southern Russia.

> The *Stavka* considered that the German-Fascist command could not rapidly transfer large strategic reserves to the region from Germany and other theaters of war, since there were none and formation of new forces required considerable time. It ruled out the possibility of the transfer of large forces to the south from the western and northwestern directions of the Soviet-German front. That also required too much time. The presence on these directions of large groupings of Soviet forces provoked understandable uneasiness on the part of the enemy, who expected an offensive:[1]

Zhukov provided a strategic rationale for the offensive.

> In our assessment of the enemy we worked on the assumption that Nazi Germany was no longer capable of executing its strategic plan for 1942. The resources it had at its disposal in the autumn of 1942 were not sufficient to achieve its objectives in the North Caucasus or the Don and Volga areas.
>
> The forces the Nazi Command could use in the Caucasus and in the Stalingrad area had been substantially weakened and depleted. The Germans had nothing more of any weight to throw into this theatre and they would undoubtedly be compelled, as after the defeat at Moscow, to take up defensive positions on all sectors.[2]

He went on to describe the Axis weaknesses, which promised to make the Soviet offensive a success.

> We knew that von Paulus' 6th Army and Hoth's 4th Panzer Army, the most efficient fighting units in the Wehrmacht, had been drawn into prolonged and exhausting battles at Stalingrad and could not complete the operation for the capture of the city; they were stuck on the approaches.
>
> On the basis of information from the Fronts the General Staff had studied strong and weak points of the German, Hungarian, Italian and Romanian forces. Compared with the Germans, the troops of the satellites were not so well armed, less experienced and less efficient, even in defence. Above all, their soldiers, and many of their officers, had no desire to die for interests alien to them in far-away Russia, to which they had been sent by Hitler, Mussolini, Antonescu, Horthy and other fascist leaders.

The enemy's position was further complicated by the fact that they had very few operational reserves in the Volga and the Don area—not more than six divisions, and these were scattered over a broad front. They could not be assembled as a strike force at short notice. We were also favoured by the operational configuration of the whole enemy front. Our troops were in an enveloping position and could with comparative ease strike out from their bridgeheads at Serafimovich and Kletskaya.[3]

Vasilevsky echoed Zhukov's view and emphasized the scope and importance of the new strategic effort.

We were now faced with an important decision: to organise and carry out a counter-offensive, moreover one which would not only radically change the situation in this region, but would lead to the crushing of the still actively operating southern flank of the enemy front.[4]

Collectively, the Soviet High Command believed that destruction of German forces in the Stalingrad region would halt the German advance into the Caucasus, win back the economically valuable Don and Kuban regions, and possibly facilitate liberation of the critical Donbas region. A successful counteroffensive could smash the armies of Germany's principal allies and significantly weaken the Axis alliance as well.

The projected Soviet counteroffensive at Stalingrad formed the centerpiece of a broader concept for a winter campaign, "the strategic aim of which was the destruction of forces of the entire southern wing of German-Fascist forces to secure the strategic initiative and create a turning point in the course of war to the Soviet Union's benefit."[5] The Soviets planned first to concentrate large strategic reserves on the Stalingrad Direction and use those reserves to attack, surround, and destroy German Army Group B around Stalingrad proper. Thereafter, Soviet *fronts* adjacent to the Stalingrad region would join the operation and attack from the middle reaches of the Don River and south of Stalingrad toward Rostov, to isolate remnants of Army Group B and cut off and destroy German Army Group A, whose forces stretched deep into the Caucasus region. Simultaneously, the *Stavka* planned a series of limited offensives in the Leningrad region and on the Northwestern and Western Directions. These offensives, conducted before and during the Stalingrad operation, would fix German forces in those regions and prevent reinforcement of German forces around Stalingrad.[6]

Planning for the Stalingrad operation, which started on 13 September while defensive fighting raged at Stalingrad and intensified throughout October and early November, was far more deliberate than that of previous operations. After initial discussions in mid-September, Zhukov, Vasilevsky, and the commander of Red Army artillery, Colonel General N. N. Voronov, inspected forces in the Stalingrad region and, when they returned to Moscow, detailed General Staff planning for the operation commenced. Both Zhukov and Vasilevsky were convinced the projected operation would produce positive results. Zhukov later wrote

> The *Stavka* and General Staff, in the course of combat operations, carefully studied intelligence information about the enemy received from the *front*s and forces, analyzed it, and reached conclusions concerning the nature of operations and his forces. They studied the considerations of staffs, *front* commanders, and types and branches of forces; and, while analyzing this data, made this or that decision. Consequently, the plan of conduct of operations on a strategic scale can arise in full scope only as a result of the lengthy creative efforts of all forces, staffs, and commanders. The basic and decisive role in the all-round planning and securing of a large strategic operation unquestionably belongs to the *Stavka* of the High Command and the General Staff.[7]

Vasilevsky confirmed *Stavka* confidence, writing

> It was well known to the Soviet High Command that, as a result of the heroic defense of our forces in regions between the Don and Volga Rivers, 6th and 4th Panzer Armies had been drawn into long, drawn-out, and, as a rule, futile battle in a narrow sector in the immediate vicinity of the city; and the flanks of that grouping were covered by weaker, over-burdened by war, Rumanian forces. The great extent of the Rumanian forces' defense sector and the lack of reserves behind them aggravated the vulnerability of the enemy defense still more.[8]

The *Stavka* planned to conduct the strategic counteroffensive with the forces of three *front*s and exploit the weakness of Rumanian forces on the German flanks. The *Stavka* created a new *front* (Southwestern) from new and existing forces and assigned it, and the Don and Stalingrad Fronts, the mission of conducting the operation. By October Vasilevsky, appointed as *Stavka* representative to coordinate operational planning, had produced a plan code-named Uranus [Uran]. The plan required the Southwestern, Don, and Stalingrad Fronts to conduct a strategic offensive to encircle and destroy all German forces in the Stalingrad region. Advancing along a 400-kilometer front, they were to penetrate Rumanian defenses on the flanks of the Stalingrad salient, penetrate into the depths, link up, and form inner and outer encirclement lines around the isolated German force. Large armored and mechanized forces were to play a key role in the operation. The Southwestern Front's 5th Tank Army, secretly deployed southward from the area east of Orel', formed the northern Soviet shock force and had the mission of attacking southward out of bridgeheads across the Don River. The 4th Mechanized and 13th Tank Corps of the Stalingrad Front were to attack northwestward from positions south of Stalingrad one day later to link up with 5th Tank Army forces west of Stalingrad and form the inner encirclement. Cavalry forces, advancing on the flanks of the two shock groups, were to form the outer encirclement line. Within days after the mobile forces had linked up, follow-on rifle units would fill in the two encirclement lines and begin the strangulation of German forces.

In every respect, this plan was more mature than earlier ones. Armed with new guidance contained in the 1942 regulations and numerous directives and instructions, Soviet forces were now, for the first time, able to exploit experiences of the first eighteen months of war and correct problems that had plagued earlier operations. That produced a quantum leap in the quality and sophistication of Soviet planning. Two areas where increased sophistication was most evident were in the related areas of deception [*maskirovka*] and intelligence. The Soviets had attempted deception in earlier operations, but with mixed success. At Stalingrad the Soviets sought to employ secret planning and integrated into the strategic plan deception measures to conceal the location and timing of the attack and the scope of offensive preparations.

Within a cloak of Draconian secrecy, the Soviets implemented deception plans to convince the Germans of Soviet intent to launch a major offensive on the Moscow axis while Soviet forces remained on the defensive in the Stalingrad area. While active diversionary measures distracted the Germans, the Soviets secretly assembled large forces to conduct the Stalingrad offensive. *Razvedka* performed the simple yet difficult task of checking the degree to which German forces were fooled by the Soviet deception. In addition, Soviet *razvedka* had the even larger task of determining all it could about the strength and disposition of defending Axis forces.

Early on 19 November 1942, Soviet Southwestern Front forces burst from their bridgeheads along the south bank of the Don River and struck defensive positions of Third Rumanian and Sixth German Armies. By midday Soviet infantry had penetrated Rumanian defenses; the 1st and 26th Tank Corps of 5th Tank Army went into action, smashing the remnants of the Rumanian defenses. The next day, forces of the Stalingrad Front attacked Rumanian forces south of Stalingrad and committed 4th Mechanized Corps in an exploitation. By 23 November the mobile forces of the two Soviet *fronts* had linked up near Kalach west of Stalingrad, entrapping most of German Sixth and part of Fourth Panzer Army in the Stalingrad pocket. Soviet forces immediately attempted to reduce the encircled German force and simultaneously extend the offensive westward with attacks against Italian and Rumanian forces defending along the Don River, while the Stalingrad Front's 51st Army erected a screen along the Aksai River, southwest of Stalingrad, to defend against German efforts to relieve the Stalingrad garrison.

While the Don and Stalingrad Fronts fought to reduce the Stalingrad pocket, the Southwestern Front, reinforced by the Voronezh Front's 6th Army and 2d Guards Army from *Stavka* reserves, planned Operation Saturn against Eighth Italian Army and Rumanian and German forces defending along the Don and Chir rivers. Originally, this operation was designed to thwart German relief attempts toward Stalingrad from the west and, ultimately, penetrate to Rostov to create an even larger encirclement of all German forces in the Don River and Caucasus regions. However, after repeated, futile attempts to crush the Stalingrad pocket, the Soviets realized they had woefully underestimated the size of the encircled force. Consequently, the *Stavka* stripped 2d Guards Army from Southwestern Front control for use at Stalingrad and delayed the commencement of Operation Saturn from 10 to 14 December. The deep objectives of Operation Saturn remained unaltered.

No sooner had planning begun in earnest for Operation Saturn and Operation Ring [*Kol'tso*] (the reduction of the Stalingrad encirclement) than, on 12 December, the Germans commenced a relief effort by LVI Panzer Corps across the Aksai River toward Stalingrad from the southwest. The *Stavka* reacted quickly to this new threat. On 13 December it halted planning for Operation Ring and ordered 2d Guards Army southward to block and ultimately defeat the German relief columns. Simultaneously, it truncated Operation Saturn into Operation Little Saturn. The new operation, scheduled to begin on 16 December, aimed at defeating Eighth Italian Army and German Army Detachment Hollidt.

This frenetic planning produced two operations.[9] The first, Operation

Little Saturn, was conducted by the Southwestern Front and part of the Voronezh Front between 16 and 27 December 1942 along the middle Don River. The operation resulted in the defeat and destruction of Eighth Italian Army and Rumanian and German forces defending along the upper Chir River. By 28 December the Germans had abandoned their relief attempt into Stalingrad from the west and were hastily attempting to erect new defenses. The second operation, the Kotel'nikovo operation, lasted from 12 to 30 December 1942. Initially, from 12 to 23 December, German forces advanced from the Aksai River to within 50 kilometers of encircled Sixth Army. Thereafter, the Stalingrad Front, reinforced with 2d Guards Army, drove German forces westward, frustrating the relief attempt. By 30 December all German hopes of rescuing the beleaguered German garrison had faded. After a long siege, on 2 February 1943, German forces in Stalingrad finally surrendered.

After frustrating German attempts to relieve encircled Sixth Army, the *Stavka* ordered its *front*s in southern Russia to undertake a series of operations and, simultaneously, to destroy the encircled force. Vasilevsky explained the General Staff rationale for these operations:

> While the Don Front was wiping out Paulus' encircled grouping in January and February 1943, several operations were underway on various sectors of the Soviet-German front, all of them were an integral part of the overall plan of the Supreme High Command for developing the strategic initiative which the Red Army had gained. . . . The liberation of our native land from the fascist invaders occurred through a series of overlapping offensive operations. In the south there was the Rostov operation from 1 January to 18 February (liberation of Rostov-on-Don); the Nalchik-Stavropol lasted from 3 January to 4 February (liberation of Stavropol); wiping out the Stalingrad grouping of Germans lasted from 10 January until 2 February; the Krasnodar-Novorossiisk operation lasted from 11 January (it only ended in May with the clearing of the enemy out of almost all the Kuban area). In the centre there was the Ostrogozhsk-Rossosh operation from 13 to 27 January (drive to the west in the region of the Don tributaries the Potudan, Tikhaya Sosna and Chernaya Kalitva); the Voronezh-Kastornaya lasted from 24 January to 17 February (liberation of Voronezh region); the Kharkov operation lasted from 2 to 26 February (driving the enemy out of the Kharkov region). In the north there was the lifting of the Leningrad siege from 12 to 30 January; destruction of the Demyansk fascist bridgehead from 15 February to 1 March. Thus, all these operations on three principal sectors were carried out by Soviet troops with maximum success in the latter half of the winter campaign of 1942–1943.[10]

The *Stavka* applied maximum pressure on the Germans and their allies by conducting a series of successive *front* operations to collapse German defenses on the entire southern wing of the Eastern Front. Initially, these operations were well planned, but as time passed each successive operation became more hasty. The last operations, begun in early February, were literally planned and conducted from the march.

In January the Soviets initiated their offensives. As had been the case in November and December 1942, the Soviets sought first to smash the forces of Germany's allies. Simultaneously, the Soviets conducted Operation Ring to reduce the Stalingrad pocket. German Sixth Army contributed to German efforts in the south by tying down seven Soviet armies of the Don Front. These Soviet armies could have had a telling effect if used to reinforce operations in other sectors of the front.

While operations to reduce Stalingrad proceeded, new Soviet offensives rippled along the front. On 13 January, the Voronezh Front struck at the Hungarian Second Army and the remnants of Italian Eighth Army along the upper Don River. In the ensuing Ostrogozhsk-Rossosh' operation, which lasted until 27 January, the Soviets destroyed Hungarian Second Army and the Italian Alpine Corps and created a major gap south of German Second Army defending in the Voronezh sector. Simultaneously, the Southwestern Front resumed a slow, grinding advance westward. Farther south, the Southern Front pushed toward Rostov while Soviet forces in the northern Caucasus pressured the by now almost isolated German Army Group A. First Panzer Army of Army Group A barely escaped through Rostov to join Army Group Don before the Soviets slammed the door shut on German forces in the northern Caucasus by seizing the city. German Seventeenth Army (of Army Group A) withdrew slowly into fortified positions on the Kuban and Taman peninsulas and around the city of Novorossiisk.

By mid-January, with the Hungarian Second Army destroyed, the *Stavka* planned a new operation to encircle and destroy German Second Army in the Voronezh area. On 24 January, the Briansk Front's 13th Army and three armies of the Voronezh Front began the Voronezh-Kastornoe operation against German Second Army. Within days, Second Army, with many of its units encircled, was forced to withdraw westward. It appeared as if the entire southern wing of German forces on the Eastern Front was about to collapse. In a burst of optimism, the *Stavka* implemented plans to accelerate the offensive and force German forces back to the Dnepr River line and perhaps even beyond. Before the Voronezh-

Kastornoe operation had concluded, the *Stavka* ordered all of its operating *front*s in the south to conduct simultaneous offensive operations to force German Army Group Don to collapse. A collapse would result in destruction of that army group and Army Group A, which still occupied extended though hard-pressed positions in the Caucasus.

While the Soviet Southern Front drove German forces back toward Rostov, the *Stavka* ordered the Voronezh and Southwestern Fronts to strike the junction of German Army Groups B and Don southeast of Khar'kov. The grand design of the *Stavka* echoed the offensive abandon evident in early 1942. The Voronezh Front was to seize Kursk, Belgorod, and Khar'kov and, if possible, push toward the Dnepr River southeast of Kiev. The Southwestern Front was to advance westward toward Izium and then swing south across the Northern Donets River, occupy Zaporozh'e and bridgeheads across the Dnepr, and ultimately reach the Sea of Azov near Melitopol', entrapping Army Group Don and isolating Army Group A in the Kuban area.

This grand design for a new and larger Stalingrad was fueled by *Stavka* optimism that the Germans were nearing collapse, by a misreading of intelligence and German intentions, and by a woeful overestimation of their own force capabilities. The new offensives (later named the Khar'kov and Donbas operations) began in late January, from the march and without extensive planning. Soviet forces swept westward to Kursk and through Khar'kov, across the Northern Donets, and toward the Dnepr River in the rear of Army Group Don. While they advanced, unit strengths eroded because of the skillful German defense and the debilitating effects of time and distance on forces operating at the end of long and tenuous supply lines. The Germans reacted by holding firmly to positions along the shoulders of the penetration at Krasnograd and Slaviansk and by rapidly shifting large forces from the Caucasus through the Rostov "gate" into the Donets Basin to counter the exploiting Soviet forces.

In one of the last major Soviet intelligence failures and the clearest case of self-deception on the Eastern Front, the Soviets permitted optimism and overconfidence to cloud judgment. Soviet intelligence detected large-scale German redeployment of armored forces westward from Rostov toward the Dnepr but steadfastly interpreted those movements as a German withdrawal to new defensive positions along the Dnepr River. Consistently, the *Stavka* and the *front* commands clung to their optimistic view as they spurred their advancing forces on, even as Soviet lower-level commanders began to suspect and fear the worst.

By mid-February the Germans had contained the Soviet advance west of Kursk and short of Poltava, but Soviet forces were nearing the Dnepr River on a broad front north and south of Dnepropetrovsk. By this time Field Marshal von Manstein of Army Group Don had nearly completed orchestrating a regroupment that was about to bring to bear the force of three panzer corps against the flanks of advancing Soviet forces. Soviet army commanders' warnings went unheeded as message after message from the *Stavka* and Southwestern Front headquarters urged their forces on. Soviet intelligence continued to misinterpret the clear evidence of major German troop concentrations south of Khar'kov and in the Donbas. A *Stavka* directive dated 11 February reiterated the Southwestern Front's mission to block a German withdrawal to Dnepropetrovsk and Zaporozh'e and demanded the *front* undertake all measures to press the German Donets group into the Crimea, to close the passages into the Crimea through Perekop and Sivesh, and then to isolate these German forces from remaining German forces in the Ukraine.[11] This directive and others underscored the *Stavka*'s belief that German forces were preparing to withdraw westward across the Dnepr River and that heavy German resistance at Slaviansk was designed to cover that withdrawal.

The advance of the Southwestern Front's armored spearhead (Mobile Group Popov) into the German rear area at Krasnoarmeiskoe reflected mistaken Soviet impressions. Even after Popov had been contained, on 19 February the lead group, 4th Guards Tank Corps, received orders reflecting Soviet misperceptions. The corps commander, General P. P. Poluboiarov, received an order from the Front Military Council that read, "I order the encirclement and destruction of the enemy at Krasnoarmeiskoe. Fully restore the situation. Do not, in any case, permit an enemy withdrawal."[12] The order typified the air of unreality permeating the *Stavka* and *front* headquarters. Within days, counterattacking German forces had decimated Popov's mobile force.

The general offensive by von Manstein's panzer corps, including the recently arrived and powerful II SS Panzer Corps, first smashed the Soviet Southwestern Front and sent it reeling back to the Northern Donets River and then, in late February and March, devoured the overextended Soviet Voronezh Front, which withdrew in confusion from Khar'kov and Belgorod to new positions covering Kursk. Both Soviet *front*s suffered grievous losses in operational failures, which were, in part, the fault of Soviet strategic planners. Shtemenko noted

This plan [the Southwestern Front's], which had arisen on the basis of misinterpretation of the enemy's actions, only appeared to correspond to the actual situation. But at the time the Front, the General Staff and GHQ as well were convinced of the correctness of their assessments and calculations. This was, of course, unforgivable, but it was a fact. The victorious reports that had been coming in from the fronts blunted the vigilance of both GHQ and the General Staff, although I must add, for truth's sake, that we did have doubts and did tell Vatutin about them, and afterwards reported them to the Supreme Commander as well in the presence of Marshal Zhukov. But this report was obviously too late.[13]

Shtemenko attributed the strategic failure to two causes.

In the final stage of the offensive of these two fronts in the winter of 1943 our forces were poorly integrated. There were virtually no powerful spearheads to deliver the main thrusts.

Finally, we were badly let down by Intelligence and made disastrous mistakes in predicting the enemy's intentions.

These were, in my view, the main causes of the failures and unrealised hopes of the winter of 1943. Although I stress again, on the whole the results of the winter campaign were successful. The Soviet Army's offensive strength had grown.[14]

The combination of strategic success from November 1942 to mid-February 1943 and operational defeats in late February and March netted Soviet strategic planners huge gains. As in 1942, however, those gains did not fully match Soviet expectations. Stalin, the *Stavka,* and the Soviet General Staff still had to learn lessons on the art of the possible. They would learn these lessons and apply them in the summer and fall of 1943.

Soviet *razvedka* and associated deception planning contributed in a major way to Soviet success at Stalingrad. Throughout the planning and preparatory period, there was a direct and important relationship between Soviet deception plans and *razvedka.* Deceptive measures would have a salutary effect in themselves, but would be most effective if means existed to validate how well German forces had taken the bait. Strategically, the High Command postured to convince the Germans a Soviet counteroffensive would occur on the Moscow-Smolensk axis. In mid-October, *Stavka* ordered *fronts* in southern Russia to engage in defensive operations only. Simultaneously, in the Moscow region, the Kalinin and Western Fronts prepared for active offensive operations against German Army

Group Center. The *Stavka* hoped the Germans would perceive these actions as a Soviet intent to renew the offensive, suspended in April 1942. German intelligence organs picked up the activity and decided that Soviet attacks were likely near Moscow.

More important, Soviet intelligence collection in the Moscow sector detected (and even overestimated) German force concentrations in that region. This led Soviet intelligence to conclude that no major southward transfers of German forces were occurring. The Soviets were equally concerned over possible German force redeployments from deep within the Caucasus or from the west. The former was clearly unlikely in light of German activity in the region. The latter could occur, but probably only after German intelligence had detected the presence of a major threat in the Stalingrad region. To confirm these judgments, throughout October and November, the Soviets employed their few long-range *razvedka* assets (principally airborne) to reconnoiter main rail and highway lines running into southern Russia. They detected no major troop movements because there were none.

Operationally and tactically, the Soviets sought to mask the major force buildup northwest and south of Stalingrad and conceal the secret movement of new shock forces (principally 5th Tank Army) into the Stalingrad region. Most deception measures were passive, since Soviet forces deliberately demonstrated a defensive posture except in the area immediately northwest of Stalingrad, where Soviet counterattacks had occurred in the recent past. Soviet intelligence had to verify the effect of operational and tactical deception and to ensure that the Germans had not detected Soviet plans and shifted large forces into the threatened sectors. Short-range air and long-range ground *razvedka* could only marginally detect movements of major enemy forces at operational depths. This problem was eased by the fact that the Germans and their allies had few operational reserves. It was even more difficult for the Soviets to detect last-minute, short-distance moves by those few German divisions available as tactical reserves, such as the 14th and 22d Panzer Divisions. The course of the offensive vividly underscored this Soviet weakness.

Soviet *razvedka* was best able to validate the results of tactical deception. The variety of means available to the Soviets for ground and air reconnaissance made it difficult for the Germans or Germany's allies to reinforce significantly tactical defenses without detection—certainly to a depth of up to 20 kilometers. The supreme test for Soviet intelligence would occur after the operations had commenced; by that time, however, the deception would have already succeeded or failed.

Soviet assessments regarding the effectiveness of intelligence operations prior to the Stalingrad offensive range from overly optimistic to starkly realistic, depending on who wrote them, in what circumstances, and when they were written. Postwar open source studies, memoirs, and articles vary in their degree of candor but generally reflect Soviet satisfaction regarding how well *razvedka* operated. Soviet classified critiques of the day also emphasized general success, but, in the spirit of self-criticism and a desire to improve procedures, they also catalogued failures that required remedying.

The memoir literature speaks with virtually one voice. *Stavka* representative Zhukov wrote

> We had learned from POW interrogations that the overall combat standard of Rumanian forces was not high. In these sectors we would enjoy considerable numerical superiority provided the Nazi Command did not regroup reserves by our offensive zero hour. Thus far, our intelligence had not discovered any signs of regrouping. Paulus' 6th Army and part of 4th Panzer Army were tied up at Stalingrad by troops of the Stalingrad and Don Fronts.
>
> Our forces were massing in the designated areas according to plan. As far as we could judge, the enemy was ignorant of our regrouping. We had taken steps to envelop all movement of troops and material with the utmost secrecy.[15]

Vasilevsky reached the same conclusion.

> In brief, our conclusions consisted in the following: The German troop grouping would basically remain as before; the main forces of the 6th and 4th Panzer Armies would continue to be involved in protracted fighting in the area of the city. The Rumanian units would remain on the flanks of these forces (that is, in the areas of our major attacks). We had not observed any more or less substantial reserves being brought up to the Stalingrad area from the interior. And we had not noted any essential regroupings taking place in the enemy troops operating there. On the whole, the strength of both sides at Stalingrad, as far as we could judge, was roughly equal at the beginning of the offensive. We would manage to assemble powerful shock groups at the points of the impending attacks of our *fronts* by calling in the GHQ reserves and taking off troops from secondary battle sectors;

this gave us a superiority in men and equipment that would enable us to count on invariable success.[16]

Stavka representative and artillery commander Voronov asked himself the rhetorical question "Did the Hitlerite Command know anything about the preparations for our offensive?" He then answered his own question, stating

> According to all information of our ground and air *razvedka*, the enemy suspected nothing. We followed the enemy with all our eyes. Observation went on around the clock. Sound *razvedka*, which detected enemy artillery and mortar batteries, worked uninterruptedly. From the skies, we systematically photographed enemy positions, especially those regions where we intended to penetrate his defenses. Generals and artillerymen wore out the seats of their pants behind stereoscopes at observation points for hours.[17]

Army commanders echoed these conclusions. General I. M. Chistiakov, 21st Army commander, wrote

> Our *razvedka* worked very actively. It established that, in the army offensive sector, units of 4th and 5th Rumanian Corps defended. The enemy defense had two belts to a depth of 15–20 kilometers. Both in the forward area and in the depth, it consisted of a system of strong points and centers of resistance, located on dominant heights. Everywhere the enemy had erected barbed-wire entanglements and established mine fields.
> Running ahead, I will tell of such an episode. At Golovski Farm we crushed a Rumanian division. The captured commander of this division was brought to me. During the interrogation I showed him our intelligence map. The Rumanian division commander gazed at it for a long time and finally, with amazement, said, "The Soviet map reflects the positions of our forces more exactly than the operational map of my staff."[18]

General P. I. Batov, 65th Army commander, when describing his intelligence efforts, noted some last-minute changes in German dispositions. Reconnaissance in force by his 304th and 24th Rifle Divisions on 10 and 12 November netted thirty-one prisoners from the Rumanian 1st Cavalry Division and thirty German prisoners. Batov suspected that German units were moving. Subsequent reconnaissances from 14 to 16 November confirmed that elements of 14th Panzer Division were, in fact, redeploying into his sector.[19]

Soviet operational studies and unit histories also insist that Soviet *razvedka* provided sufficient intelligence information for sound planning and successful conduct of the operation. Although, in general, events bore this out, the fact was that this was the first major offensive in which the Soviets employed a coordinated intelligence collection effort. Many of the component parts of that system were incomplete, and personnel involved in operating each part were still inexperienced in preparing for large-scale offensive operations. Classified Soviet critiques of all aspects of *razvedka,* compiled shortly after the operation, provided an accurate appreciation of how well the intelligence system functioned.[20] In general, though they supported the favorable postwar views of the participants, the critiques also highlighted many problems that had to be solved in the future.

During the course of these operations, Soviet intelligence organs were severely tested. It was one thing to prepare for an offensive over an extended period while the front was relatively static. It was an altogether different matter to conduct intelligence work while the situation was in a state of flux. Between 19 November and 30 December, Soviet intelligence forces had to support simultaneously the conduct of the Stalingrad operation, prepare for the Middle Don and Kotel'nikovo operations, and then support the conduct of each of these operations. Soviet intelligence organizations employed the same basic techniques they had used in preparing for the Stalingrad operation. Whenever possible, they altered their procedures to correct deficiencies apparent in earlier phases, but these corrections were limited by the paucity of available time and the rapidly changing situation. Within time constraints the Southwestern and Stalingrad Fronts planned for the Middle Don and Kotel'nikovo operations in much the same fashion as they had planned the Stalingrad operation. For the latter this was very difficult, for it had just passed responsibility for reducing the Stalingrad pocket to Don Front control.

*Front*s employed their longer-range air and radio assets to conduct operational *razvedka* by monitoring movement of German operational and tactical reserves. They were assisted in this effort by the general Soviet presumption that the Germans would attempt relief missions and by geography, which dictated the regions those attempts would have to emanate from. The adjacent Voronezh and North Caucasus Fronts assisted this effort by using their long-range aviation assets. *Front*s employed shorter-range troop, artillery, engineer, and combat *razvedka* assets to prepare for and conduct operations in their respective sectors. Soviet commanders and staffs also confronted the new challenge of conducting *razvedka* on the march, particularly in support of deep-operating mobile forces. Here again, the primary Soviet concern was the location and movement of German reserve units—in particular, panzer corps and divisions that could disrupt Soviet offensive efforts.

Soviet *razvedka* in the Stalingrad operation was a marked improvement over that of earlier operations. If the goal of intelligence is to provide an accurate enough picture of the enemy to achieve victory, then Soviet *razvedka* must be judged to have been adequate. Certainly, the Germans contributed to their own precarious situation and eased the task of Soviet intelligence. By choosing to operate both in the deep Caucasus and in the Stalingrad region, the Germans so strained their manpower and material resources that, to defend their extended flanks, they were forced to rely on poorly trained and under-equipped Axis allies. This was an invitation for Soviet attack. Because of their overextension, the Germans lacked operational reserves and could create them only by thinning out some other sector of the front, with all the incurrent risks. This situation partially solved the most serious Soviet *razvedka* problem of attempting to conduct long-range surveillance of the deep German operational rear with inadequate air, agent, and radio assets. The Germans themselves created propitious circumstances for their defeat, circumstances that also eased the task of Soviet *razvedka*.

A number of positive conditions besides poor German strategy assisted Soviet intelligence efforts in the autumn. After eighteen months of war, the Soviet command cadre had developed a keen appreciation for the value of *razvedka* and the effects of intelligence failures. All were familiar with what had happened at Khar'kov in May 1942, and all realized this could not be permitted to happen again—they could no longer trade away another 1,000 kilometers in order to restore a stable front. At Stalingrad, Soviet commanders and staffs understood what had to be done and, to an increasing extent, how to do it. Equipped with new and thorough regulations based on analysis of vast war experience, they had only to implement the regulations' provisions. Events proved that this was no mean task. At Stalingrad, the Red Army contained the nucleus of an articulated force structure necessary to carry out required *razvedka* tasks. The course of operations demonstrated that additional personnel training at all levels, and more equipment, was required to achieve full combat expectations. That, quite naturally, would also take time.

Equally important was the fact that the *Stavka*, General Staff, and *front*s had the time necessary to plan the operation thoroughly, a luxury they had not enjoyed a year before at Moscow. The one-month preparatory period permitted a studied Soviet approach to the problem of mounting a strategic offensive, and Soviet performance vividly demonstrated the value of that planning time. The planning process itself was the subject of study and analysis after the operation, a process that, in time, produced even greater dividends as the Soviets overcame problems evident in the Stalingrad operation. It was no coincidence that the Soviet system for analyzing war experiences emerged in the context of the Stalingrad operation.

Soviet *razvedka* performance was uneven but markedly better than that of the previous year. Strategic *razvedka* was still weak, due in part to the fragility of strategic collection systems and in part to lingering misperceptions on the part of the General Staff and *Stavka*—misperceptions that tinged strategic estimates. The High Command, *front*s, and armies had a crude air *razvedka* system and force structure, but a combination of factors (including German air superiority, equipment shortages, and communications problems) inhibited system performance. Air *razvedka* was only partially effective. It detected many important German troop movements and concentrations in the deep German rear before and throughout the operation, but it could neither determine with any certainty unit identification nor precisely detect the direction of movement or ultimate destination of these units. Fortunately for the Soviets, there were few German reserves to detect.

A Soviet agent and reconnaissance-diversionary structure functioned during the Stalingrad operation but seems to have had only marginal effect on the operation's outcome. Moreover, no substantial partisan organization existed in southern Russia to emulate contributions of the partisans during the winter campaign of 1941 and 1942 or to anticipate the extensive partisan warfare that would rage throughout central and northern Russia in 1943 and 1944. A few specialized radio *razvedka* units attempted radio intercepts in late 1942. These, as well as regular communications units in the force structure, were able to log the identity of enemy units. However, the range of these Soviet units was limited to the tactical and shallow operational depths.

At operational depths, Soviet intelligence relied on a combination of air, agent, reconnaissance-diversionary, radio, and long-range troop *razvedka*. Although each means was subject to severe limitations, used in combination they were able to "sense" and sometimes clearly detect changes in German dispositions and major troop movements. This was evident in all three operations. However, *razvedka* information was not exact enough to tell *precisely* where these units were moving. Consequently, the Stalingrad Front located German 22d Panzer Division by engaging it. Later, the Southwestern Front, having detected reserves moving to Rossosh' and Kantemirovka, met and identified those reserves (German 385th Infantry and 27th Panzer Divisions) in combat south of the Don. Later in the same operation, 24th Tank Corps fell victim to German reserves (11th and 6th Panzer Divisions) at Tatsinskaia after Soviet air intelligence reports had earlier detected general German troop movements west of Tormosin. In short, collection systems were incomplete and thus imprecise. At Stalingrad this impeded but did not halt or abort operations. More refined systems were essential in the future lest the reverse be the case.

In comparison with its earlier performance, Soviet tactical *razvedka* made striking progress at Stalingrad. This happened in part because the General Staff and higher commands knew it was absolutely necessary to solve the problem of penetrating enemy defenses and so paid tremendous attention to the problem and in part because Soviet commanders now had the ability and the will to effect positive changes. Consequently, despite equipment problems, artillery *razvedka* worked particularly well in the attack of 19 and 20 November. That the Soviets achieved 30 percent of total targets identified is impressive when one realizes most of these were in penetration sectors. Difficulties encountered along the middle Don resulted not from lack of proper procedure or target identification but rather from fog and bad weather, which curtailed planned observed fire. Engineer *razvedka* was effective and also proved its worth, particularly in the November operation.

The tactical-scale reconnaissance in force preceding offensive operations also proved effective. It upset the stability of Axis defenses, clarified enemy firing and defensive systems, and improved jumping-off positions for main attacks. On several occasions they also induced complacency on the part of enemy units, which felt they had successfully repelled an offensive and gained a respite for further combat. In time, however, the Soviets realized reconnaissance in force could become an attack indicator in its own right. They also learned that reconnaissance in force conducted unevenly across the front too many days prior to an offensive could defeat its own purpose if the enemy shuffled forces prior to the attack. This was part and parcel of a learning process that prompted further Soviet improvements of these techniques.

Soviet *razvedka* was most effective during preparatory periods prior to major offensives. It was markedly less effective once operations had begun and during fluid combat. The Soviets also had difficulty in organizing *razvedka* while planning operations on the march. This recurring problem would have deadly consequences later in the winter during operations around Khar'kov and in the Donbas. In short, Soviet employment of *razvedka* at Stalingrad was a successful, if modest, beginning. Experiences at Stalingrad, both positive and negative, provided Soviet commanders and staffs with a blueprint for future improvements. The challenge to the Soviets was to act on that blueprint so that they could continue to achieve success in the future.

During the second stage of the winter campaign, beginning about 1 January while intelligence collection remained fairly efficient, analysis of that data again weakened. In essence, the old malaise of 1941 and early 1942 resurfaced: a tendency for Stalin and higher commands to permit subjective perception and even wishful thinking to override objective analysis. Initial operations incorporated detailed *razvedka* and deception plans. Later, as increasingly overtaxed and exhausted Soviet units sought to deliver that last blow required to produce German collapse, operations were characterized by adequate intelligence collection but poor interpretation of data and lax implementation of deception.

Although the Soviets had displayed considerable skill at tactical and operational *razvedka* during and after the Stalingrad offensive and had standardized *razvedka* procedures to a considerable extent, the efficacy of those measures depended to a large degree on thorough planning. Thoroughness was a direct product of available time. Thus, where planning time was short or nonexistent, although *razvedka* collection was adequate, the processing of the data tended to be sloppy and the information was often misinterpreted. This became apparent in the frantic Soviet drive across southern Russia in late January and February 1943. Although Soviet units individually conducted *razvedka,* it is doubtful Soviet *front* and armies planned *razvedka* operations on the scale of those used at Stalingrad. The principal sources of intelligence in both operations were airborne means and agents, which apparently kept track of German troop movements in the operational depths while troops in contact and ground *razvedka* determined German tactical dispositions.

The mood of optimism within the *Stavka* and General Staff persisted from the beginning of the operation and was based upon hard intelligence and the collective impression on the part of the Soviets of the immense damage done to the forces of Germany and her allies since 19 November. German Sixth, Italian Eighth, and Hungarian Second Armies had been erased from the German order of battle in the East. Fourth Panzer Army and Second Army had been badly chewed up, and the remainder of German forces had suffered grievous losses. Surely, the Soviets reasoned, the trickle of reinforcements from the West could not compensate for these losses.

In a sense, attitudes and actions of the Soviet High Command in the winter of 1942 and 1943 were a repeat, on a grander scale, of similar *Stavka* behavior prevalent during the winter of 1941 and 1942, when the *Stavka* misread intelligence indicators and assigned unrealistic missions to overextended armies. That rashness and inability even to consider the necessity for restraint surfaced again in February 1943. As Soviet forces advanced, the *Stavka* reverted to traditional offensive form and continually ignored the warnings of commanders who sensed impending disaster. *Stavka* optimism also colored Soviet assessments of intelligence, which was collected in adequate quantities, but which was misinterpreted, since the High Command and the *fronts* placed their own rosy interpretation on German intentions. Information received from western sources, although sketchy, tended to reinforce Soviet impressions.

Both the Southwestern and Voronezh Front commanders believed they were witnessing, on all sides, the withdrawal of German forces toward the Dnepr River and safety. The Southwestern Front staff, in particular, erroneously assessed the large German regrouping, which it detected as the beginning of a German withdrawal. *Front* headquarters used that assessment to continue to rationalize the pursuit. Lieutenant General S. P. Ivanov, *front* chief of staff, and Major General A. S. Rogov, *front* chief of reconnaissance, signed an intelligence estimate that noted the concentration of large German armored units in the Krasnograd and Krasnoarmeiskoe region after 17 February, but they judged that these concentrations were designed "to strike a blow to liquidate a penetration of Soviet forces and to free communications for a withdrawal of forces in the Donbas territories across the Dnepr."[21] No partisan or agent reports contradicted this impression. The estimate concluded that "all information affirms that the enemy will leave the territory of the Don basin and withdraw his forces beyond the Dnepr." Vatutin, Southwestern Front commander, underscored that judgment by stating, "Without a doubt the enemy is hurrying to withdraw his forces from the Donbas [to] across the Dnepr."[22] He was so convinced of this German intent that he ignored repeated warnings from his army commanders that troop fatigue, equipment shortages, and growing enemy strength made it impossible to conduct simultaneous offensives in all sectors of the front. Instead, he insisted on pressing to fulfill his mission of encircling and destroying the entire German Donbas group before the beginning of the spring thaw.

On the eve of the German counteroffensive (the afternoon and evening of 19 February and the morning of 20 February), Soviet air reconnaissance observed large German tank concentrations near Krasnograd, noted the forward movement of equipment from Dnepropetrovsk, and detected the regrouping of tank forces from the east between Pokrovskoe and Stalino toward Krasnoarmeiskoe.[23] Nevertheless, in an estimate dated 20 February at 1600, the Southwestern Front chief of staff assessed the movements of German XXXXVIII Panzer Corps as a withdrawal from the Donbas to Zaporozh'e. Based on that conclusion, Vatutin ordered his forces to continue their advance and demanded that the *front* mobile groups "fulfill their assigned mission at any cost."[24] According to 17th Air Army's official history, "Air *razvedka* carried out continuous observation of the withdrawal and regrouping of enemy forces and foresaw in timely fashion the approach and concentration of fresh enemy tank forces and infantry."[25] However, the higher commands consistently continued to misjudge German intentions regarding these regrouped forces.

Southwestern Front's optimism affected the attitude and actions of the Voronezh Front as well. A steady stream of information sent from the Southwestern to the Voronezh Front confirmed German intentions to withdraw and encouraged the Voronezh Front to speed up its offensive. German SS Panzer Corps' abandonment of Khar'kov on 16 February and its withdrawal to Krasnograd simply reinforced that view. Golikov, the Voronezh Front commander, later admitted his error, stating, "It is necessary to recognize that at this stage I had an incorrect evaluation of the intent and capabilities of the enemy."[26]

As it had done earlier in the war, the *Stavka* and General Staff reinforced the *front* commanders' optimism and compounded their mistakes. On 21 February, Lieutenant General A. N. Bogoliubov, deputy chief of the Operations Section of the General Staff, said, "We have exact data that the enemy in the evening is withdrawing in dense columns from the Donbas," when, in fact, those dense columns were about to participate in a violent counterattack.[27] These miscalculations by *Stavka* and *front* persisted well after the Germans had commenced their counteroffensive, and the misperceptions hindered Soviet ability to deal with the attacks. Only on 23 February, days after the devastating German counterstroke had begun, did the air of unreality enveloping the *Stavka* and Southwestern Front headquarters evaporate. By then it was too late, for Soviet forces were reeling back to the Northern Donets River after suffering heavy losses. Subsequently, in early March, Manstein mauled the Voronezh Front and seized Khar'kov and Belgorod before Soviet reinforcements and the spring thaw brought operations to a halt.

The events of February and March had a sobering effect on the Soviet High Command. Once and for all, it ended the Soviet tendency to launch strategic offensives designed to succeed at all costs. Henceforth, the Soviets would interpret intelligence data more cautiously and resist the natural impulse to let preconceptions rule over objective data. Also, they took a more jaundiced and prudent view of information provided by western or "special" sources. A period of sober reflection on the part of the Soviets began, which endured to July 1943. That period was probably the most productive in the entire war for the Soviets in terms of force reorganization and analysis and inculcation of war experience into Red Army combat theory and practice. In the late spring and early summer of 1943, the Soviets created the basic force structure that would endure until war's end and drafted the directives and regulations that incorporated lessons learned at Stalingrad and during the winter. Soviet combat performance at Kursk and thereafter attested to the effectiveness of Soviet study and analysis. In the realm of *razvedka* and deception, the legacy of that analysis soon became clear.

The Summer-Fall Campaign, July–December 1943

In March 1943, after three months of almost constant combat, an operational lull began on the Eastern Front, during which German planners pondered ways to regain the strategic initiative by capitalizing on their March victories (see map 8). Ultimately, they focused their attention on the Kursk Bulge, which, if defended, seemed to offer German forces an opportunity to bleed the Red Army white, without having to engage in arduous operations over long distances. Hitler's operational orders Number 5 and Number 6 of 13 March and 15 April 1943 provided the planning guidance for Operation Citadel, which the Germans would launch against Soviet forces in the Kursk Bulge.[28] Hitler initially chose 3 May as the attack date, but almost immediately problems of force preparation produced delay after delay. Finally, despite the growing apprehension of many German commanders, Hitler designated 5 July as the final attack date. The Germans amassed around Kursk the most impressive armored armada yet assembled for a single attack. Considering the fact that, up to July 1943, no German strategic offensive had ever failed to achieve immediate tactical and operational success, the Soviet High Command had real cause for concern.

Stavka planners also debated military strategy for the summer of 1943. Stalin wished to resume the offensive to preempt German actions, while

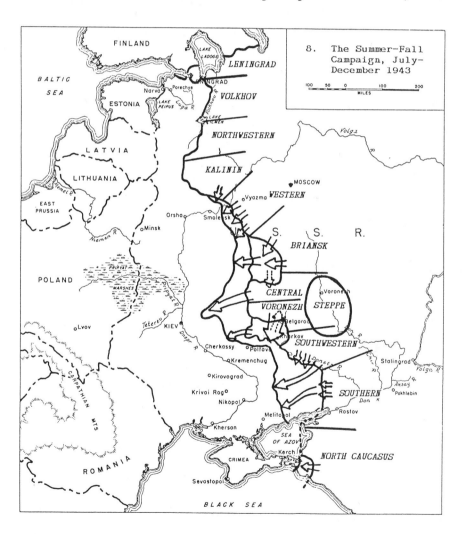

8. The Summer–Fall Campaign, July–December 1943

Zhukov, Vasilevsky, and the General Staff urged the Red Army to assume a defensive posture initially, while the Germans expended their offensive strength. Then, they argued, Soviet forces could launch a strategic offensive with a reasonable chance of success. On 8 April Zhukov wrote to Stalin:

> I consider it inexpedient for our troops to launch a pre-emptive offensive in the near future. It would be better for us to wear down the enemy on our defenses, knock out his tanks, bring in fresh reserves, and finish off his main grouping with a general offensive.[29]

On 12 April in Moscow, Zhukov, Vasilevsky, and the chief of the General Staff's Operations Department, Antonov, armed with messages of support from *front* commanders, convinced Stalin of the necessity for an initial defensive phase of the summer strategic offensive. Shtemenko, first deputy of the Operations Department, wrote

> Ultimately it was decided to concentrate our main forces in the Kursk area, to bleed the enemy forces here in a defensive operation, and then switch to the offensive and achieve their complete destruction. To provide against eventualities, it was considered necessary to build deep and secure defenses along the whole strategic front, making them particularly powerful in the Kursk sector.[30]

The resulting strategic plan required the Voronezh and Central Fronts to defend the Kursk Bulge, flanked on the north by the Briansk Front and on the south by the Southwestern Front. In the rear, the *Stavka* formed a large strategic reserve, the Steppe Military District, which would ultimately become the Steppe Front. Since throughout April Soviet planners were uncertain where the main German thrust would occur, they ordered all five *fronts* to erect strong defenses. Initially, Steppe Military District forces formed around the nucleus of 5th Guards Tank Army east of Khar'kov, in positions from which they could deploy to meet any German thrust. By mid-May, a clearer intelligence picture permitted the *Stavka* to focus planning on the Kursk sector. As reported by Zhukov:

> The final decision concerning the deliberate defense was accepted by the *Stavka* at the end of May and beginning of June 1943 when it became known, in fact in all its details, about the German intention to strike the Voronezh and Central Fronts a strong blow by the use of large tank groups and new "Tiger" tanks and "Ferdinand" assault guns.[31]

The *Stavka* assigned initial defensive missions to all *fronts* but, at the same time, ordered them to prepare two major offensives, the first to begin during the German attack and the second to follow shortly after the German offensive had ended. The *Stavka* ordered extensive *razvedka* measures to determine German intentions and dispositions, and it also ordered strict deception measures to conceal the assembly and redeployment of the strategic reserve—the Steppe Military District. During the defensive phase of the operation, the Soviets ordered *fronts* in other sectors to undertake diversionary attacks timed to draw German operational reserves away from the point where the Soviet counterstrokes would occur. The Soviets also planned preemptive air and artillery counterpreparations to disrupt the final stage of German deployment. Thus, for the first time in the war, the *Stavka* formulated a general strategic plan incorporating extensive *razvedka* and deception measures to assist the initial defense and to conceal preparations for subsequent offensive operations.

Specific *front* missions reflected the strategic plan. The Voronezh and Central Fronts erected substantial defenses within the Kursk Bulge and, while concealing as many of their forces and preparations as possible, prepared to meet and defeat potential German assaults on Kursk from the north and south. Other *fronts* on the flanks defended along other critical axes and prepared counterstrokes as well. The Steppe Military District deployed at sufficient depth to cover all strategic axes. And, if the attack materialized around Kursk, it prepared to displace northward secretly, to occupy assembly areas east of Kursk, back up the two forward *fronts*, repulse German penetrations, and launch a major counterstroke on the Belgorod-Khar'kov axis after the defensive phase at Kursk had ended. The Briansk Front and left wing of the Western Front postured to support the Central Front's defense and to prepare a major offensive against German forces at Orel'. The offensive was to begin as soon as the Central Front had halted the German advance. The Southwestern and Southern Fronts prepared diversionary attacks in the Donbas and along the Mius River. Zhukov described the purpose of the attacks: "In order to tie down enemy forces and forestall maneuver of his reserves, individual offensive operations were envisioned on a number of directions in the south of the country, and also on the northwestern direction."[32]

Thus, Soviet strategic planning called for an initial deliberate defense, followed by a massive counteroffensive, extensive use of *razvedka,* and implementation of a comprehensive strategic deception plan.[33] While initial defensive operations unfolded, large troop concentrations would secretly assemble and launch a massive counterstroke against German forces at Orel', to support the Kursk defenders. Within days after the Soviets had halted the German advance, a second secret force regroupment would take place, followed by a second massive Soviet counterstroke toward Belgorod and Khar'kov. During the interval between the first and second counterstrokes, the Southern and Southwestern Fronts would conduct diversionary offensives across the Northern Donets and Mius rivers into the Donbas. Preparations for these diversions would occur during the German offensive phase, and it was intended that the Germans detect those offensive preparations (which they did). Success in all aspects of the strategic plan depended, in part, on the accuracy of Soviet intelligence.

The German offensive began on 5 July, and the *Stavka* patiently waited until German offensive intentions were vividly clear. Only then did it dispatch orders to its reserve armies to concentrate at the decisive point and halt the German drive, which by then had suffered greatly in its attempt to hack its way through deep Soviet tactical defenses. On 6 July, Commander of the Steppe Military District Colonel General I. S. Konev ordered 5th Guards Tank Army forward to support the Voronezh Front. The next day the tank army began a two-day 250-kilometer forced march northward. On 9 July the tank army received new orders, which propelled it to its fateful meeting with II SS Panzer Corps at Prokhorovka. That night Konev received orders redesignating the Steppe Military District forces as the Steppe Front. The orders read

2. Include in the Steppe Front 27th Army with 4th Guards Tank Corps, 53d Army with 1st Mechanized Corps, 47th Army with 3d Guards Mechanized Corps, 4th Guards Army with 3d Guards Tank Corps, 52d Army with 3d, 5th, and 7th Guards Cavalry Corps, 5th Air Army and all reinforcing units, rear service units and institutions of the Steppe Military District.
3. Armies of the front will deploy in accordance with verbal orders given by the General Staff.
4. Movement of forces will be carried out only at night.
5. Command post of the Steppe Front from 12 July will be in the Gorianovo region.

STAVKA of the High Command

J. Stalin

Antonov[34]

Within a week other strategic reserve armies (3d Guards Tank, 4th Tank, 11th) moved forward toward the Orel'-Kursk sector. While multiple

Soviet armies reinforced the Kursk salient, others initiated counteroffensive action at Orel'.

By 12 July the German offensive had exhausted itself and ground to a halt. Thereafter, the Soviet counteroffensive developed according to plan. The first counterstroke began on 12 July against German Army Group Center northwest of Orel' and expanded on 13 July as the Soviet Central Front went into action south of Orel'. On 17 July the Southern and Southwestern Fronts commenced major diversionary assaults across the Mius and Northern Donets rivers against Army Group South. Finally, on 3 August, the Voronezh and Steppe Fronts, after a major regrouping, assaulted Army Group South's position around Belgorod, to which German forces had withdrawn after their defeat at Kursk.

By mid-August, the series of thrusts and counterthrusts that constituted the offensive phase of the Soviet Kursk operation expanded into a major strategic effort focused on the Southwestern Direction but involving the entire Red Army. Vasilevsky explained the strategic intent:

> The Soviet Supreme High Command put into effect the strategic plan that had been drawn up earlier and adopted for the summer and autumn campaign of 1943, taking advantage of the favourable situation resulting from Kursk. It now decided swiftly to widen the front of the offensive by Soviet troops in the South-Western direction. Tasks were set the Central, Voronezh, Steppe, South-Western and Southern Fronts of routing the main forces of the enemy at one of the central sectors and on the entire southern flank of the Soviet-German front, liberating the Donbas, the left bank of the Ukraine and the Crimea, breaking through to the Dnieper and seizing a bridgehead on its right bank. It was envisaged that the Central, Voronezh and Steppe Fronts would advance to the middle reaches of the Dnieper, while the South-Western and the Southern Fronts would gain the lower reaches. At the same time, an operation was planned to the north and south; it was planned to use the main forces of the Western and the left flank of the Kalinin Fronts to defeat the 3rd Panzer and the 4th Field Armies of the German "Centre" group, to get as far as Dukhovshchina, Smolensk and Roslavl so as to shift the front farther away from Moscow, to enable us to liberate Byelorussia and deprive the fascists of any chance to transfer forces to the south, where the main objective of the campaign was being decided. The North Caucasus Front in cooperation with the Black Sea Fleet and the Azov Flotilla were to wipe out the enemy from the Taman peninsula and seize a bridgehead at Kerch. Thus, the GHQ planned to launch a general offensive on a front from Velikie Luki to the Black Sea.[35]

The extent of the plan was evidenced by the tremendous scale and complexity of its component operations.

This ambitious plan, far-reaching in design and in the number of forces taking part in it, was to be put into effect during the following operations: Smolensk from 7 August to 2 October (with the capture of Smolensk and Roslavl, the beginning of the liberation of Byelorussia); the Donbas between 13 August and 22 September (liberation of the Donbas); operation for liberating the Dnieper's left bank in the Ukraine—between 25 August and 30 September (breaking through to the Dnieper); Chernigov-Pripyat— between 3 August and 1 October (liberation of Chernigov region); Bryansk—between 1 September and 30 October (advance from the Central Russian Uplands to the Desna basin); Novorossiisk-Taman—between 10 September and 9 October (complete liberation of the Caucasus); Melitopol—between 26 September and 5 November (arrival at the Crimean isthmus); Kerch landing (seizing a bridgehead in the Eastern Crimea).[36]

At Stalin's insistence, the Fall phase of the offensive was to consist of numerous direct blows delivered across a broad front. (Zhukov argued for conduct of envelopments in more limited but critical sectors of the front, such as the Donbas.)[37] No two blows were to be simultaneous. Instead the timing was staggered to support the main thrust toward Kiev. Vasilevsky described the reason for the time phasing:

> As we see, not one of these operations was to begin or end at the same time. They were to overlap one another in time, being consecutive only in a very general sense. This would force the enemy to split up his reserves, bringing them from one sector to another, trying to block the enormous breaches being made in his front by Soviet troops first in one place and then another.[38]

To control the massive Soviet offensive, the *Stavka* assigned representatives to groups of *fronts* operating on each major strategic direction. Zhukov supervised the Voronezh and Steppe Fronts on the critical Kiev Direction, Vasilevsky did likewise in the south with the Southwestern and Southern Fronts, and Voronov coordinated the *fronts* participating in the Smolensk operation.

The *Stavka* concept capitalized on the staggered nature of the assaults to deceive the Germans regarding attack timing and priority of effort. In addition, the offensive simultaneously hindered the Germans' ability to shift forces laterally across the front and exploited the situation when the Germans did shift reserves. The broad-front form of attack compounded the German problem of establishing defensive priorities and made it difficult for the Germans to detect concealed Soviet operational regroupings. By attacking on a broad front, however, the Soviets inevitably dispersed their own efforts and failed to achieve the concentrations by which Zhukov had hoped to achieve decisive results in more selected sectors. During the operations the Soviets employed operational deception with mixed success.

The forward lunge of Soviet forces, which began across the broad expanse of the Eastern Front in late August and September 1943 from Velikie Luki south to the Black Sea, by the end of September had propelled Soviet *front*s to the eastern borders of Belorussia, the Dnepr River, and the lower Tavria. The hard-pressed German army sought desperately to restore a coherent defense line midst the rapidly deteriorating situation. Quite naturally, the attention of German commanders focused on terrain features whose presence could act as a backbone for new defenses. Along the critical central and southern portions of the front, the Dnepr and Sozh rivers were natural barriers where German forces might make their next defensive stand. In late September, German forces raced for sanctuary on the western banks of these rivers, often scarcely hours ahead of their Soviet pursuers. In isolated sectors Soviet forces won the race and were able to insert small units into cramped but nevertheless threatening enclaves on the far bank. For the most part, however, the Germans successfully erected defenses on the west bank of the rivers; cordoned off those small Soviet bridgeheads; and tried, usually in vain, to eradicate them.

By 1 October, Soviet forces in the north reached a line running from west of Velikie Luki southward, east of Vitebsk and along the Sozh and Dnepr rivers, past Kiev to Melitopol'. German forces clung to bridgeheads on the eastern bank at Gomel' and Zaporozh'e while the Soviets held tenaciously to tenuous footholds on the west bank at numerous locations but most threateningly near Chernobyl', north of Kiev; at Bukrin, south of Kiev; and at Mishurin Rog, between Kremenchug and Dnepropetrovsk. The Soviet High Command understood that the summer-fall offensive could not be brought to a fitting end without achieving a major breach in these river obstacles, bridgeheads from which new and more powerful offensives could be launched in the winter of 1944.

At the end of September and beginning of October, the *Stavka* assigned new missions to its forces.

> The forces of the northwestern direction were expected to destroy the defending enemy group and prevent their withdrawal to Dvinsk and Riga.

On the western direction it was planned to destroy the central enemy group, reach the line Vil'no, Minsk, Slutsk, Sluch' River and liberate regions of the Pre-Baltic and eastern Belorussia. The *fronts* of the southwestern direction were to liquidate the Hitlerite bridgeheads on the Dnepr, inflict defeat on their southern group, and reach the line Mogilev-Podol'sk, Rybnitsa, and Kherson.[39]

As had been the case during the drive to the Dnepr, the main direction remained toward Kiev, where the Voronezh Front, cooperating with the Central Front's left wing, was to liquidate German forces in the Kiev region, liberate the capital of the Ukraine, and then develop the offensive to Berdichev, Zhmerinky, and Mogilev-Podol'sk.[40] The Steppe Front was to enlarge its bridgehead at Mishurin Rog, while the Southern and North Caucasus Fronts eradicated German bridgeheads east of the Dnepr River, in the Tavria, and on the Taman Peninsula.

By early October advancing Soviet *fronts* and opposing German forces had been in almost constant combat since early July, and exhaustion had taken its toll on both sides. The Soviets now sought to exploit the momentum of their strategic offensive by concentrating their exhausted forces to achieve decisive penetration of the Dnepr River barrier. Soviet critics noted the Soviet problem:

> The subsequent course of events demonstrated that not all missions assigned to *fronts* were successfully fulfilled in 1943. The penetration of the enemy defensive lines demanded considerable forces and weaponry which the *fronts* were clearly lacking in the concluding operations of 1943.[41]

Given this situation, success was even more dependent on careful planning, accurate intelligence, and skillful deception.

The culminating stage of the summer-fall campaign unfolded along the banks of the Dnepr River around Kiev where, through a combination of deception and combat skill, Soviet forces broke through the German defensive "Eastern Wall" along the banks of the Dnepr. Vasilevsky related the intent and nature of the ensuing strategic operation:

> Such was the situation in the early part of November that the GHQ's main attention had to be focused in the Kiev sector. The arrival of Soviet troops in the area of Kiev created a threat from the north to the entire southern enemy grouping on the Soviet-German front. Yet attempts by the command of the 1st Ukrainian Front to take the city in October by launching

its main attack to the south of the city from the Bukrin bridgehead with an auxiliary attack from the north from the Lyutezh bridgehead had brought no success, since the enemy had concentrated their main forces there. The GHQ was obliged to amend its decision on 25 October and order the Front to regroup its main forces towards Lyutezh so as to launch the major attack there. As a result, the mission was accomplished, and Kiev was taken on 6 November. Only then did the situation become more conducive to a further offensive by Soviet troops to the west and southwest. Pursuing the enemy, the 1st Ukrainian Front captured the important railway junction of Fastov on 7 November and on 13 November it liberated Zhitomir.[42]

In the successful Kiev operation, the Soviets secured a strategic bridgehead across the Dnepr River. Subsequently, Soviet forces parried German attempts to eradicate the bridgehead and, on 24 December, orchestrated the Zhitomir-Berdichev operation, in reality the first phase of the new winter campaign, which dashed German hopes of restoring the Dnepr River defense line.

In July 1943 Soviet forces had seized the strategic initiative on the Eastern Front by their planned counteroffensive at Kursk. They maintained the initiative by conducting active operations across the central and southern portions of the front throughout the late summer and fall and capped their offensive successes in November by seizing significant bridgeheads across the Dnepr River barrier—the vaunted German Eastern Wall. In the course of six months, Soviet forces eased the German stranglehold on Leningrad, cleared the Kalinin and Smolensk regions to the eastern extremities of Belorussia, occupied and pierced the Dnepr River line, and isolated German forces in the Crimea. As a result of its losses, the German army was no longer capable of conducting even limited strategic offensives. It could, however, still conduct a credible defense, if the Soviets permitted them to do so. The principal Soviet task in 1944 was to maintain the strategic initiative and avoid the specter of positional war, which, some Germans hoped, could deny the Soviets victory by bleeding her armies and by destroying her will to prevail.

Improved Soviet skill at intelligence collection and analysis, greater restraint in allowing subjective judgments to override objective assessments, and increasingly effective deception at all levels contributed to Soviet strategic success in the summer-fall campaign. Soviet assessments throughout the spring reflected the maturing intelligence picture. In fact, the performance of Soviet intelligence at Kursk typified similar efforts during the remainder of the summer-fall campaign.

On 8 April Zhukov dispatched to Stalin an extensive strategic appreciation concerning prospective German operations and the advisable
Soviet response.

> To Comrade Vasilyev [Stalin's code name]
> 5:30 a.m., April 8, 1943
> I hereby state my opinion on the possible movements of the enemy
> in the spring and summer of 1943 and our plans for defensive actions in
> the coming months.
> 1. Having suffered serious losses in the winter campaign of 1942/
> 1943, the enemy would not appear to be able to build up big reserves by
> the spring to resume the offensive on the Caucasus and to push forward
> to the Volga to make a wide enveloping movement around Moscow.
> Owing to the inadequacy of large reserves, in the spring and first half
> of the summer of 1943 the enemy will be forced to launch offensive
> operations on a smaller front and resolve the task facing him strictly in
> stages, his main aim being the taking of Moscow.
> Proceeding from the fact that, at the given moment, there are groupings
> deployed against our Central, Voronezh and South-Western Fronts, I be-
> lieve that the enemy's main offensives will be spearheaded at these fronts,
> in order to rout our forces on this sector and to gain freedom for his
> manoeuvres to outflank Moscow and get as close to it as possible.
> 2. At the first stage, having gathered as many of his forces as possible,
> including at least 13 to 15 tank divisions and large air support, the enemy
> will evidently deal the blow with his Orel-Kromy grouping in the enveloping
> movement around Kursk from the north-east and likewise with the Bel-
> gorod-Kharkov grouping from the south-east.
> An additional attack on Kursk from the south-west aimed at dividing
> our front must be expected from the west, from the area around Vorozhba
> between the rivers Seim and Psyol. The enemy will attempt by means of
> this operation to defeat and surround our 13th, 70th, 65th, 38th, 40th, and
> 21st Armies, his ultimate purpose at this stage being to reach The River
> Korocha-Korocha-Tim-River Tim-Droskovo line.
> 3. At the second stage, the enemy will attempt to come out on the
> flank and in the rear of the South-Western Front, his general direction
> being through Valuiki-Urazovo.
> To counter this offensive, the enemy may deal a blow at the Lisichansk
> area on a northern, Svatovo-Urazovo sector.
> In the remaining sectors the enemy will strive to reach the Livny-
> Kastornoye-Stary and Novy Oskol line.
> 4. At the third stage, after the corresponding regrouping, the enemy
> will possibly try to reach the Liski-Voronezh-Yelets front and, taking cover

in a south-eastern direction, may launch an offensive as part of the wide enveloping movement around Moscow from the south-east via Ranenburg-Ryazhsk-Ryazan.

5. In his offensive operations this year the enemy may be expected to count chiefly on his tank divisions and air force since his infantry is at present considerably less well prepared for offensive action than it was last year.

At the present time, the enemy has as many as 12 tank divisions lined up along the Central and Voronezh Fronts and, by taking in three or four tank divisions from other sectors, he could pitch as many as 15 or 16 tank divisions with some 2,500 tanks against our Kursk grouping.

6. If the enemy is to be crushed by our defensive formations, besides measures to build up the anti-tank defences on the Central and Voronezh Fronts, we must get together 30 anti-tank artillery regiments from the passive sectors as rapidly as possible and redeploy them as part of the Supreme Command's reserves in the areas threatened; all the regiments of the self-propelled artillery must be concentrated in the Livny Kastornoye-Stary Oskol sector. Even now it would be desirable for some of the regiments to be placed under Rokossovsky and Vatutin as reinforcements and for as many aircraft as possible to be transferred to the Supreme Command's reserves to smash the shock groupings with massed attacks from the air coordinated with action by tank and rifle formations and to frustrate the plan for the enemy's offensive.

I am not familiar with the final location of our operational reserves; therefore I believe it expedient to propose their deployments in the Yefremov-Livny-Kastornoye-Novy Oskol-Valuiki-Rossosh-Liski-Voronezh-Yelets area. The deeper reserve echelon should be deployed around Ryazhsk, Ranenburg, Michurinsk, and Tambov.

There must be one reserve army in the Tula-Stalinogorsk area.

I do not believe it is necessary for our forces to mount a preventive offensive in the next few days. It will be better if we wear the enemy out in defensive actions, destroy his tanks, and then, taking in fresh reserves, by going over to an all-out offensive we will finish off the enemy's main grouping.

"Konstantinov" [Zhukov's code name][43]

In his appreciation, Zhukov highlighted the most critical attack indicator: the movement and concentration of German armored forces.

Zhukov's assessment was reinforced by those of *front* commanders and chiefs of staff who in early April forwarded their appreciations for *Stavka* consideration. Shtemenko summed up the resulting General Staff view on German intentions:

The question as to "where" was not then too difficult. There could be only one answer—in the Kursk Salient. This was where the enemy had their main strike forces, which represented two possible dangers for us; a deep outflanking thrust round Moscow or a turn southwards. On the other hand, it was here, against the enemy's main concentration, that we ourselves could use our manpower and weapons to the greatest effect, particularly our big tank formations. No other sector, even if we were very successful there, promised so much as the Kursk Salient. This was the conclusion eventually reached by GHQ, the General Staff and the Front commanders.[44]

A subsequent 12 April *Stavka* meeting agreed that Kursk was the most likely Soviet target. Meanwhile, on 23 April, the *Stavka* ordered the Steppe Military District to erect a safety net of reserve armies deep in the rear from Elets through Voronezh, then south of the Don River to Millerovo. Simultaneously, the *Stavka* ordered all *front*s to be vigilant against the German practice of mounting diversionary attacks elsewhere across the front.[45] On 20 April, the Soviet agent Rado (code-named Dora) in Switzerland relayed intelligence that set 14 June as the date of the offensive but observed, "Only modest operations were planned." Subsequent messages over the next nine days from Dora indicated postponement of the offensive from early May to 12 June.[46]

On 2 May, as defensive preparations proceeded apace, intelligence indicators produced the first of several *Stavka* warnings that an attack might materialize in the near future. Zhukov noted

The Supreme Command had carried out thorough intelligence and aerial reconnaissance which had gained reliable information on the enemy flows of troops and ammunition towards the Orel, Kromy, Bryansk, Kharkov, Krasnograd and Poltava sectors. This confirmed the correctness of our forecasts in April. The Stavka and General Staff became increasingly of the opinion that the German forces might mount an offensive in the next few days.[47]

The 2 May warning order coincided closely with Soviet receipt from the British of a 25 April Ultra intercept, which summarized an Army Group South assessment of Soviet dispositions and anticipated actions. On 30 April the British passed this assessment to the Soviets, along with a warning of an impending German attack on Kursk.[48] Soon, however, available Ultra material decreased in quality and quantity.

Although the attack did not materialize, the *Stavka* heightened force readiness and on 5 May issued a directive that provided the evidence for increased vigilance and mandated conduct of a preemptive air offensive. It read

> Recently considerable movement of enemy forces and transport has been noted into the Orel, Belgorod, and Khar'kov regions as well as movement of forces to the front lines. This forces us to expect active enemy operations in the near future.
>
> The *Stavka* of the High Command draws your attention to the necessity of
>
> 1. Full implementation of the plan to employ frontal aviation to destroy enemy aviation and disrupt the work of rail lines and highways.
> 2. Maximum attention to *razvedka* of all kinds, in order to reveal the enemy grouping and intentions. In these days without fail we must have prisoners daily, especially in important front sectors. . . .
>
> A. Vasilevsky, Antonov[49]

Consequently, on 8 May the *Stavka* sent the following directive to the Briansk, Central, Voronezh, and Southwestern Fronts:

> According to certain information, the enemy may begin an offensive between 10 and 12 May in the Oryol-Kursk or the Belgorod-Oboyan direction, or in both directions at once. The GHQ instructs you to have all troops of both the first line of defence and the reserves in full combat readiness by the morning of 10 May on order to meet the possible enemy attack. Pay particular attention to aviation readiness so that you can not only repel the enemy air attacks in the event of the enemy launching an offensive, but you can gain air superiority from the very first moment of his active operations.
>
> J. Stalin, A. Vasilevsky[50]

The *Stavka* dispatched a similar message to the Steppe Front.

> Speed up as much as possible the manning of the military district troops and, by the morning of 10th May, have all your available troops in full combat readiness both for defence and for active operation on GHQ instructions. Pay particular attention to the readiness of the air force meeting possible attacks by enemy aircraft on our airfields and troops.[51]

Characteristically, Stalin still harbored thoughts of conducting some sort of preemptive action. After extensive deliberations with his advisors and commanders, however, Stalin finally agreed to an initial defensive phase, but only after deciding to incorporate into the strategic plan extensive preemptive air activity and planned counteroffensives to begin after the German assaults had been halted. Although the German offensive had not materialized, by mid-May Stalin and the *Stavka* pressed on with their mixed defensive-offensive efforts. The first of those preemptive actions occurred between 6 and 13 May, when Soviet air units struck at German airfields. Once again in late May, the *Stavka* sensed an impending attack. This prediction was based, in part, on reports by Zhukov of the situation confronting the Voronezh and Central Fronts. Regarding the latter, on 22 May Zhukov reported

To Comrade Ivanov [Stalin's code name]

The situation on the Central Front on May 21, 1943 was as follows:

1. By May 21 reconnaissance of all kinds has established that before the Central Front the enemy has 15 infantry divisions in the first line and 13 divisions, including three panzer divisions, in the second line.

There is, moreover, information about the concentration of the 2nd Panzer Division and the 36th Motorised Infantry Division south of Orel. The information about these two divisions requires verification.

The enemy's 4th Panzer Division, formerly deployed west of Sevsk, has been moved somewhere. Besides, there are three divisions, two of them panzer, in the Bryansk and Karachev area.

Consequently, as of May 21 the enemy can operate with 33 divisions, six of them panzer divisions, against the Central Front.

The Front's instrumental and visual reconnaissance has detected 800 artillery pieces, mainly 105-mm and 150-mm guns.

The enemy keeps the bulk of his artillery opposite the 13th Army, the left flank of the 48th Army and the right flank of the 70th Army, i.e., in the Trosno-Pervoye-Pozdeyevo sector. Behind this main artillery grouping there are 600–700 tanks on the Zmeyevka-Krasnaya Roshcha line. The bulk is concentrated east of the River Oka.

In the area of Orel, Bryansk and Smolensk the enemy has concentrated 600–650 warplanes. The main enemy air grouping is in the Orel area.

Both on the ground and in the air the enemy has been passive in the last few days, confining himself to small-scale air reconnaissance and occasional minor artillery attacks.

In his forward line and his tactical depth, the enemy is digging trenches and intensively fortifying his positions in front of the 13th Army, in the Krasnaya Slobodka-Senkovo sector, where he already has a second defence line beyond the River Neruch. Observation reveals that the enemy is building a third defence line in this sector, 3–4 kilometres north of the Neruch.

Prisoners say the German Command knows about our grouping south of Orel and our planned offensive, and that German units have been warned. Captured airmen claim that the German Command is itself preparing for an offensive and concentrating aviation for this purpose.

I personally visited the forward lines of the 13th Army, observed the enemy defences from various points, watched his activity, and talked with divisional commanders of the 70th and 13th Armies, with commanders Galanin, Pukhov and Romanenko, and came to the conclusion that in the forward line the enemy was not making direct preparations for an offensive.

I may be mistaken. It may be that the enemy is camouflaging his preparations for an offensive very skilfully. But an analysis of the deployment of his armour, the inadequate density of infantry formations, absence of heavy artillery groupings as well as the dispersion of reserves lead me to believe that the enemy will not be ready to launch an offensive before the end of May.[52]

According to Vasilevsky, Stalin again had fleeting thoughts of preemptive action.

On 20 May the General Staff, on the basis of freshly received information on enemy movements, warned the fronts with Stalin's permission that the Nazi offensive was expected no later than 26 May. After the first warning, when it had not been confirmed, the military council of the Voronezh Front regarded this as being due to a certain wavering on the part of the foe, perhaps even a rejection of the whole idea of an offensive; it therefore asked Stalin to decide on the question of whether to launch the initial blow at the enemy. Stalin took a serious interest in this proposition and it took all that we—Zhukov, myself and Antonov—could do to dissuade him from it.[53]

Moskalenko, commander of 40th Army, affirmed that the principal indicator of German intentions on both occasions in May was troop movements, writing, "Unusual troop movements were detected on the enemy side twice in May."[54] In addition, intensified troop *razvedka* produced a new batch of prisoners, which undoubtedly echoed rumors circulating in the German camp concerning an impending offensive. Heavy air activity associated with the Soviet air offensive of 6 through 13 May produced new air *razvedka* data confirming heavier German troop movements forward. This scare, however, also passed; and, by the end of the month, the entire *Stavka* resolved itself to the conduct of an initial defensive phase. As reported by Zhukov:

The final decision concerning the deliberate defense was accepted by the *Stavka* at the end of May and beginning of June 1943 when it became known, in fact in all its details, about the German intention to strike the Voronezh and Central Fronts a strong blow by the use of large tank groups and new "Tiger" tanks and "Ferdinand" assault guns.[55]

Zhukov and Vasilevsky supervised preparation and conduct of the Kursk strategic operation. *Front* and army commanders in the Kursk Bulge exerted tremendous efforts to create deeply echeloned and firepower-intensive defenses while ensuring the secrecy of the preparations. *Razvedka* and deception measures were extensive. Building upon the experiences of earlier operations, the Central, Voronezh, and Steppe Front staffs prepared detailed *razvedka* and deception plans, which exploited all intelligence collection assets and included concealment of preparations, creation of false troop concentrations, simulation of false radio nets and communications centers, construction of false air facilities and false aircraft, and dissemination of false rumors along the front and in the enemy rear area.[56] These plans also included collation of information from all intelligence sources, secret movement of reserves, hidden preparations for counterattacks and counterstrokes, and concealed locations of command posts and communications sites.

As defensive planning progressed, tension built within the *Stavka*. Vasilevsky later reflected

> As a result of constant and very careful military observation of the enemy on both the Voronezh and the Central Fronts, as well as the information being received from all forms of intelligence, we knew precisely that the Nazis were fully prepared for the offensive. And yet for some reason or other the offensive did not come. It was this "for some reason or other" that gave us some anxiety and knocked some people out of their stride.[57]

In early June, to confirm that an attack was not imminent, the General Staff's operations section again ordered *front*s to focus *razvedka* assets on German force dispositions, particularly panzer units. This order may have been prompted in part by a 6 June Werther agent report that forward movements of motorized units of Second and Fourth Panzer Armies had been cancelled on 28 May.[58] An air of distrust surrounded the Soviet reaction. The 6 June order produced a reassuring assessment. "Five days were allowed and when they had elapsed, reassuring reports came back that there had been no change at the front and the enemy's tank concentration was still the same."[59] In fact, actual German dispositions reflected the accuracy of this assessment for German panzer forces remained in assembly areas, the bulk of which were in the Khar'kov area. Anxiety produced renewed calls for offensive action by some commanders (Vatutin); but, regardless, the *Stavka* held firm to its plans.

After 20 June German troop movements had convinced most members that the attack would come in the near future. Vasilevsky and Zhukov thought it would occur during the week after 22 June, but, again, the time passed without incident, although intelligence indicators mounted. This warning, however, also turned out to be premature, as confirmed on 23 June when agent Lucy (Rudolph Rossler) reported from Lucerne, "The very latest news from Fuehrer headquarters . . . [is that] the German attack against Kursk, contemplated since the end of May is no longer planned."[60] Hard on the heels of Lucy's news, Werther also sent a message (23 June) which read

> OKW does not wish to provoke a large-scale Russian offensive in the central sector under any circumstances. Therefore one considers the German preventive attack planned for May-early June in the southern sector no longer serves a purpose . . . Soviet build-up in the Kursk area since early June is now so great that German superiority there no longer exists.[61]

In essence, Werther stated the offensive would not occur. Within ten days, however, German offensive indicators involving troop movements mounted to such an extent that a new warning was warranted. Zhukov described the impact of those indicators:

> The situation finally became clear in the last few days of June, and we realized that the enemy would mount an offensive in the coming days precisely here in the Kursk area and nowhere else.
>
> Stalin telephoned me on June 30. He ordered me to remain on the Orel sector to coordinate the operations of the Central, Bryansk, and Western Fronts.
>
> "Vasilevsky is in command on the Voronezh Front," said the Supreme Commander.[62]

Zhukov added that on 2 July, "the *Stavka* warned the commanders of the Fronts that the enemy's offensive was anticipated between July 3 and July 6."[63]

Vasilevsky provided a more complete description of the measures he immediately undertook.

> On the night of 2 July the information received at General Staff from our intelligence section told us that in the next few days, at any rate no later than 6 July, the enemy's offensive on the Kursk Front was bound to begin. I instantly reported this to Stalin and asked permission to warn the Fronts at once. I then read to him the prepared draft GHQ directive: "From existing information, the Germans may launch an offensive on our front between 3 and 6 July. The GHQ orders you as follows: 1. To strengthen intelligence and observation of the enemy for the purpose of exposing his intentions in time. 2. To see that the troops and air force are ready to repel a possible enemy attack. 3. To report on the instructions issued."
>
> Stalin approved the text of the directive during the night of 2 July and it was despatched to the commanders of the Western, Bryansk, Central, Voronezh, South-Western and Southern Fronts. I set off on the same day for the Voronezh Front. By evening I was at Nikolayev's (code name for Vatutin) command post.[64]

On 29 June German forces had begun forward deployment of forces for the 5 July offensive. Movements associated with these final preparations were substantial and literally dwarfed movements that had prompted previous Soviet alert orders. From 29 June through 1 July, SS Panzer Division "Totenkopf" of II SS Panzer Corps moved north from assembly areas south of Khar'kov into positions in the tactical depth west of Belgorod. The remaining divisions of the corps assembled north of Khar'kov; III Panzer Corps deployed 7th Panzer Division to positions northeast of Khar'kov and moved 19th Panzer Division from the Barvenkovo area into positions near Khar'kov. Simultaneously, XXXXVIII Panzer Corps moved both Panzer Grenadier Division Grossdeutschland and 11th Panzer Division into assembly areas 60 kilometers from the front and 3d Panzer Division to new positions west of Khar'kov. In addition, the 328th Infantry Division moved into assembly areas south of Khar'kov.[65]

These extensive troop movements prompted Zhukov's final warning, confirming what was already abundantly clear. Soviet *razvedka,* probably agent and air, but perhaps also radio, detected the scope and direction of redeployments sufficiently to determine once and for all the general sectors where the blows would fall. During the ensuing three days (2 through 4 July), German XXXXVIII, III, and II SS Panzer Corps completed their large-scale deployment into the tactical dispositions of forces mounting the attack. At the same time, German panzer corps finished their concentration into attack positions south of Orel'. The scale of these movements was staggering, involving as it did the movement and assembly of over 1,500 armored vehicles plus countless supporting vehicles into positions west and south of Belgorod and almost 1,200 armored vehicles on a narrow front south of Orel'. It was at this juncture that Soviet tactical *razvedka* organs began receiving a flood of reports, which ultimately resulted in the 2 July *Stavka* alert order for an attack expected from 3 through 6 July.

An intelligence report prepared on 3 July by Moskalenko's 40th Army indicates the degree of detail concerning German concentration available to Soviet commanders defending south of Kursk.

Information About the Enemy in the 40th Army Sector on 3.7.43
1. Three German infantry divisions defend in the first line in the army sector.
   a) 57 ID—division commander Lt. Gen. Pikko. It defends a sector of 18 kms, with three regiments in the first line. . . .
   b) 255 ID—division commander Lt. Gen. Poppe. It defends a sector of 17 kms. . . .
   c) 332 ID—division commander Lt. Gen. Shaefer. Two regiments defend against our army in a sector of 18 kms.

   The indicated formations include in their composition 120 field guns and 77 mortars. All types of *razvedka* have disclosed the existence of 8 batteries of 150-mm (29 guns), 25 artillery batteries of 105-mm (83 guns) and 20 batteries of 75-mm (78 guns). A total of 54 batteries—190 guns. Besides these, there are 27 separate mortars. The greatest density of enemy artillery is in the Pochaevo, Kasilovo, and Nikitskoe regions. Apparently the artillery of a reserve tank division located in the Borisovka, Graiveron area also operates in this region.

2. Enemy motor—mechanized force grouping:
   a) According to aviation [*razvedka*] an unidentified tank division with up to 200 tanks operates in the Sumy, Nizh, Syrovatka, Bol. Bobrik area.
   b) From 20.6 to 26.6.43 aviation detected up to 20 tanks in the Starosel'e area and up to 15 tanks at Slavgorod (10–20 km

southeast of Krasnopel'e). Whom they belong to has not been established.

c) On the line Novo-Berozovka, Kazatskoe (north of Tomarovka) 100 tanks belonging to tank division SS "Reich" are operating in the infantry combat formation, with an immediate reserve of up to 40 tanks in the forest west of Blizhnii (southwest of Belgorod) and up to 60 tanks belonging to tank division SS "Deathshead" are in the Streletskii, Krasnoe, Belgorod area.

3. Immediate and operational infantry reserves in the army sector have not been identified. . . .

5. Enemy aviation:
Aviation has detected up to 100 aircraft at field aerodromes at Belopol'e, Lebedin, Graivoron, Borisovka, and Mikoianovka, presumably from the Khar'kov aerodrome center, which conducts *razvedka* of our combat formation. . . .[66]

This report generally conformed to actual German dispositions and, with like reports, provided adequate data upon which to base the 2 July alert order. As indicated, air and troop *razvedka* played a major role. Radio intercept probably contributed to precise identification of German units.

Even as late as early July, after concentration of the German armored armada had been completed and after the Germans had conducted their 4 July preoffensive reconnaissance west of Belgorod, the Soviet command, having determined the general timing of the attack and the general attack sectors, still lacked refined data concerning what unit would attack where and where the precise main attack axis was. The chief of the Voronezh Front Operational Department, Major General V. A. Svetlichnyi, later wrote:

The staff of the Voronezh Front, having known about the beginning of the enemy offensive, did not undertake necessary measures to strengthen the defense of 6th Guards Army [on the Oboian axes], since it considered that he [the enemy] would deliver the main attack on Stary Oskol and part of his force in Oboian.[67]

Lieutenant General M. E. Katukov, 1st Tank Army commander, echoed the uncertainty, commenting that he anticipated the attack could materialize from Suzhda, Rakitnoe, Belgorod, or Korocha toward Oboian.[68] This inability to detect precisely the direction of the main German attack explained why the Germans made their greatest offensive progress in the Voronezh Front sector. The events of 3 through 4 July, described by Vasilevsky, confirmed the information of 2 July.

> All was quiet on the Voronezh and the Central Fronts on 3 July, as it had been on all preceding days. But at 16.00 on 4 July the enemy carried out his reconnaissance in force on a wide sector of the Voronezh Front with approximately four battalions supported by 20 tanks, artillery and aircraft (some 150 sorties). All attempts by the enemy to drive a wedge into our forward line were repulsed. A prisoner captured during the battle, a German from the 168th Infantry Division, let us know that the soldiers had been issued with battle rations and a portion of schnapps, and that they were to launch an offensive on 5 July. From a telephone conversation with Zhukov I found out that this was confirmed by enemy deserters who had come over to us on the Central Front on July 4.[69]

The cumulative data obtained from troop *razvedka,* combined with information obtained from operational and strategic means and technical data from artillery and engineer *razvedka,* alerted the Soviets. On 29 June, a Central Front intelligence summary concluded that the Germans had occupied jumping-off positions for the offensive. Daily summaries for 30 June and 1, 2, and 3 July repeated the warning. Suddenly, on 4 July, the Soviets noted all activity had sharply halted.

> On the enemy side, where we expected the offensive, suddenly all was quiet. Nothing could be observed in front of Central Front forces. The field of battle was lifeless. Enemy firing activity fell off. On the Voronezh Front to the left it was the same. Moreover, operational *razvedka* [agent, air, radio] determined that tanks, vehicles, and tractors stretched along roads running east and west in the Donbas, 150–200 kilometers south of Khar'kov. It seemed as if from the Kursk bulge all were rushing back and heading for the Donbas. However, these and other measures conducted by the enemy, not only did not deceive our *razvedka* but also alerted them even more. All forces and means of *razvedka* of units, formations and large formations intently followed the enemy actions.
>
> Hour after hour passed and in the enemy camp as before quiet ruled. What did it mean? Why did the enemy act so unusual? That question also extremely interested officer-*razvedchiks* and commanders at all levels.
>
> There were of course hypotheses and proposals in search of the truth.
>
> Finally we decided. You see, it was all in order. In the course of the last five days the enemy had moved his forces and equipment to the forward edge and regrouped in preparation for the offensive.

> On the night of 4 July the enemy had occupied jumping-off positions
> for the attack. Therefore on 4 July no regrouping or movement of forces
> from the depths could be detected. You see, the enemy needed at least
> one day to rest, inspect, and prepare the personnel of his subunits and units
> for the attack.
>
> Such a conclusion was written in the intelligence summary of the
> Central Front for 4 July. In particular it said that the enemy had finished
> his force concentration and was preparing to go over to the offensive,
> which was expected to occur in one–two days.[70]

Despite this assessment, the Soviets still did not know the precise
time of the offensive or the precise main attack axes. Based on this
summary and a like summary prepared by the Voronezh Front, all forces
were directed "to strengthen all types of *razvedka* to establish the exact
time of the enemy offensive."[71] This order reinforced similar orders issued
by the *Stavka* on 2 July, which mandated intensification of air *razvedka*
and seizure of prisoners. In response to these orders, the Soviets intensified
aerial *razvedka* and sweeps, searches, and ambushes organized by first
echelon rifle divisions.

One of the many groups consisted of a sergeant and fourteen men
from the 15th Rifle Division, which at about 2200 hours seized a prisoner
from the German 6th Infantry Division. Interrogation of the prisoner
revealed that the attack would occur at 0200 on 5 July.[72] One Soviet
assessment focused on this single, seemingly inconsequential episode to
generalize about the importance of low-level troop *razvedka*.

> It is not difficult to note, that the prisoner sapper of the 6th German
> Infantry Division, his testimony in the interrogation, and conclusions
> reached by our commands had not only tactical or operational, but also
> strategic importance.[73]

As a result of this intelligence, the Soviets responded early on 5 July
with a preemptive artillery counterpreparation, which preceded the German offensive by only a matter of hours. By nightfall on 5 July, the front
was aflame. The long-awaited German Kursk offensive had begun.

It is clear that ample information was available to the Soviets regarding
German intentions to launch a summer offensive. Precedent alone indicated the Germans would do so. Moreover, by late April 1943, a variety
of indicators pointed to the likelihood of an attack in the vicinity of Kursk,
including geography, the disposition of German operational reserves as
determined by air and agent *razvedka*, and information provided by Ultra.

All played a part in shaping Soviet decisions to add a defensive phase to plans for a summer offensive.

Between early May and late June, *razvedka* data permitted the Soviets to refine their estimate and reach the conclusion that the most likely direction of German attack would be along the Orel' and Belgorod axes toward the base of the Kursk Bulge. Throughout the period, however, the Soviets remembered past experiences and remained cautious in their assessments. In fact, Soviet dispositions as late as 5 July reflected an intent to defend every major axis along which German forces might advance. There were good reasons for this caution, among which were a healthy Soviet appreciation of German deception capabilities; respect for the ability of the Germans to move forces quickly between sectors; and skepticism born of experience regarding the veracity of intelligence sources, information, and assessments. On several occasions, but most notably in the spring of 1942, the Soviets had been deceived by the Germans regarding where the strategic blow would occur, with tragic consequences. More recently, in February 1943, the Soviets badly misread accurate intelligence indicators, which led to their subsequent defeat in the Donbas. From these and other unfavorable but enlightening experiences, the Soviets were determined to cover all eventualities while exploiting intelligence whenever possible.

The Soviets were also skeptical of some of the intelligence data they received. Information from the Swiss agent network—in particular, Werther's transmissions—ostensibly based on OKW information, was contradictory and often unreliable. The Soviets tended to note it but accorded it little value. Dora, Lucy, and Werther provided valuable material regarding overall enemy intentions—as did Ultra, but only during early spring. Thereafter, the information either dried up entirely or contained little detail necessary to make operational or tactical assessments. In the end, by their own resolve and by habit, the Soviets relied upon what they themselves had developed—an intricate network of *razvedka* sources that covered the entire combat spectrum and that they understood and, hence, tended to trust. Ultimately, this was the most important source of intelligence data upon which the Soviets based their assessments in May and June and, finally, their judgments prior to the German attack in July.

While undertaking a massive and systematic *razvedka* effort to refine their defensive capability and prepare for subsequent offensive action, the Soviets also erected an immense safety net to avoid repetition of the disasters of 1941 and 1942. They prepared an initial defense that could adequately check a German thrust along every potential German axis of advance. This is not apparent in most general Soviet sources, nor have Western accounts realized the unique configuration of Soviet strategic deployments.

Razvedka, in close concert with deception, played a significant role in the Soviet strategic defense at Kursk and during the strategic counteroffensive that followed. Soviet intelligence assessments by late April were accurate enough for the *Stavka* to decide to organize an initial defensive phase in the summer of 1943 and, at the same time, incorporate into that plan significant offensive measures and a complex strategic deception plan. Despite the accurate strategic *razvedka* assessments, the Soviets avoided earlier mistakes by treating the assessments skeptically and by creating powerful defenses on every major potential strategic axis the Germans could employ. Thus, throughout the planning phase, they took into account potential German deception like that which had been so effective in the spring and summer of 1942.

Having created a strategic safety net, the Soviets focused on operational and tactical *razvedka* to refine their appreciation of German intentions. These measures, focused primarily on detecting German troop movements, produced the warnings of May and June and, ultimately, of the actual German attack in July. Careful and patient control over strategic reserve units enabled the Soviets to redeploy those forces and commit them to combat at the most critical times and in the most important sectors. *Razvedka* thereby detected and helped thwart the German offensive. Subsequently, *razvedka* provided the requisite information for successful implementation of the strategic deception plan. To a far greater degree than before, the Soviets were able to monitor German troop units in the operational and strategic depths. This increased sophistication in *razvedka* was absolutely vital for such an equally sophisticated deception plan to succeed. Succeed it did—in large part due to improved Soviet intelligence.

At Kursk the Soviets successfully detected German strategic, operational, and tactical intent, while masking to a considerable degree their own counteroffensive intent. This combination of factors spelled doom for German offensive plans in the summer of 1943 and, more important, ultimately sealed the fate of German fortunes on the Eastern Front as a whole.

As the Soviet strategic offensive developed into the fall, *razvedka* continued playing the positive role it had played at Kursk. While keeping track of German dispositions and movement of dwindling German operational reserves, intelligence, to an increasing extent, verified the effectiveness of deception planning. Intelligence contributed to several notable deception and combat successes. During the Chernigov-Pripiat' operation in September, Marshal K. K. Rokossovsky's Central Front detected a major gap in the left flank of German defenses covering Sevsk and Glukhov. Through the use of careful deception, Rokossovsky rapidly shifted his 13th Army and 9th Tank Corps from his right flank to his left flank, tearing a hole in German defenses and prompting precipitous German withdrawal to the Dnepr. A similar intelligence success enabled Vatutin's Voronezh Front to commit 3d Guards Tank Army into another gap in German defenses, and the tank army dashed to the Dnepr River south of Kiev. In both instances, however, in light of the rapidly changing situation, deep intelligence was weak, and this caused failures toward the end of the operation as the Soviets lost track of German units. On 24 and 25 September the Soviets attempted to seize a bridgehead across the Dnepr River near Velikii Bukrin, using airborne forces. Soviet intelligence, however, failed to detect the arrival of German forces in the region (in particular 19th Panzer Division, which had moved rapidly south from Kiev). The poorly executed night airborne drop landed midst German units and understandably failed to achieve its objectives. The Soviets ended up in possession of a small bridgehead seized by forward units of 3d Guards Tank Army but were unable to expand it to strategic proportions.

During late September and October 1943, a short stalemate existed along the Dnepr River. The Soviets held small bridgeheads at numerous points, but no single bridgehead of sufficient size to mount a major operation to breach the Dnepr River line. In early November another major intelligence success in conjunction with a masterful deception operation broke the deadlock. Vatutin secretly shifted 3d Guards Tank Army and other units from the Velikii Bukrin bridgehead northward into the Liutezh bridgehead north of Kiev. Soviet intelligence confirmed that the Germans had failed to detect the movement. On 3 November 1943 Soviet forces broke out of the bridgehead, seized Kiev, and—after heavy fighting—secured a strategic bridgehead west of the city. Subsequently, in mid-December, a major Soviet deception plan drew German reserves away from a new projected main attack sector of the reinforced Voronezh Front. The new Soviet offensive—Zhitomir-Berdichev, which commenced on 24 December—struck weak German defenses and paved the way for a subsequent advance of 120 kilometers. This operational success, facilitated by effective intelligence and deception, provided the strategic bridgehead from which Soviet forces commenced their winter campaign in January 1944.

Throughout all of these fall operations, *razvedka* organs operated in accordance with procedures employed at Kursk and achieved commensurate results. As was the case at Kursk, effective intelligence collection and analysis proved to be an important factor contributing to Soviet strategic success.

Summary

The principal strategic aim of the Soviet armed forces in 1943 was to secure and maintain the initiative by using all types of strategic operations (defensive and offensive), by carefully employing field forces on critical strategic directions, by judiciously using strategic reserves, and by implementing ambitious strategic deception plans. The dominant form of strategic operation was the strategic offensive, exemplified by the two Soviet general counteroffensives conducted at Stalingrad and Kursk, and subsequent development of those counteroffensives. Each counteroffensive, which was launched by a group of *fronts* and directed by a *Stavka* representative, was larger in scale than any earlier counteroffensive, and each involved simultaneous or successive blows [*udary*] across a broad front. The winter offensive, conducted on the heels of the Stalingrad counteroffensive, involved four *fronts* and eighteen combined-arms armies advancing in a 700- to 900-kilometer-wide sector to a depth of 120 to 400 kilometers. The summer offensive at Kursk involved ten *fronts*, forty combined-arms and five tank armies, operating on a 2,000-kilometer front to a depth of 600 to 700 kilometers. Although the winter offensive fell short of its ambitious objectives, the summer offensive succeeded in its aims.

The Soviet 1943 strategic defense and offensive at Kursk, unlike that at Moscow in 1941, did not occur along the entire front. Rather, it occurred on one strategic direction and involved an initial strategic defense by a group of *fronts*. Sufficient time existed to prepare and fully man a deeply echeloned and fortified defense extending over 100 kilometers deep and to prepare a deception plan involving the conduct of diversionary operations and secret movement of reserves. The year 1943 also saw the rise of a strategically important partisan movement, which disrupted the German rear areas and tied down a considerable number of German troops.

Throughout the period, the *Stavka* continued the practice it inaugurated at Stalingrad: It employed a representative of the *Stavka* to coordinate operations by groups of *fronts*. When required, *front* commands were reorganized or new *fronts* created to satisfy changing strategic requirements. In earlier years no single unifying plan had provided a basis for a campaign, but this situation changed in the second period of the war. The Stalingrad operations took place in the context of broader strategic aims, and subsequent operations were envisioned in at least outline form. The rapid development of the offensive, however, blurred the intended strategic aim and ultimately produced confusion and defeat. During the latter stages of the operation, Stalin and, to some extent, other *Stavka* members and staff personnel, reverted to earlier bad habits. They stubbornly insisted on continuing the operation despite unsettling intelligence reports. They chose to follow subjective judgment rather than objective fact, just as had been the case in the winter of 1941 and 1942. Similarly, they ignored the eroded strength of their forces and again fell victim to the mistake of seeking strategic ends dysfunctional with the forces at hand. These lessons were not lost on the High Command. In the future, forces and means would be better balanced against desired ends. This became a marked characteristic of the summer-fall campaign.

The summer-fall campaign plan was more mature than that which governed winter operations. The *Stavka* and General Staff planned in advance, and in some detail, for the defensive and offensive phases of the Kursk operation. They also sketched out the principal aims and lines of operations for the subsequent drive to the Dnepr. In part, the improved predictability of planning was due to maturing intelligence collection and analysis.

Razvedka planning was coordinated by the *Stavka* and implemented by detailed operational and tactical planning at every command level. The *Stavka* and General Staff prepared general appreciations of German strategic intentions based on reports from *razvedka* sources and then gave *fronts* the task of planning further intelligence collection. *Front* and army *razvedka* plans were formal documents that focused all intelligence activities by specifying who would conduct it, where, by what means, and to what end. They included tasks for all air, agent, signal, special, and ground intelligence collection means available to respective commanders. At the same time, the High Command passed down to *front* all intelligence data received from its specialized collection means. This process was governed by the 1942 regulations and subsequent amendments issued in 1943.

In 1943, army and *front* headquarters staffs organized their efforts in accordance with the new directives and regulations (see Appendix A). By April new principles of intelligence collection, processing, and analysis had emerged, and the Soviets had fashioned a logical system for the conduct of *razvedka*. Success, however, depended in large part on the efficiency of each collection means, on the creation of reliable communications means, and on efficient staff operations required to convert raw data into meaningful estimates that could be acted upon. In the first two years of war, collection problems associated with each means had often frustrated the Soviets; by the spring and summer of 1943, tighter procedures and extensive experience had solved many of the more nagging problems.

By spring 1943, a command and staff system had evolved to carry out centralized *razvedka* specified by regulations, directives, and instructions.

> *Front* commanders, while defining the aim of *razvedka,* as a rule, pointed out what basic strength must be devoted to it and what information and in what time limits it must be obtained. The chief of staff specifies the *razvedka* missions decreed by the commander; establishes the sequence of their fulfillment; and, while specifying the directions (regions) in which to concentrate necessary forces, determines the forces for *razvedka* of the most important objectives.[74]

Intelligence departments [*razvedyvatel'nyi otdel,* or RO] of *front*s organized all *razvedka* activity supervised by the Chief Intelligence Directorate, the GRU, of the General Staff, which provided *front*s with strategic intelligence data. *Front* ROs worked out projects required by the plan, *razvedka* orders for subordinate armies and staffs of subordinate branches and types of forces, and directives for subordinate partisan detachments. Thereafter, ROs supervised collection of intelligence data, processed materials, prepared necessary reports and estimates, and kept commanders and operations departments informed of the intelligence situation.[75]

Prior to April 1943 the functions of *razvedka* and *kontrrazvedka* [counterintelligence] had been collocated in *front* and army headquarters, carried out by the *osobyi otdel'* (OO) [Special Department] and *razvedyvatel'nyi otdel'* (RO) [Razvedka Department], respectively. To increase the prestige and power of counterintelligence agencies, on 19 April 1943 the Defense Commissariat reorganized the OOs into *otdel kontrrazvedka* (OKR), which were shifted in subordination from the NKVD to the Commissariat of Defense (NKO).[76] Henceforth, they were directly responsible to one of the assistant commissars of defense. These counter-*razvedka* organs came to be known by the acronym SMERSH (*smert' shpionam* [death to spies]. The extensive activity of these organs in dealing with enemy agents in the Soviet rear area and in assisting intelligence and *maskirovka* efforts by engaging in disinformation are beyond the scope of this paper; nevertheless, they probably made major contributions.

The *front* intelligence staff planned and organized air, agent, radio, and troop *razvedka* by using specialized intelligence subunits under its control and assets of subordinated commands. In addition, *front*s employed partisan detachments to conduct operational *razvedka* at greater depths in the enemy rear. Specialized long-range air reconnaissance units assigned to *front* air armies employed visual and photographic techniques to gather intelligence at strategic and operational depths while army air *razvedka* units used primarily visual observation at tactical and shallow operational depths (50 to 100 kilometers). Long-range air *razvedka* observed rail and highway nets deeper in the enemy rear to determine the scale and direction of troop movements. Both long-range and regular air reconnaissance units surveyed tactical and operational assembly areas and other objectives in the enemy rear, but they paid particular attention to principal enemy defense lines, artillery firing positions, headquarters, supply installations, and reserve positions that could affect the development of the German offensive. Air *razvedka* data were passed to the staff that controlled the air assets and, if combat was under way, to all lower headquarters through regiment by clear-text radio transmission.

Front staff departments controlled agent and special *razvedka* by reconnaissance-diversionary teams deployed from commando (destroyer) brigades and partisan *razvedka* through the staff department that had formulated the planned use of each asset. *Front* staff departments processed the intelligence information and, when appropriate, passed it to army headquarters. Specialized radio units at *front* level organized and conducted radio *razvedka* by intercepting enemy radio transmissions, by conducting limited radio location, and occasionally by jamming enemy radio transmissions. Communications units at army level and lower organized eavesdropping activities and, whenever possible, attempted to tap into enemy wire communications as well. Radio *razvedka*, used extensively for the first time at Stalingrad, sought to obtain information on enemy strength and dispositions, the location of major army force groupings, and the time and location of artillery and air strikes.

Armies and subordinate headquarters conducted ground *razvedka* by means of observation, troop *razvedka,* and large-scale conduct of combat *razvedka*—specifically, reconnaissance in force. Ground *razvedka* served primarily to "illuminate" enemy tactical positions to determine the identity and nature of enemy forces and the location of specific enemy defensive lines, weapons positions, and troop assembly areas. Soviet concern for ground *razvedka* reflected the belief that careful study of tactical positions could produce an intelligence mosaic that would assist in accurate assessments of enemy attack intentions and preparations. Consequently, the Soviets paid special attention to refining their ground *razvedka* techniques, which could supplement and verify information obtained in increasing amounts from more refined technical collection means. The most basic means of ground *razvedka* was planned observation of enemy defenses. Commanders and staffs at every level organized extensive observation post networks manned by personnel specially trained in observation techniques and equipped with a variety of observation devices. Army first-echelon divisions and regiments created the most important segment of the observation post (OP) network.

In addition, armies, divisions, and regiments extensively employed small combat groups dispatched into enemy defensive positions to conduct sweeps, ambushes, and raids to obtain intelligence data. By summer 1943 these measures were facilitated by the proximity of opposing force positions and by the vast experience gained in conducting such operations in the first two years of war. Small groups of five to eight men conducted sweeps and ambushes to seize prisoners, documents, and enemy weapons. Smaller groups of three to five men conducted diversionary and reconnaissance missions deeper in the enemy rear to perform the same missions and also to locate, reconnoiter, and sometimes destroy enemy command posts, communications facilities, and logistics installations. Larger reconnaissance detachments from *front* and army conducted deeper operations against stronger objectives in the operational depths and cooperated with partisan detachments. Normally, these larger forces were controlled by the ROs of armies and *front*s. In addition, artillery and engineer staffs planned and conducted extensive artillery and engineer *razvedka,* fully integrated with other means.

During the second period of war, intelligence served as a basis for planning and verifying critical deception plans. As was the case with strategic planning, the role of intelligence grew throughout this period. There emerged a direct relationship between the quality of intelligence collection and analysis and the success of strategic plans in general and deception plans in particular. At Stalingrad sound tactical intelligence data combined with correct operational and strategic assessments to pave the way for an effective secret operational regrouping of forces and an effective operational deception plan. After the winter campaign developed, weaker intelligence on the march and subjective judgments by High Command personnel hindered effective deception and, in part, produced the operational failures of February through March.

Effective intelligence during the summer and fall of 1943 permitted the High Command to plan effectively for the Kursk operation and subsequent operations and to implement the Soviets' first successful strategic deception. Although local tactical failures and operational difficulties demonstrated that the quality of intelligence was not uniformly high across the front, in the main it was effective enough to support accomplishment of most aspects of Soviet strategic deception. The performance of intelligence in the service of military strategy and deception throughout late 1942 and 1943 clearly demonstrated its future potential. It was the task of the *Stavka* and General Staff to analyze the contributions of intelligence and ensure that the results of that analysis were exploited for the benefit of Soviet strategic planning in the future.

4 The Third Period of War

Context

The Soviets opened 1944 with the first of a series of successive strategic offensives that would continue unabated until war's end. The January offensives at the extremities of the Eastern Front against German forces around Leningrad and at Krivoi Rog and Nikopol', south of the Dnepr River, gave way in early spring to the multi-*front* Korsun'-Shevchen-kovskii encirclement operation. Unlike previous springs, the Soviets ignored the thaw [*rasputitsa*] and continued a series of successive *front* offensive operations, which liberated the right bank of the Ukraine and brought Soviet forces to the Rumanian borders by the end of April. While Soviet armies chopped away at the German northern flank, ultimately driving Finland from the war, a multi-*front* offensive in June 1944, using successive encirclement operations within a brilliantly conceived strategic deception plan, crushed German Army Group Center in Belorussia and penetrated to the East Prussian borders. A subsequent blow in the Ukraine brought Soviet forces deep into Poland; they held bridgeheads across the Narev and Vistula rivers north and south of Warsaw. In August, reflecting Soviet strategic concerns, the Soviets launched a series of successive offensives into and through the Balkans that drove Rumania from the war and propelled Soviet forces into Hungary and Yugoslavia while other Soviet *front*s continued to grind up German forces in the Baltic region.

The Soviets opened 1945 with a series of simultaneous strategic operations extending from the Baltic to the Balkans. The East Prussian and Vistula-Oder operations propelled Soviet troops to the Baltic Sea and across the Oder River, only 60 kilometers from Berlin, while in the south

Soviet forces parried a German counteroffensive at Budapest and then continued the advance into Austria. After conducting operations in February and March 1945 to clear German forces from the flanks of the Soviet main thrust, the Soviets commenced the titanic, almost ceremonial struggle to conquer Berlin and liquidate the Nazis in their own lair, thus ending the Great Patriotic War. However, combat for Soviet forces was not over. In August 1945, responding to requests for assistance from their allies, the Soviets organized and conducted their largest-scale strategic operations of the war (in terms of space), which crushed Japanese forces in Manchuria and won for the Soviet Union a place in subsequent negotiations for peace and postwar reconstruction in the Far East.

The Winter Campaign, December 1943–April 1944

In November and December 1943, the *Stavka* and General Staff considered their options for continuation of the ongoing strategic offensive into the winter (see map 9). Based on what had recently occurred, there was every reason for optimism. Vasilevsky noted

> By the end of 1943 the leaders of the country and the armed forces faced the urgent question of a third winter campaign. The military and political position of the Soviet Union had been considerably consolidated by that time. The successful completion of the summer and autumn campaign of 1943 had brought the liberation of the left bank of the Ukraine and the Donbas, the isolation of enemy troops in the Crimea, the smashing of their defences on the Dnieper and the seizing of sizeable strategic bridgeheads on the river's right bank, as well as the extensive partisan movement behind the enemy lines and the existence of powerful strategic reserves at GHQ disposal. All this had created conditions conducive to new, large-scale offensive operations. The liberation of Kremenchug, Dnepropetrovsk, Zaporozhye, Cherkassy and Kiev was a big setback to the enemy. We had freed half of all the territory of the country occupied by the enemy. The Red Army had destroyed the offensive might of Hitler's Wehrmacht and forced the enemy to switch to defence along the entire Soviet-German front. The war had entered a stage when we could now directly tackle the question of completing the liberation of all Soviet soil.[1]

The *Stavka*, however, realized it had achieved success in 1943 by applying pressure to German forces along the entire Eastern Front and collapsing German defenses in specific sectors. This had been a costly solution to the strategic problem in terms of casualties, and a continuation of that strategy in 1944 across the same extensive front could produce a diffusion of military efforts, continued heavy losses, and possible stalemate. Deputy Chief of the General Staff Shtemenko described *Stavka* strategic planning in mid-December 1943:

> The simultaneous offensives by the Soviet Armed Forces along the whole front from the Baltic to the Black Sea, which had been characteristic

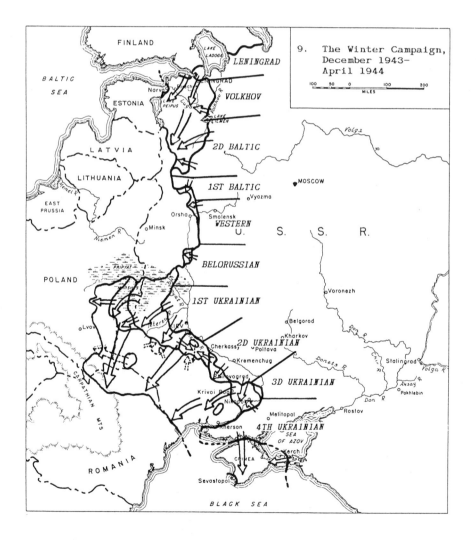

9. The Winter Campaign, December 1943– April 1944

of the autumn 1943 plan, were now unfeasible. The realities of the war compelled us to abandon simultaneous offensives in favour of powerful consecutive operations or, as we used to say and write in those days, strategic blows, which would be more suited to the new situation.[2]

Large German forces still existed near Leningrad, in Belorussia, on the right bank of the Ukraine, and in the Crimea. Destruction of any of these groups in rapid fashion would require a tremendous concentration of effort, although the absence of large German strategic and operational reserves eased the Soviet problem somewhat. However, the Germans did possess reserves in corps and division strength which, if used properly, could thwart Soviet offensives in a particular operational sector. Shtemenko articulated the Soviet solution to the strategic dilemma:

> In order to pierce the enemy front, break it up on a wide sector and prevent its restoration, Soviet strategists had to plan with a view to creating more powerful concentrations than the enemy's. The role of tanks, artillery and aircraft must be enhanced to make each of these concentrations a predominantly attacking force. There would have to be massive reserves that would allow us to build up a decisive superiority of forces on the chosen sector rapidly enough to take the enemy by surprise. Their reserves, on the other hand, could best be dispersed by alternating our blows and delivering them in areas far apart from one another.[3]

For such a strategy to succeed, while avoiding the large casualties of earlier years, the *Stavka* had to improve its ability to shift strategic reserves secretly from one sector to another and to employ them effectively in well-planned operations.

During the winter campaign the *Stavka* planned to conduct operations across the entire front in staggered fashion. It sought to clear German forces from the Leningrad region and develop the offensive in southern Russia to liberate as much of the Ukraine as possible, and the Crimea. The main strategic offensive would occur in the south where the bulk of Soviet reserves were deployed. There the 1st, 2d, 3d, and 4th Ukrainian Fronts were to destroy German Army Groups South and A. Zhukov outlined the priority tasks of the winter campaign.

> After an in-depth and comprehensive analysis, the Supreme Command decided in the winter campaign of 1944 to mount an offensive on a front running from Leningrad all the way down to the Crimea.

According to our plan, the major offensive operations were to be launched in the South-Western theatre of war in order to liberate the entire Ukraine west of the Dnieper, and the Crimea. It was decided to totally smash the siege of Leningrad, and to push the enemy out of the entire Leningrad Region. On the North-Western Direction the troops were to reach the boundaries of the Baltic Republics. The Western Direction was ordered to liberate as much of Byelorussia as possible.

When the actions of Soviet forces in the winter of 1944 were planned, it was also decided to concentrate the principal effort on the 1st, 2nd, 3rd, and 4th Ukrainian Fronts so as to build up a greater superiority over the enemy in those sectors and to swiftly smash the forces of Army Groups South and A.

As for the other Fronts in the north, north-west and west, the Supreme Command decided to deploy fewer forces so as not to divert them from the main sections on the front.[4]

The Soviet winter campaign would commence almost simultaneously against the German northern flank in the Leningrad area and from the Dnepr bridgeheads. On the Northwestern Direction the Leningrad, Volkov, and 2d Baltic Fronts would strike Army Group North and drive German forces back to the eastern border of former Estonia. On the Southwestern Direction the 1st and 2d Ukrainian Fronts would attack Army Group South and drive it toward the Carpathians while the 3d and 4th Ukrainian Fronts drove German forces from the Krivoi Rog and Nikopol' regions of the eastern Ukraine. Thereafter, the 3d Ukrainian Front would attack westward toward Odessa in tandem with 1st and 2d Ukrainian Fronts operating to the north and 4th Ukrainian Front operating to clear German forces from the Crimea.

As Shtemenko described, the offensive would unfold in three stages.

According to the plan of campaign, the earliest offensive (January 12) was to be launched by the Second Baltic Front. On January 14, it would be joined by the Leningrad and Volkhov Fronts. This joint operation of the three fronts was known as the "First Blow." Ten days later (on January 24) the main offensive, in the Ukraine, was to begin. Our operations here were designated the "Second Blow." The "Third Blow" was to be delivered in March–April, when Odessa would be liberated by the Third Ukrainian Front, after which the enemy forces in the Crimea would be crushed by the onslaught of the Fourth Ukrainian Front. After this the plan envisaged an offensive on the Karelian Isthmus and in Southern Karelia.[5]

Shtemenko reiterated the purposes of Soviet strategy:

> This system of alternating blows at widely separated targets fully justified itself. The enemy was forced to swing his forces from one sector to another, including the distant flanks, and thus lost them bit by bit.[6]

The principal Soviet offensive on the Southwestern Direction took the form of ten distinct operations, some sequential and some almost simultaneous, collectively named the Right Bank of the Ukraine Operation. The first, which began in late December 1943 (Zhitomir-Berdichev), represented both a culmination of the Kiev operation to secure a strategic bridgehead across the Dnepr and the commencement of the new strategic offensive. Subsequently, through the winter, Soviet forces conducted nine more operations, organized chronologically into two phases, as follows:

Phase One
Kirovograd: 5–16 January 1944 (2d Ukrainian Front)
Korsun'-Shevchenkovskii: 24 January–17 February 1944 (1st and 2d Ukrainian Fronts)
Rovno-Lutsk: 29 January–11 February 1944 (1st Ukrainian Front)
Nikopol'-Krivoi Rog: 30 January–29 February 1944 (3d and 4th Ukrainian Fronts)

Phase Two
Proskurov-Chernovtsy: 4 March–17 April 1944 (1st Ukrainian Front)
Uman'-Botoshany: 5 March–17 April 1944 (2d Ukrainian Front)
Bereznegovataia-Snigirevka: 6–18 March 1944 (3d Ukrainian Front)
Odessa: 26 March–14 April 1944 (3d Ukrainian Front)
Crimea: 8 April–12 May 1944 (4th Ukrainian Front)

While the Soviets were conducting their main blows in the Ukraine and a secondary blow in the Leningrad region, forces on other directions would engage in limited offensive action. On the Northwestern Direction Soviet forces were to distract German attention and forces from the Leningrad area and then capitalize on Soviet success at Leningrad by advancing to the border of the Baltic states. Forces on the Western Direction were to mount limited objective attacks into eastern Belorussia.

The *Stavka*'s objectives were twofold. First, it sought to mask to as great a degree as possible the direction of the main strategic thrusts—a difficult problem, for geography and prior offensive operations made

Soviet intentions obvious. Second, and more important, the Soviets hoped to shift forces secretly between *fronts*, operating on main strategic attack directions to achieve surprise and keep German forces off balance. *Razvedka* and deception would play a considerable role in the initial operations. As operations developed into the depths and the direction of the Soviet strategic main thrust became apparent to the Germans, deception would naturally become more difficult and the role of intelligence would change. Henceforth, advantage would accrue to that force that could best conceal its tactical and operational regroupings and keep close track of changes in the enemy's operational and tactical dispositions. In essence, as the arena of conflict shrank, intelligence would have to sharpen to accord that small, but decisive, advantage required as the operational direction of attack changed. The yardstick for measuring advantage would now be marked in kilometers, hours, and days rather than weeks. To be successful, intelligence had to provide a basis for deception on that scale.

Planning for the first blow, near Leningrad, began in September 1943, almost four months before the operation commenced. Between 9 and 14 September the Leningrad and Volkhov Fronts outlined proposed offensive schemes to the *Stavka,* and on 29 September the *Stavka* ordered the *fronts* to begin preparations for the new offensive. The *Stavka* concept required the Leningrad and Volkhov Fronts "to destroy German Eighteenth Army, liberate the Leningrad region, and prepare to conduct successive offensive operations to liberate the Soviet Baltic republics."[7] Assisted by an effective deception plan, the Soviet attacks, which began on 14 January, made considerable initial progress. After the Soviets committed their reserves, the front collapsed, ultimately forcing the Germans to withdraw from the Leningrad area to the "Panther" position covering the approaches to the Baltic states.

Farther south, in early January, while the 1st Ukrainian Front struggled with counterattacking German forces north of Vinnitsa in the Zhitomir-Berdichev operation, Konev's 2d Ukrainian Front sought to break the stalemate north of Krivoi Rog by enlarging its already substantial lodgement south of the Dnepr River. Prior to early January Konev, Malinovsky (3d Ukrainian Front), and Tolbukhin (4th Ukrainian Front) had focused their efforts on crushing German Sixth Army in the Krivoi Rog and Nikopol' areas, but to no avail. Consequently, on 20 December Konev requested permission to go on the defensive temporarily to regroup and refresh his forces prior to resuming offensive operations toward Krivoi Rog in early January. The *Stavka* consented and established 5 through 7

January as the dates of the new offensive. On 29 December, in light of the 1st Ukrainian Front's spectacular progress west of Kiev, the *Stavka* altered Konev's mission by ordering him to reorient his armies 90 degrees from a southerly to a westerly direction and concentrate on the Kirovograd direction. At this time Zhukov was responsible for coordinating the actions of 1st and 2d Ukrainian Fronts and Vasilevsky the 3d and 4th Ukrainian Fronts.

Konev formed two shock groups to strike north and south of Kirovograd. The northern group (5th Guards Army and 7th Mechanized Corps) and the southern group (7th Guards Army and 5th Guards Tank Army) were to penetrate German defenses and envelop the city from the north and east. Three other armies would tie down German forces on the *front*'s northern flank. The *front* directive, issued on 2 January, ordered armies to regroup, concentrate, and attack on 5 January.[8] Despite the fact that the Germans detected a portion of the Soviet regrouping, on the appointed date Konev began the Kirovograd offensive. Although his southern group made only limited progress, his northern group ruptured German defenses north of the city. Konev quickly reinforced his northern group. The combined force swept southwest, enveloped Kirovograd, and linked up with 5th Guards Tank Army, which had finally broken the stalemate on Konev's southern front, and thrust westward to Kirovograd. Early on 8 January Kirovograd fell. Assisted by deteriorating weather, German forces finally stabilized the front 20 kilometers west of the city.

The 1st and 2d Ukrainian Fronts' advance to Berdichev and Kirovograd set the stage for the Korsun'-Shevchenkovskii operation, which the Soviets have since called the "new Stalingrad on the Dnepr," a major operation designed to eliminate the German salient protruding to the Dnepr River in the Kanev and Korsun'-Shevchenkovskii region. The salient formed naturally as a result of the preceding operations and Hitler's reluctance to abandon territory, in this case the last remaining segment of the previously formidable Dnepr River Eastern Wall. By design, the Korsun'-Shevchenkovskii operation was to be a classic envelopment of the exposed salient occupied by two army corps of German First Panzer and Eighth Armies.

In late December, the *Stavka* formulated a concept for the joint 1st and 2d Ukrainian Front operation. But, because of delays associated with the Kirovograd operation, it repeatedly amended the concept. Finally, on 12 January, a *Stavka* directive ordered the two *front*s to encircle and destroy the enemy group in the Zvenigorodka-Mironovka salient by closing the left flank units of the 1st Ukrainian Front and the right flank units of the 2d Ukrainian Front somewhere in the Shpola region, because only such a union of 1st and 2d Ukrainian Front forces could produce the capability of developing the shock force necessary to reach the Southern Bug River.[9]

The 1st Ukrainian Front was to attack on 26 January and the 2d Ukrainian Front on 24 January because of the different distances to their objectives. These plans probably involved diversionary activity by other *fronts*, in particular the 3d and 4th Ukrainian Fronts. The ensuing two-front operation resulted in the encirclement of two German army corps by 3 February. In subsequent operations a significant portion of these German corps was destroyed.

Three days after operations had commenced on the left flank of Vatutin's 1st Ukrainian Front, 13th and 60th Armies, on the *front* right flank, went into action near Rovno. The operation was designed to capitalize on German fixation on fighting to the east and take advantage of local terrain conditions to surprise German forces defending Rovno. Because the northern part of the region was swampy, forested terrain and Soviet forces there were overextended, the German command did not expect an offensive in the region. Thus, the 1st Ukrainian Front's right flank armies faced a weak German defense organized around strong points along the main roads manned by Corps Detachment C, containing remnants of several German divisions. Vatutin ordered 13th Army to attack toward Rovno and Lutsk and assigned it two cavalry corps (1st Guards and 6th Guards) to spearhead the advance. To achieve surprise, the army concentrated the bulk of its forces 20 kilometers from the forward area and planned to launch its attack from the march. 13th Army's left flank corps were to strike frontally and then envelop Rovno, while neighboring 60th Army units attacked German positions farther south at Shepetovka.[10]

On 27 January 13th and 60th Armies began their assault toward Rovno against heavy resistance. Simultaneously, on 13th Army's right flank, 1st Guards and 6th Guards Cavalry Corps conducted a secret night march. On the following day they attacked the German rear area. Only on 31 January, when the two cavalry corps had reached the outskirts of Lutsk and Rovno, did the Germans realize the seriousness of the situation. After subsequent heavy fighting Lutsk fell on 2 February and Rovno shortly thereafter. Soviet seizure of Rovno further complicated the complex task of German Army Group South, already under attack at Korsun' and about to be attacked again in the Krivoi Rog area. It also severed the army group's rail connections northward. The successful offensive secured positions out of which Soviet forces would commence a major offensive in March against the rear of Army Group South. It was but one facet of the continuously shifting pressure applied on German forces—the pressure that would ultimately produce a collapse of its entire defense in the Ukraine.

The final Soviet assault on German Army Group South during the December-January wave of offensive activity occurred in the Nikopol'-Krivoi Rog region, where the Soviets had seized one of their first footholds across the Dnepr and where subsequent progress had been extremely limited because of heavy German resistance. The Soviets had maintained heavy pressure on German forces in the area and had launched periodic diversionary attacks by the 3d and 4th Ukrainian Fronts to divert German attention from the more critical sectors farther north, to tie down German forces (coincidentally also playing upon Hitler's concern for holding the area), and to make whatever gains possible. Throughout December 1943 and January 1944, the Soviet attacks in the region had suffered from the natural difficulty of effecting secret regroupments in confined spaces. Now, as late January approached, the Soviet High Command ordered preparations for a final operation to capitalize on success elsewhere and—once and for all—to clear the great bend of the Dnepr and liberate Nikopol' and Krivoi Rog. The High Command was immeasurably assisted in that task by the ongoing fight in the Korsun' area, which drew German reserves from the Nikopol' and Krivoi Rog regions.

The interrelationship of all operations south of the Dnepr was apparent from a message that Vasilevsky sent to the *Stavka* on 29 December.

> The successful development of the operation of the front forces of Nikoleyev [Vatutin], and chiefly—the serious defeat of the main enemy group on that direction and our fundamental decision to direct the main forces of Stepin [Konev] on Kirovograd and further to Pervomaisk—forces us to reconsider the plan of operations of the Third and especially the Fourth Ukrainian Front.[11]

Vasilevsky concluded that German forces were likely to begin withdrawing from the Nikopol' area and therefore urged renewed attacks on the area on 10 through 12 January. The *Stavka* approved his proposal, but the attacks achieved only minimal gains and were halted by 17 January. Vasilevsky submitted a new plan, along the same lines as the first, for a reinforced attack on 30 January. Vasilevsky's new concept required Malinovsky's 3d Ukrainian Front to attack with 46th and 8th Guards Armies backed up by 4th Guards Mechanized Corps toward Apostolovo and the Dnepr River to link up with 4th Ukrainian Front whose 3d Guards, 5th Guards, and 28th Armies and 2d Guards Mechanized Corps were to crush German forces defending the Nikopol' bridgehead. To deceive the Germans regarding the location of the main attack, Malinovsky planned to begin his operation on his flanks in 37th and 6th Armies' sectors.[12]

On 30 January 37th and 6th Armies began their diversionary assaults to draw German reserves (two panzer divisions) into their sector. The next day the *front* main force struck. 8th Guards Army penetrated German defenses and 4th Guards Mechanized Corps advanced to exploit. By 5 February Soviet forces had advanced 45 to 60 kilometers and secured Apostolovo. Heavy fighting ensued up to 24 February, when Soviet forces finally secured Krivoi Rog.

By mid-February the first phase of the Right Bank of the Ukraine Operation had been completed. German forces had been driven back from the Dnepr River from the Pripiat' marshes to south of Nikopol'; the 1st, 2d, and 3d Ukrainian Fronts were poised along a front running from Lutsk through Dubno, Shepetovka, Zvenigorodka, and Kirovograd to Krivoi Rog and the lower stretch of the Dnepr River. The *Stavka* consulted Zhukov, Vasilevsky, and the *front* commanders concerning upcoming operations. In previous years it had been at this point that operations had ground to a halt, mired in the mud of the spring *razputitsa* [thaw]. The Germans had every reason to believe and hope that this would be the case in 1944. But it was not to be the case. Vasilevsky summed up the *Stavka* position, stating

An analysis of the strategic situation at the front, the state of the enemy troops and the constantly mounting Soviet resources gave the Supreme High Command grounds for concluding that it was both possible and expedient to continue the offensive of the Ukrainian fronts without any breathing space, so as to dismember the German fascist troops by simultaneous powerful blows on a wide front from the Polesye area to the mouth of the Dnieper and, having destroyed them piecemeal, to complete the liberation of the right bank of the Ukraine.[13]

The *Stavka* ordered the 1st Ukrainian Front to strike southward through Chertkov to Chernovtsy, the 2d Ukrainian Front to advance through Uman' to Bel'tsy and Iassy, and the 3d Ukrainian Front to advance through Nikolaev to Odessa. The *Stavka* reinforced Vatutin's *front* with 4th Tank Army and shifted forces from 4th to 3d Ukrainian Front. In the growing gap between Rokossovsky's Belorussian Front and the 1st Ukrainian Front, it created the new 2d Belorussian Front, with orders to strike westward toward Kovel'. Unlike the first phase of operations in the Ukraine, during the second phase the *front*s would attack almost simultaneously, on 4 March (1st Ukrainian), 5 March (2d Ukrainian), and 6 March (3d Ukrainian). On the northern flank 2d Belorussian Front would join the offensive on 15 and 16 March.

The *Stavka* assigned *front*s their missions on 18 February, and in the last five days of February the *front*s assigned missions to subordinate armies. The *Stavka* directive included a deception plan to mislead the Germans concerning the principal strategic direction of advance. Since November the main strategic attack direction had been toward Kiev, Berdichev, and Vinnitsa. That had been the case during the Kiev and Zhitomir-Berdichev operations. Now the *Stavka* shifted the main attack to the right wing of the 1st Ukrainian Front, toward the Dnestr River and Chernovtsy on the Prut River. To conceal the westward regrouping of forces, the *Stavka* ordered deception measures to simulate a continuation of the main effort toward Vinnitsa. This task fell to Vatutin as he formulated his *front* plan. The 18 February *Stavka* order to Vatutin, in part, read

> . . . 1 Ukrainian Front . . . prepare an offensive operation including in the *front* shock group forces of 13, 60, 1 Gds Army, 3 Gds TA and 4 TA.
>
> Strike a blow from the front Dubino, Shepetovka, Lyubar to the south with the mission of destroying German groups in the Kremenets, Staro-Konstantinov, Ternopol' areas and secure the line Berestechko, Brody, Ternopol', Proskurov, Khmel'niki.
>
> Subsequently, have in view, while firmly securing your flank toward L'vov, attacking in the general direction of Chertkov to cut off the southern group of Germans from their path of retreat to the west in the sector north of the Dnestr River.[14]

After meeting on 23 February with *Stavka* representative Zhukov, Vatutin formulated a plan to strike with 13th, 60th, and 1st Guards Armies, backed up by 3d Guards and 4th Tank Armies, from the sector Torgovitsa-

Shepetovka-Liubar southward toward Ternopol' and Chertkov. 18th and 38th Armies, on the *front* center and left flank, would launch supporting attacks. 3d Guards and 4th Tank Armies were to go into action in 60th Army's sector; initially, 1st Tank Army would remain in *front* reserve on the left flank. The plan was drafted by Vatutin and, after his death at the hands of anti-Soviet partisans in early March, by Zhukov, who was appointed his successor.[15] Vatutin's deception plan called for active measures to simulate preparations for a main attack in 38th Army's sector on the *front* left flank and measures to mask the massive regrouping required by the operation. In essence, the Soviets embarked on a race to regroup their forces, based on their intelligence data.[16] Zhukov won the race to regroup, and on 4 March his forces struck. Within days 3d Guards and 4th Tank Armies had ripped a huge hole through the German front, and by 7 March the tank armies were approaching Proskurov. While Soviet attacks developed, the regrouping went on, and between 6 and 14 March 1st Tank Army shifted 250 kilometers westward and concentrated southwest of Shepetovka.

On 7 March the Germans commenced heavy counterattacks northwest of Proskurov and north of Ternopol', which ended the rapid progress of the Soviet offensive. Consequently, Zhukov proposed to the *Stavka* a new plan to continue the offensive south toward the Dnestr River, using 1st Guards and 60th Armies spearheaded by 4th Tank Army and the newly regrouped 1st Tank Army. Zhukov's aim was to capitalize on the success achieved farther east by 2d Ukrainian Front by reaching Kamenets-Podol'skii and cutting off the withdrawal routes of German First Panzer Army. He proposed the new phase begin on 20 March. The *Stavka* agreed but changed his *front* objective to the city of Chernovtsy, deeper in the German rear.[17] Zhukov's new attack began on 15 March, with a diversionary thrust by 13th Army toward Brody and L'vov on the right flank to conceal his intent to thrust south with his main force. Meanwhile 1st Tank Army secretly deployed forward and joined the regrouped *front* main forces near Proskurov. On 21 March, Zhukov's main thrust toward the south began, ending German speculation as to where the main Soviet attack would be directed. 1st and 4th Tank Armies plunged into the German rear, ultimately cutting off First Panzer Army. 1st Tank Army reached the Dnestr River on 24 March. Meanwhile, Zhukov regrouped 3d Guards Tank Army and 1st Guards Army and on 22 March commenced another sudden attack northwest of Proskurov.

In the ensuing weeks Zhukov and von Manstein played a game of chess with their forces, with the fate of encircled First Panzer Army at stake. By the end of the month, First Panzer Army successfully broke out westward and linked up with German relief forces dispatched from southern Poland. Manstein's plan for the breakout succeeded, but disputes with Hitler cost the army group commander his job. Soviet success in the 1st Ukrainian Front sector quickly translated into success in other *front*s' sectors as well. The Soviets quickly capitalized on the risk von Manstein had taken when he shifted the bulk of his army group reserves westward and dispatched reinforcements to the Ukraine in First and Fourth Panzer Armies' sectors. A day after the 1st Ukrainian Front began its offensive, Konev's 2d Ukrainian Front struck toward Uman' against weakened German Eighth Army.

Konev's mission, contained in the 18 February *Stavka* directive, was

to prepare an offensive operation including in the *front* shock group forces of 27, 52, 4 Gds. Army, 5 Gds TA, 2 and 6 Tank Armies.

Deliver the blow from the sector Vinograd, Zvenigorodka, Shpola in the general direction of Uman to destroy the German Uman group and secure the line: Ladyzhin, Gaivoron, Novo Ukrainka.

Subsequently continue the offensive to reach the Dnestr River in the sector Mogilev-Podol'sk-Yagorlyk.

The offensive is to begin 8–10.3[18]

Konev conducted his main attack with 27th, 52d, and 4th Guards Armies from Zvenigorodka toward Uman' with 2d, 5th Guards, and 6th Tank Armies conducting the exploitation operation. 7th Guards and 5th Guards Armies launched supporting attacks on the left flank toward Novo-Ukrainka, and 40th Army covered the right flank. Konev's offensive emanated from the southern portion of the Korsun'-Shevchenkovskii battlefield. The 5 March Soviet assault quickly penetrated German defenses. Shortly thereafter, the Germans initiated a long fighting withdrawal westward toward the Southern Bug River and ultimately the Dnestr River.

Meanwhile, 3d Ukrainian Front offensive planning went on as its forces widened their bridgehead across the Dnepr River west of Nikopol' and fought to seize a bridgehead over the next major water obstacle defended by German Sixth Army, the Ingulets River. The original *Stavka* order of 18 February required the *front* to gain a foothold over the Ingulets River by 2 March and insert 6th Army and 5th Shock Army into the bridgehead to outflank German defenses from the south.[19] Events, however, turned out differently. 46th Army and 8th Guards Army's advance developed more favorably than expected, and the two armies secured bridgeheads over the Ingulets south of Krivoi Rog, while 6th Army and 5th Shock Army lagged behind. Quickly, Malinovsky ordered 46th Army and 8th Guards Army to attack from their bridgeheads and moved 23d Tank Corps northward to exploit in 46th Army's sector and I. A. Pliev's Cavalry-Mechanized Group to attack in 8th Guards Army's sector. Pliev's group was to advance through German defenses and then turn south in the German rear to outflank German Sixth Army. The 3d Ukrainian Front's flank armies were to tie down other German forces.

The regrouping occurred very quickly over soggy terrain but achieved considerable surprise when 8th Guards and 46th Armies began their 6 March assault. That evening Pliev's group suddenly joined the slowly developing attack and drove deep into the German rear. Subsequently, German Sixth Army was encircled and began a tortuous process of extracting itself from battle and withdrawing westward. Within days, German Sixth Army joined Eighth Army to the north in a delaying action westward across the Ukraine—an action that did not stop until late April along the borders of Rumania. In the course of that withdrawal, Soviet forces conducted yet another operation to liberate the city of Odessa. Soon the 4th Ukrainian Front began an operation that reconquered the Crimea.

Throughout the winter offensive the Soviets focused their efforts on the German southern flank. Unlike the summer-fall offensive, when they had mounted major operations against the German center, in the winter the central sector remained relatively stable while the Soviets conducted a major thrust around Leningrad. The degree to which this was dictated by future Soviet strategic planning for operations against German forces in Belorussia in the summer of 1944 or by the difficulty of fighting in the center is conjecture. It is clear that Soviet resources were sufficient only to ensure success in the south. While the Soviet offensive unfolded in the Ukraine, diversionary activity occurred in the center in the form of the Belorussian Front's operations at Mozyr and Rogachev in January and February 1944.[20] These operations tied down German units but threatened no serious consequences. Creation of the 2d Belorussian Front in February and its subsequent operations around Kovel' also fell into the category of a diversion and measure designed to improve the Soviet position for future offensives.[21]

The Soviets used deception with good effect in the Right Bank of the Ukraine Operation, in particular during its first phase. The timed, staggered nature of the operations, somewhat reminiscent of Soviet practices during the Kursk period, kept the Germans off balance and prevented them from detecting the primary Soviet strategic attack direction and from shifting reserves to counter the Soviet thrusts.

Initially, the Soviets secretly shifted large strategic reserves into the Kiev bridgehead and rent German defenses on the left flank of Army Group South, thus attracting German reserves to that region. Subsequently, the Soviet offensive focus shifted slightly eastward toward Korsun' and Kirovograd, where the Soviets exploited secret regroupings within the 1st and 2d Ukrainian Fronts to damage German Eighth Army and First Panzer Army. No sooner had German reserves adjusted to the new Soviet thrust than Soviet forces capitalized on the weakness of the German flanks by striking at Rovno, Krivoi Rog, and Nikopol'. In the trying weather and terrain, where deception failed to conceal fully the Soviet regroupings, the Germans simply could not move forces rapidly enough to stave off initial defeats. German response timing lagged behind the timing associated with Soviet planning and implementation of plans and never caught up. Unable to anticipate, the Germans forever reacted— in most cases, too late.

In phase two of the operation, the Soviets concealed a major strategic regrouping for a period sufficient to mount a devastating attack on Army Group South's left flank near Shepetovka. This sealed the fate of German forces throughout the Ukraine. It also demonstrated the beneficial effects of deception in the hands of a force whose numerical superiority was steadily growing. Soviet intelligence collection and analysis had a salutary effect on Soviet deception efforts and operations as the winter campaign unfolded. Several vivid examples attest to the effectiveness of *razvedka* in support of strategic plans.

One of the most successful Soviet deception operations took place prior to the 1st Ukrainian Front's Zhitomir-Berdichev operation in December 1943. In early November, Soviet forces had broken out of the Liutezh bridgehead, seized Kiev and Zhitomir, and established a strategic bridgehead on the west bank of the Dnepr River. Thereafter, from mid-November to mid-December, German Army Group South conducted a series of counterattacks to eradicate the bridgehead. The initial counterattack struck Soviet forces in the Fastov region and failed to make progress.

Subsequently, on three occasions German panzer forces shifted their attack axis westward in search of a weak point in Soviet defenses. By mid-December, after repeated failure to crush the Soviet defenders, the Germans launched a last series of attacks near Korosten, northwest of Kiev. As these counterattacks developed, the Soviet 1st Ukrainian Front secretly regrouped and concentrated its forces for an offensive near Brusilov, southwest of Kiev, against a sector weakly defended by German forces. Soviet success in the new offensive depended directly on the ability to keep their attack preparations secret and to monitor the movement of German forces. This was the task of Soviet *razvedka*.

From the very beginning of the German counterattacks, intelligence correctly assessed when and in what strength each blow would fall, although not always the precise location. Colonel-General K. V. Krainiukov, 1st Ukrainian Front commissar, recalled

> On 19 November the Military Council reported to Stalin that all types of *razvedka* established that 31 enemy divisions, including 10 tank divisions, were operating in front of the 1st Ukrainian Front. The report presumably indicated that the main enemy attack evidently would be struck by 10–12 divisions from the Zhitomir region along the Zhitomir-Kiev road. A secondary attack was expected along the Belaia Tserkov-Kiev road.[22]

These sectors were where the first German counterattacks materialized. In his memoirs, Moskalenko, 38th Army commander, provided additional details regarding *razvedka*. Referring to the German regrouping before the final counterattack near Korosten, he noted

> In an account of troop *razvedka* in that period, 38th Army reported, "As a result of active operations by scouts [*razvedchiki*] and by the securing of controlled prisoners, the following regrouping was determined on the army's front: 3.12.43 the enemy withdrew from the army sector of the front 1st Panzer Division, 7th Panzer Division and SS Panzer Division 'Adolf Hitler,' and transferred them to another sector, castled SS Panzer Division 'Reich' north of Kocherovo, introduced 8th Tank Division withdrawn from the region north of Zhitomir into the first line of defense and withdrew 2d Panzer Grenadier Division into reserve."[23]

The army then tracked the movement of these divisions into new assembly areas. As reported by 38th Army at 1800 on 5 December:

Radiorazvedka determined the shift of the following staff communications centers: 7th Panzer Division from Iosefovka to Ivanovichi (20 km west of Cherniakhov), 8th Panzer Division from Tsarevka to Iosefovka and 48th Panzer Corps from Popel'nia to the Vilsk region (15 km northwest of Zhitomir). One of the radio stations, presumably from the network of SS Panzer Division "Adolf Hitler," shifted from Morozovka to the Zhitomir region. The staff of 4th Panzer Army transferred from the Belaia Tserkov region to the Berdichev region.[24]

As a result of this intelligence, two German counterattacks—the first from 6 to 14 December toward Malin and the second from 19 to 22 December from Korosten—were blocked and defeated. The same intelligence reports noted that German strength in the secondary sector from Malin to Radomyshl' was three to four divisions and in the Brusilov sector, where the Soviets intended to attack, was up to four divisions. In 38th Army's tactical sector, intelligence drew an accurate picture of German dispositions using reconnaissance-diversionary forces and conducting engineer and artillery *razvedka*. Moskalenko described one such mission:

> Thanks to the dispatch of a small reconnaissance group up to 10 kilometers in the enemy rear, and from information received from "tongues" [*iazikov,* or prisoner debriefs], we succeeded in rather fully revealing the enemy [force] grouping, the system of fire and weak places in the defense, flanks and gaps. An important role in this was played by personal observation conducted daily by division, corps, and army commanders and by chiefs of artillery.[25]

A fortuitous event then confirmed earlier Soviet intelligence judgments. Shortly before the 24 December Soviet attack, a Soviet scout obtained a German operational map, which showed German dispositions prior to the regrouping and estimated Soviet troop locations. It demonstrated that German intelligence had failed to detect any of the Soviet preattack regrouping.[26]

During the three days prior to the offensive, the Soviets conducted extensive reconnaissance in force throughout the attack sector and in secondary and defensive sectors as well. This action confirmed the results of earlier intelligence, provided details of the German tactical defense, and permitted last-minute Soviet adjustments to their attack dispositions. A history of 18th Army reported

In order to verify information about the enemy and his defensive system, from 21–23 December reconnaissance in force was conducted in the army sector. In and south of the Rakovichi sector, scouts of the 129th Guards, 395th and 117th Guards Rifle Divisions seized prisoners and documents, belonging to subunits of SS Panzer Division "Reich" and 8th Panzer Division.[27] .

The Germans reacted by firing heavy artillery concentrations, which, in turn, revealed German firing positions and permitted Soviet refinements of their artillery preparation and assault plans.

Moskalenko's army similarly conducted reconnaissance in force. At 1500 on 21 December, all rifle divisions on secondary axes conducted reconnaissance in force with reinforced rifle companies. The following day they employed reinforced rifle battalions on the same axes, and on 23 December all divisions on all axes again used reinforced battalions to carry out reconnaissance in force. Moskalenko described the results:

> Reconnaissance in force confirmed that the enemy continued to occupy defensive positions and maintained mobile tank reserves in the tactical depths. As soon as our detachments penetrated into the combat formation of the defense, he quickly employed counterattacks by tanks and self-propelled guns, reinforced by a considerable quantity of infantry. From all of this we reached the following conclusions: that a shortage of infantry forced the enemy to strengthen the soundness of his defense by counterattacks from the depth. During the reconnaissance in force, we were able to define precisely the outlines of the enemy forward region and targets for our artillery.[28]

On 24 December the fruits of Soviet intelligence activity became evident. The Soviet attack tore through German defenses, and, within two days, two Soviet tank armies were racing into the operational depths. Even after the attack, intelligence continued playing a role, in particular, keeping track of German mobile reserves. Again radio interception played a significant role, as Moskalenko noted.

> Already on 24 December we knew about it [the movement of German reserves]. At midday I telephoned the *front* commander and reported that *radiorazvedka* established the transfer of 48th Panzer Corps and its three panzer divisions—1st, 7th, and SS "Adolf Hitler"—to the Zhitomir region.[29]

Moskalenko related similar examples as the operation developed into late January and Soviet forces advanced on Berdichev and Vinnitsa. When approaching Zhitomir, one of Moskalenko's corps intercepted radio traffic of German 19th Panzer Division and entered that division's radio net. It sent 19th Panzer a message ordering it to penetrate south of Zhitomir. Moskalenko added, ''I will never forget this unusual Christmas. From 19th Panzer we received a radio message, 'Attacked by 30 enemy tanks. Out of fuel. Help, Help, Help!' After that communications ceased.''[30] For all of the positive examples of intelligence, Moskalenko cited some negative ones as well. For example, later in the operation, German defenses stiffened, and Moskalenko noted, ''Prepared enemy defense lines in the army sector were not detected'' until Soviet forces came upon them unexpectedly.[31]

In late December and early January, German Army Group South transferred First Panzer Army from the Krivoi Rog area to the Vinnitsa-Uman' sector to deal with the burgeoning crisis. Again Soviet intelligence detected the movement.

> Their [First Panzer Army's] transfer . . . was fixed by our aviation and radiorazvedka. As it was determined, especially active disembarkation occurred at stations near Vinnitsa, Zhmerinka, and Khristinovka, where, on separate days, twenty or more enemy trains with troops, equipment, and ammunition arrived.[32]

Soon after, ''All types of *razvedka* determined that 30 enemy divisions, including 17 infantry, 10 tank (1, 6, 7, 8, 16, 17, 19, 29, SS 'Adolf Hitler,' SS 'Reich'), one (20) motorized and 2 artillery, confronted the 1st Ukrainian Front.''[33] As the German counterattacks developed and forced Soviet forces onto the defense, intelligence reports continued to define the scope of German activity. On 14 January troop and aviation *razvedka* detected large tank concentrations forming for the attack and unloading at railheads. Soon after:

> Radiorazvedka determined by radio location the transfer of radio stations of SS Panzer Division ''Deaths Head'' from Kirovograd (2d Ukrainian Front) to the Tal'noe region (the sector of 40th Army). There the Hitlerites were preparing a secondary strike to support the salient around Zvenigorodka and Boguslav. The staff of enemy 48th Panzer Corps dislocated to the region southwest of Lipavits, where it launched the main attack in the sector of 38th and 1st Tank Armies.[34]

Later, new intelligence reports from prisoners of war confirmed the arrival in the 1st Ukrainian Front sector of 72d, and 88th Infantry Divisions and 6th, 17th, 11th, and, finally, 3d Panzer Divisions.[35]

These examples of intelligence collection in the Zhitomir-Berdichev operation demonstrated the scope of Soviet intelligence activities. Subsequent regrouping of forces on both sides, Soviet planning, and the flow of combat itself lent credence to the data. These intelligence capabilities, in large measure, explain why the Soviets had such apparent success with deception in this and other operations and why their strategic plans achieved the success they did. Similar examples of intelligence collection existed for all subsequent operations in the strategic Right Bank of the Ukraine Operation, but perhaps the most revealing in terms of Soviet intelligence capabilities relate to the largest and most decisive of the operations, the Proskurov-Chernovtsy operation.

In late February 1944, after German forces had been driven from the banks of the Dnepr deep into the Ukraine, the *Stavka* shifted the focus of its operations in the Ukraine to its right flank. After a major secret regrouping of forces from the Vinnitsa region, the 1st Ukrainian Front was to attack from the Dubno-Shepetovka sector southward toward the western Bug and Prut rivers to isolate and destroy German forces in the Ukraine. As had been the case in the Zhitomir-Berdichev operation, Soviet intelligence was to verify the deception plan and support the offensive by tracking the movement of German forces. Again the Soviets achieved considerable success before and during the initial phase of the operation and experienced problems only when its forces had penetrated deep into the German rear. The Soviets were able to regroup secretly two tank armies (3d Guards and 4th) in the Shepetovka area, although the Germans did detect the final stages of movement and responded by regrouping their forces. The Soviets, however, had several days' advantage, during which they penetrated German defenses in a broad sector. The appearance of German reinforcements did surprise the Soviets. One source noted, "One must note that our *razvedka* did not succeed in revealing that regrouping in timely fashion. The appearance of six new panzer divisions in that sector of the front was detected by 1st Ukrainian Front *razvedka* only during the early phases of the operation."[36]

Moskalenko, whose 38th Army attacked in a secondary sector and whose task was to deceive the Germans into believing his army would make the *front* main attack, provided more details concerning *razvedka*. Moskalenko's tactical intelligence organs were able to pinpoint the composition, nature, and strength of German forces and reserves on his front.[37] The Soviets exploited their advantage by penetrating German defenses and advancing about 80 kilometers to the Proskurov region, where German counterattacks brought the advance to a halt. 1st Tank Army then regrouped into the region and, on 21 March, the Soviet advance resumed. In the course of several days' fighting, Soviet 1st and 4th Tank Armies plunged south, seized Chernovtsy, and encircled German First Panzer Army. However, a faulty Soviet intelligence assessment permitted First Panzer Army to cut its way westward out of encirclement and join with II SS Panzer Corps, sent from southern Poland to relieve the beleaguered German force.

Zhukov recalled the basic misjudgment made when Soviet forces had the German force loosely encircled:

> As I retrospectively analyze the whole operation today, I think that the 1st Tank Army should have been turned from the Chertkov-Tolstoye area to the east to strike at the surrounded group. But we had reliable intelligence from various sources that the surrounded enemy intended to attempt a breakthrough southward across the Dniester to the Zaleshchiki area. At the time this seemed an extremely reasonable and likely way of action.[38]

Other sources criticized Soviet forces on the inner encirclement line for conducting insufficient *razvedka*.[39] Soviet intelligence had been correct in its initial judgment regarding German intentions to break out to the south. What it did not discover was Hitler's reluctant approval on 25 March of von Manstein's request to move the army westward. Nor did Soviet intelligence detect in timely fashion the German relief force assembled to assist First Panzer Army's breakout. One source stated, "In particular, a shock group was created in the Bol'shovtsy region consisting of 9th and 10th SS Panzer Divisions, the 100th Light Division, and the 367th Infantry Division. One must note that our *razvedka* did not detect the concentration of these units in timely fashion."[40] Moskalenko cites evidence that indicators were present regarding the potential relief effort. He quotes the 1st Ukrainian Front combat journal for 26 March, which noted, "*Radiorazvedka* noted initial operations of an unidentified panzer division in the Zolochev region." The following day the journal read, "The enemy on the line Zolochev, Zborov, Koniukhi have concentrated up to two panzer divisions, which are assembling from the west. . . . *Radiorazvedka* for the first time noticed the operation of a communications

center of an unknown panzer division in the Remizovtse (south of Zolochev) and Koniukhi regions." A last entry on 28 March stated, "Up
to two regiments of infantry were noticed in the Zolochev region, and
up to 100 vehicles moved from Zolochev through Berezhany to Pod-
gaitsi."[41] These reports were not reflected in Zhukov's 29 March order
to block the movement of First Panzer Army south toward the Dneister.
Zhukov later wrote, "As we subsequently found out from captured documents," the Germans had really assembled a sizable relief force.[42]
Zhukov did not comment on the subsequent escape of First Panzer Army
except to say, "Neither I nor the Front headquarters were able to absolutely
ascertain the numbers of the units that broke out. Various figures were
cited, but the final count was probably a great many more than the several
dozen infantry-carrying tanks our troops reported at the time."[43]

Initially, Soviet intelligence worked effectively in the operation to
accord temporary advantage to Soviet commanders. The same applied to
the second phase of the operation, which began on 21 March. Subsequently, while intelligence collection functioned adequately, analysis
failed, primarily because of misinterpretation by the *front* commander,
Zhukov. A Soviet critique of the operation as a whole stated

> As a result of the decisive blow to the south by forces of the 1st
> Ukrainian Front, in cooperation with forces of the 2d Ukrainian Front, a
> large group of enemy forces were squeezed in the region north of Kamemets-
> Podol'skii and, in the course of battle, suffered heavy losses. However,
> our forces did not succeed in destroying them. The main reasons for this
> failure were inadequacies in control of forces, mistakes by the *front* com-
> mander, poor *razvedka* and also difficulties in moving and maneuvering
> forces and resupplying materiel technical means, resulting from the spring
> thaw [*razputitsa*].[44]

On balance, throughout the winter campaign, Soviet intelligence
worked well, and collection steadily improved despite the often difficult
weather. More often than not, where failure or partial successes occurred,
as in earlier days of the war, it was a result of faulty judgment on the
part of high-level commanders. Despite these deficiencies, intelligence
served to provide a sound underpinning for the series of successive and
simultaneous *front* operations. In particular, in the many instances where
deception succeeded, the successes were due as much to Soviet *razvedka*
success as to German intelligence failure.

As the winter campaign came to an end, two new realities emerged. The first was the fact that Soviet offensive successes had reduced the length of the Eastern Front considerably. This meant the Soviets would face more contiguous German defenses in the future which, in turn, would again elevate the importance of operational as well as strategic deception. Second, and perhaps more important, the patterns of Soviet operations throughout the winter left an indelible imprint on the minds of German planners. The Soviet offensive focus had been on the south—through the Ukraine, toward southern Poland and Rumania. This posed a dilemma to German planners and an opportunity for their Soviet counterparts. The dilemma for the Germans was determining whether Soviet attention would continue to focus on the south. The Soviets had the opportunity to exploit the German dilemma by playing upon it. If the Soviets could convince German planners that the south was indeed their focus, the Soviets could make major progress elsewhere.

The Summer-Fall Campaign, June–October 1944

The Soviet winter campaign continued well into the spring. The successive and, finally, simultaneous *front* operations across southern Russia ultimately drove German forces from the Ukraine. By late April the offensive momentum had ebbed, and the Soviets faced the task of deciding where to focus their next strategic efforts (see map 10). There were several enticing options, including an offensive southward into the Balkans to reap considerable political as well as military rewards, an offensive across central and eastern Poland to the Baltic Sea to entrap both German Army Groups Center and North, an offensive into the Baltic States and Finland, and an offensive against the so-called Belorussian Balcony (which jutted westward north of the Pripiat' marshes). The goal of the Belorussian offensive would be to crush German Army Group Center; penetrate into Poland and East Prussia; and, perhaps, reach the Baltic Sea and isolate German Army Group North as well. The offensive would clear German forces from Belorussia and facilitate future operations through Poland and East Prussia on the direct route to Berlin. The Soviets selected the Belorussian option because, as Shtemenko noted

Repeated analysis of the strategic situation gave us the growing conviction that success in the summer campaign of 1944 was to be sought in

Byelorussia and the Western Ukraine. A major victory in this area would bring Soviet troops out on the vital frontiers of the Third Reich by the shortest possible route. At the same time more favorable conditions would be created for hitting the enemy hard on all other sectors, primarily, in the south, where there was already a strong build-up of our forces.[45]

In choosing this option, the Soviets capitalized on the deception potential of the other options by preparing an extensive strategic deception to conceal their intentions and major force regroupings. *Razvedka* had the imposing task of supporting those ambitious plans.

10. The Summer Fall Campaign, June–October 1944

During April the *Stavka*, General Staff, and *Stavka* representatives developed a campaign concept, giving priority to an offensive in Belorussia and working out the sequencing of the summer's operations. The summer-fall campaign would begin in early June, with the Leningrad Front attacking toward Vyborg on the Karelian Isthmus. Soon after, the Karelian Front would commence operations north of Lake Ladoga. When German attention shifted north, four Soviet *front*s would strike in Belorussia, and after German reserves had sped north from eastern Poland to deal with these Soviet attacks, the 1st Ukrainian Front would attack toward L'vov and the Vistula River in eastern Poland. Simultaneously, the 2d Baltic Front would attack German Army Group North in the Baltic. After defeating German forces in Belorussia and eastern Poland, the Soviets would cap their success with a two-*front* offensive into Rumania, which by then should have been denuded of German reserves.

> The summer phase of the campaign included five distinct operations:
> Karelian Isthmus–south Karelia: 10 June–9 August 1944
> Belorussia: 23 June–29 August 1944
> L'vov-Sandomierz: 13 July–29 August 1944
> Lublin-Brest: 18 July–2 August 1944 (technically part of the Belorussian operation but in reality a link between that operation and the L'vov-Sandomierz operation)
> Iassy-Kishinev: 20 August–7 September 1944

Each operation would exploit the success of earlier operations. Thereafter, operations would continue into the fall, based on the existing situation in late August.

During preliminary planning the *Stavka* reorganized its *front*s to match the requirements of the upcoming offensive, which would be far more powerful than those that had occurred during the winter across the Ukraine.[46] Soviet success in the campaign depended directly on the ability to regroup and concentrate strategic and operational reserves secretly across wide sections of the front.[47] These movements had to be concealed because the strategic deception plan required that the Germans identify these forces in incorrect locations. It was equally important for Soviet intelligence to track the movement of German operational reserves.

Soviet offensive success in the winter campaign and the strategic positioning of Soviet forces in late spring facilitated Soviet use of strategic deception on an unprecedented scale. The Soviet strategic deception plan capitalized on German fears of future Soviet offensive operations against central and southeastern Europe by accentuating Soviet intent to continue operations into southern Poland and Rumania. The *Stavka* ordered all *front*s in the south to remain active and openly demonstrated the presence of the bulk of Soviet tank armies in that region. Vasilevsky later wrote

> In order to strengthen this view the Soviet command left the bulk of its tank armies in the south. Throughout daylight hours feverish ''defensive'' work would be in progress among the troops of the central sector of the Soviet-German front (on the southern sector the defensive work would be done at night).[48]

The *Stavka* ordered these forces to conduct limited objective attacks during May to convince the German command that this was the region of continuing Soviet strategic interest. Consequently, on 1 May 2d Ukrainian Front launched an attack with 27th and 2d Tank Armies across the Prut River toward Iassy, which culminated in a Soviet defeat at Tyrgu-Frumos but which perpetuated German concerns for their position in Rumania and kept German reserves rooted to Rumania. Similar Soviet efforts in the western Ukraine deceived the Germans regarding a June offensive. At the end of April the *Stavka* ordered all *front*s to go on the defense (except those specifically conducting deception) while it planned the summer offensive.

Thus, the Soviet concept for the 1944 summer-fall campaign was grander in scale than that of 1943, and it was offensive in nature from the very start. Rather than a single strategic thrust, it envisioned a series of powerful successive multi-*front* strategic operations along several strategic directions to destroy several German army groups. The strategic deception plan was also more ambitious. In 1943 the Soviets had concealed one *front* in strategic reserve and then employed it in a counteroffensive. Elsewhere, individual armies within *front*s had regrouped to maintain the momentum of the attack. In 1944 the Soviets planned to regroup large strategic reserves between *front*s and strategic directions while also shifting armies within *front*s. Since deception plans at all levels were far more sophisticated, the task of *razvedka* to verify them would be more challenging.

As had been the case in winter, the opening act of the impending summer drama began north of Leningrad, where the Soviets hoped to drive Finland from the war, divert attention from Soviet offensive preparations elsewhere, and politically embarrass the Germans by defeating one of her allies. The *Stavka* ordered the Leningrad and Karelian Fronts to secure the Karelo-Finnish region and the Karelian Isthmus northwest and north of Leningrad. The offensive began on 10 June and developed according to plan. By 20 June Soviet forces had secured Vyborg, and the next day the Karelian Front commenced operations north of Lake Ladoga, ultimately forcing the Finns to sue for peace. The Vyborg and Karelian operations were clearly peripheral and had only limited effect on the more important operations which, on 23 June, began to unfold farther south.

Preliminary planning for the critical Belorussian operation was completed on 30 May, when the *Stavka* approved the plan. *Stavka* representatives Vasilevsky and Zhukov coordinated subsequent detailed planning for the operation, which was to begin between 15 and 20 June. The *Stavka* concept for the Belorussian operation required simultaneous penetration of German defenses in six sectors and initial encirclement and destruction of forward enemy armies in the Vitebsk, Bobruisk, Orsha, and Mogilev regions. Subsequently, the converging blows of three *fronts* in the direction of Minsk would encircle and destroy the main group of Army Group Center. Soviet forces would then advance to the western borders of the Soviet Union. Once Soviet success against Army Group Center was assured, the 2d and 3d Baltic Fronts would expand the offensive to the north with attacks toward Riga against Army Group North, and the Belorussian Front's left wing would advance into central Poland.

During the first phase of the strategic operation, the 1st Baltic and 3d Belorussian Fronts would operate against German Third Panzer Army, which was defending the Vitebsk sector. The 3d Belorussian Front would strike German Ninth Army at Bobruisk, and the 2d Belorussian Front would attack German Fourth Army at Mogilev and Orsha. Subsequently, the three *fronts* would march on Minsk to encircle German Fourth Army. After Minsk had fallen, the left wing of the 1st Belorussian Front would commence the Lublin-Brest operation to the south, and the 1st Ukrainian Front would begin a major operation toward L'vov and the Vistula River in eastern Poland. Success in the first phase of the operation depended largely on the secret movement into the region of large forces, including 6th Guards Army to reinforce the 1st Baltic Front, 28th Army to reinforce the 1st Belorussian Front, and 5th Guards Tank Army to exploit in 3d Belorussian Front's sector. Concealing such a massive redeployment posed serious problems and required extensive strategic and operational deception. Simultaneously, Soviet intelligence had to guarantee that the deception plan worked and that regrouped German forces would not interfere with the operation.

The Soviet offensive, which commenced on 23 June, achieved immediate success. Within days German Third Panzer and Ninth Armies were encircled and largely destroyed, and, by early June, Soviet forces had seized Minsk and destroyed the better part of German Fourth Army. German Army Group Center was a shambles and could do little more than conduct a fighting withdrawal westward as the Germans transferred reserves northward from Poland and Rumania to stem the advancing Soviet tide.

Within two weeks after the successful Belorussian operation had begun, Soviet forces to the south benefited from the same strategic deception plan, this time in a location where the German High Command had originally expected the Soviet offensive. The Germans, in light of what had occurred in Belorussia, were unable to deal with the new thrust, which the Soviets called the L'vov-Sandomierz operation. The L'vov-Sandomierz operation, which commenced on 13 July 1944, took place within the context of the Belorussian operation, which had begun on 23 June, and the Lublin-Brest operation, which would begin on 18 July. All three massive operations formed a trinity tied together by a mutual strategic deception plan and simple timing. Each was conditioned by the other; each, in turn, had its effect on the other.

The overall strategic deception plan served all three operations but gave first priority to the Belorussian operation. Initially, the plan called for creating offensive concentrations in the western Ukraine (opposite L'vov) in 1st Ukrainian Front's sector and in the southern Ukraine (opposite Rumania) in the 2d and 3d Ukrainian Fronts' sectors. The *Stavka* deployed three tank armies (1st Guards, 3d Guards, 4th) to the western Ukraine and three (2d, 5th Guards, 6th) to southern Ukraine. Then it secretly moved 2d Tank Army and 8th Guards Army into the Kovel' area, behind the left wing of the 1st Belorussian Front and 5th Guards Tank Army northward to Smolensk. While German forces concentrated against perceived threats to southern Poland and Rumania, the Soviets struck in Belorussia. By 11 July the Soviets had destroyed German Army Group Center, taken Minsk, and drawn German reserves northward from southern Poland. Then, on 13 July, Konev's 1st Ukrainian Front attacked toward L'vov, using internal deception to feign an attack from its left flank but actually attacking from its center and right flank. When German reserves shifted to halt this new Soviet penetration, on 18 July the left wing of the 1st Belorussian Front struck farther north, using its secretly deployed 8th Guards Army and 2d Tank Army to spearhead an advance toward Lublin. All three thrusts, in Belorussia and then subsequently toward L'vov and Lublin, were the product of a single plan, which wrought havoc on German defenses from Vitebsk to the Carpathian Mountains.

Orchestrating the second major offensive was the task of Konev's 1st Ukrainian Front. On 24 June 1944 the *Stavka* directed Konev to

> prepare and conduct an offensive operation to destroy enemy groups on the L'vov and Rava-Russkaya direction . . . and reach the line Khrube-shuv-Tomashuv-Yavorov-Galich, by delivering two blows: the first—from the region south-west of Lutsk in the direction of Sokal'-Rava-Russkaya and the second—from the Tarnopol' region to L'vov. In order to secure the blow on the L'vov direction, an offensive was outlined by a portion of the front left wing on Stanislov.[49]

Konev decided to attack in two sectors 60 to 70 kilometers apart. The northern attack from the Lutsk region toward Rava-Russkaia would be mounted by 3d Guards and 13th Armies, backed up by 1st Guards Tank Army and a cavalry-mechanized group. The southern attack, from the Ternopol' region toward L'vov, would be launched by 60th and 38th Armies, supported by 3d Guards Army, 4th Tank Army, and a second cavalry-mechanized group.

Konev deployed 1st Guards and 18th Armies on a 220-kilometer front southward to the foothills of the Carpathian Mountains, with orders to support and cover the flank of the *front*'s southern attack and to simulate the *front* main attack as part of his deception plan. The most challenging task Konev faced was to regroup five rifle and three tank armies over a considerable distance and then concentrate them secretly. For example, 1st Guards Tank Army had to move over 500 kilometers and 4th Tank Army over 250 kilometers. To conceal this regroupment and mask of-fensive preparations, Konev's *front* deception plan simulated concentra-tion of two tank armies and one tank corps on the *front* left flank, in 1st Guards and 18th Army's sectors. This deception concealed Konev's north-ern concentration, but only partially hid the scope of the southern re-groupment.

Konev's northern thrust began on 13 July, when 3d Guards and 13th Armies penetrated German defenses east of Rava-Russkaia. Farther south, opposite L'vov, German resistance was heavier, and the initial Soviet attack made only limited progress. Ultimately, after conduct of a full penetration operation, the Soviets punched through German defenses opposite 60th Army and immediately committed 3d Guards and 4th Tank Armies to drive through the narrow corridor. Meanwhile, in the north, 3d Guards and 13th Armies completed their penetration, and the cavalry-mechanized group moved forward to exploit. On 15 July 1st Guards Tank Army's forward detachment, the reinforced 1st Guards Tank Brigade, advanced in 3d Guards Army's sector to help complete the penetration and secure the commitment of all of 1st Guards Tank Army for an advance westward on Porytsk (toward Vladimir-Volynsk).[50] Konev allowed 1st Guards Tank Brigade to continue its attack toward Porytsk, but he ordered the remainder of 1st Guards Tank Army to shift its advance southward through 13th Army's penetration after his intelligence had detected German operational reserves (16th and 17th Panzer Divisions) moving north to block the anticipated Soviet advance to Porytsk. Subsequently, 1st Guards Tank Army rapidly advanced southwest into the German rear north of L'vov.

Subsequent operations attested to 1st Guards Tank Army's deception success. Outflanked from the north, German resistance also broke east of L'vov; 3d Guards and 4th Tank Armies penetrated into the depths, bypassed L'vov and, together with 1st Guards Tank Army, began a race toward the Vistula River. The race ended in early August, with Soviet forces occupying bridgeheads across that major strategic obstacle.

By mid-July the German defenses in the central sectors of the Eastern Front were a shambles. Soviet forces had dealt Army Group Center a devastating blow, seized Minsk, and were advancing toward Vilnius and Baranovichi. Farther south, Soviet forces had pierced German defenses opposite and north of L'vov and were threatening to envelop German forces defending the city. At this juncture, on 18 July, the left wing of the 1st Belorussian Front unleashed the third major thrust of the Soviet strategic offensive toward Lublin and the Vistula River.

In accordance with earlier planning, on 7 July, after completion of the Bobruisk operation and at a time when the center and right wing of Rokossovsky's 1st Belorussian Front were advancing on a broad front toward Baranovichi and Minsk, the *Stavka* ordered Rokossovsky to prepare the Lublin thrust. The directive assigned Rokossovsky the following mission:

With the arrival of the right flank armies approximately to the distant approaches to the city of Brest, conduct a successive offensive operation with a shift of the main forces into the sector of your left wing, and in cooperation with the right wing of the 1st Ukrainian Front destroy the Lublin-Brest enemy group and reach the Vistula on a broad front.[51]

Rokossovsky planned his *front*'s main attack from the Kovel' area toward Lublin with three rifle armies, 2d Tank Army, and three mobile corps, while two armies on his *front*'s right flank advanced on Brest to catch German forces withdrawing from southern Belorussia in a pincer and destroy them. The massive regrouping of forces within the left wing of the *front* involved movement of 8th Guards and 2d Tank Armies, three mobile corps, and numerous supporting units previously used to support the 1st Belorussian Front attack in Belorussia. Rokossovsky's deception plan relied on the operational situation to the north and south to distract German attention from his offensive preparations and to cover necessary redeployments, which began in mid-June and continued to the very eve of the attack. Intelligence closely monitored German troop movements.

On 18 July Rokossovsky's main assault force struck German forces defending the Kovel' direction, and within hours the German tactical defenses had been ripped apart. On 20 July, while rifle forces approached the Western Bug River, 2d Tank Army moved forward and the next day began an operational exploitation that propelled it to the outskirts of Warsaw. At the same time, 8th Guards Army was breaching the line of the Vistula River at Magnushev.

The Lublin-Brest operation was the third act of a four-act drama that had begun on 23 June. The theme behind that drama was deception in the form of an intricate mosaic of operational and tactical measures unified by a coherent strategic plan. The Soviet strategic deception plan worked well, in particular in Belorussia and in the Kovel' sector, and Soviet intelligence confirmed that German reserves remained where they had been in May. However, stubborn German fixation on a probable Soviet offensive in southern Poland persisted and, while conditioning Soviet success in Belorussia, confounded part of Konev's deception planning.

By early August the five Soviet *front*s that had smashed German strategic defenses between Vitebsk and the Carpathian Mountains struggled along an extended front from the Northern Dvina River to the upper Vistula River. As in 1943, as the main thrust grew in scale, Soviet *front*s on the flanks capitalized on German defeats on the main strategic direction.

On the northern flank, the Baltic Fronts attacked in time-phased sequence from south to north in what is known as the Baltic strategic offensive. The 1st Baltic Front went into action north of the Northern Dvina River on 4 July. In short order, the 2d and 3d Baltic Fronts joined battle, and the three *fronts* drove toward the Baltic coast and Riga against heavy German resistance. This series of operations endured well into the fall— an unspectacular, slow, broad *front* advance measured in kilometers per week. Although progress was slow, the operations distracted the Germans from what was about to occur in the south.

Meanwhile, in the south, along the Rumanian borders, the front had been quiet since early May, when the Germans had considered it to be a prime location for a new major offensive. That offensive had not materialized. On the contrary, while the Germans waited expectantly for an attack, the Soviets had thinned out their front, dispatching army after army northward and leaving the 2d and 3d Ukrainian Fronts with only one tank army (6th) and a reduced complement of rifle forces. By then the Germans were well aware of the havoc wrought by these forces elsewhere. Unknown to the Germans, however, the *Stavka* had chosen German forces in Rumania as its final target in the fourth act of the summer strategic offensive drama.

Planning for the projected Soviet operation in Rumania began on 15 July 1944. The *Stavka* approved Malinovsky's (2d Ukrainian Front) and Tolbukhin's (3d Ukrainian Front) plans in early August and ordered them to destroy German Army Group South Ukraine's forces in the Iassy, Kishinev, and Bendery regions and subsequently advance to Fokshany, Galats, and Ismail. The Black Sea Fleet was to cooperate with the 3d Ukrainian Front and conduct amphibious landings along the Rumanian Black Sea coast. The two *fronts* were to conduct their main attacks in the most vulnerable enemy sectors: the 2d Ukrainian Front between the Tyrgu-Frumos and Iassy strongpoints of German Eighth Army, a region defended largely by Rumanian troops, and the 3d Ukrainian Front south of Bendery at the junction of German Sixth and Rumanian Third Armies.

Malinovsky's main attack force of two rifle armies was backed up by 6th Tank Army and a tank corps. On his right flank two armies would launch a secondary attack supported by a cavalry-mechanized group, and on his left flank, one army would advance up the Prut River to sever the communications between German Eighth and Sixth Armies. Tolbukhin's main attack force consisted of three armies backed up by two mechanized corps. Another army on the right flank would first simulate a main attack and then conduct a secondary attack toward Kishinev while forces on the *front* left flank would cooperate with the Black Sea Fleet in encircling and destroying Rumanian Third Army. Massive regrouping was necessary, and both Malinovsky and Tolbukhin developed complex *front* deception plans to conceal regrouping and confuse the Germans regarding Soviet attack intentions and locations. *Razvedka* successfully confirmed that German dispositions did not change before the 20 August attack. Within one week after the assault, Army Group South Ukraine had suffered a fate similar to that of Army Group Center—the destruction of Sixth Army and two Rumanian armies and the utter collapse of the German front in Rumania. An Axis retreat ensued—a retreat that would not halt until Soviet forces had penetrated Bulgaria and swung west to enter the plains of Hungary.

By the end of August 1944, the major offensive stage of the Soviet summer-fall strategic offensive had run its course. In the central sector of the Eastern Front, the three Belorussian fronts fought along the East Prussian borders, approached the Narev River north of Warsaw, and clung to tenuous bridgeheads across the Vistula River south of the Polish capital city. During July and August German reserves gravitated to the central sector to contest every kilometer of ground and, if possible, hold Soviet forces out of the German heartland of East Prussia and east of the Narev and Vistula barriers. Bitter fighting raged throughout September and into October. Worn-down Soviet forces at the ends of frayed logistical umbilicals sought to improve their positions for another winter offensive against equally worn and heavily attrited German forces, who now fought more out of desperation than conviction. Soviet forces fought their way into the Augustov forests west of the Neiman River, to the gates of Warsaw. There 2d Tank Army, after its victorious march through Lublin to the Vistula, suffered heavy damage at the hands of Model's counterattacking panzers. The Soviets fought their way into bridgeheads over the Vistula River at Magnushev, Pulavy, and Sandomierz. In the Narev and Vistula bridgeheads, the Soviets dug in and fended off counterattack after counterattack by German panzer forces trying to drive them back across the rivers. By mid-October quiet had set in on the Warsaw-Berlin axis as both sides licked their wounds and prepared for the inevitable resumption of the Soviet offensive.

Meanwhile, Soviet attention shifted to the flanks where fighting continued to rage. In the Baltic region the three Baltic *front*s launched offensive after offensive and slowly drove German forces back from their

"Panther" line toward Tallin and Riga. The well-constructed German defenses and the shrinking size of the front combined to thwart any hope for a rapid Soviet advance. The city of Riga became a magnet, attracting the offensive efforts of the Soviets until mid-October, when a sudden secret Soviet maneuver shifted the focus of battle and propelled Soviet forces to the Baltic coast, cutting off Army Group North in the Courland pocket. In the south, the Soviets capitalized on their August destruction of the bulk of Army Group South Ukraine by seizing Bucharest and forcing Rumania to switch her wartime allegiance. Soon after, Soviet forces crossed the Danube into Bulgaria and, in October, forced the Bulgarians to join the Allied cause. In mid-October the 2d Ukrainian Front swung west across the Carpathians into eastern Hungary, and the 3d Ukrainian Front stood poised for a thrust into southern Yugoslavia to seize Belgrade and destroy Germany's position in the Balkan peninsula.

In the transitional period between the summer offensive of 1944 and the winter offensive of 1945, the Soviet advance in the Baltic and into southeastern Europe were strategic diversions, although with definite concrete objectives of their own. A thrust into the Danube basin threatened not only Germany's military position but also its already weakened political and economic state. Germany's last ally (Hungary) would certainly abandon her should Budapest fall, and the Balaton oil fields and food supplies of the Hungarian plain were essential for continuation of the German war effort. Hitler knew this and had long stressed the value of the southern peripheral (in fact, since 1942). The Soviets knew he would defend it.

More important, continued Soviet attacks into the Danube basin would inexorably draw German reserves from the central portion of the front and weaken the Germans there, thus improving Soviet chances for a decisive drive during the winter along the main strategic approach to the Oder River and Berlin. Thus, Soviet operations on the flanks in the fall of 1944 were necessary preconditions for what would occur in the center in January 1945. Zhukov, in his memoirs, noted

In the opinion of the General Staff, the offensive would have to be initiated by our Southern Fronts on the Vienna sector. This would inevitably compel the German command to move considerable forces from our Western Fronts in order to reinforce their South-Eastern strategic direction, which was crucial for the fate of south and south-east Germany.[52]

In late October, the *Stavka* surveyed the situation along the Eastern Front, especially regarding Soviet offensive capabilities in the central sector, and concluded that further offensives without refitting and rest would be futile. Thus, as Shtemenko recorded, "On the night of November 4, 1944, a directive was issued ordering the Third and Second Byelorussian Fronts to go over to the defensive. A few days later similar instructions were sent to the right wing of the First Byelorussian Front."[53]

At the same time the *Stavka* was determining the general phasing of its upcoming winter campaign, without delineating when the main attack would occur. Clearly, the first stage would involve continuation of what Shtemenko called the "old line of advance—the southern flank of the Soviet-German front in the Budapest area." Shtemenko affirmed Zhukov's judgment, writing

> We knew that the enemy were particularly sensitive in East Prussia and Hungary. If hard pressed they would be sure to throw in reserves and troops from sectors that were not under attack. This would lead to a serious weakening of the whole Western Sector, where the decisive events were to take place.[54]

Within this context, in October Soviet forces in the Baltic region prepared operations to isolate German Army Group North, while in the Balkans Malinovsky's 2d Ukrainian Front planned operations to secure the Hungarian plains and Budapest.

By the end of September 1944, the Leningrad Front had cleared virtually all of Estonia of German forces except the Baltic coastal islands. The 1st, 2d, and 3d Baltic Fronts had reached the close approaches to Riga although German resistance had stiffened, bolstered by extensive prepared defenses covering the approaches to the city. Shtemenko, then working with Bagramian, the 1st Baltic Front commander, later noted

> Progress was slow, however, on the main Riga line of advance. Once again it proved impossible to split up the enemy's concentration, which made a fighting withdrawal to prepared positions 60–80 kilometers from Riga. Our troops had to gnaw their way methodically through the enemy's defenses, driving them back meter by meter.
>
> With the operation going like this there could be no quick victory, and we were sustaining heavy losses. . . . The enemy was even counter-attacking. . . .
>
> Everything indicated that the enemy were determined to maintain Army

Group North's link with East Prussia at all costs, so that they would be able to withdraw their troops from the Baltic area by land if necessary.[55]

In these circumstances, on 24 September the *Stavka* changed the direction of attack of its *fronts*, in particular the 1st Baltic Front toward Memel' and the Baltic seacoast.

The *Stavka* ordered the Leningrad Front and Baltic Fleet to complete the liberation of Estonia and the 3d and 2d Baltic Fronts to seize Riga and clear the Baltic coast of Germans. The 1st Baltic and part of the 3d Belorussian Front were

> to prepare and conduct a powerful blow on the Memel' direction and cut off the entire enemy Baltic group from East Prussia, and also create the prerequisites for successive blows against him to destroy fully all German Fascist forces on the Baltic direction.[56]

The *Stavka* ordered the 2d Baltic Front to shift two armies southward to replace two other armies, which would then move south of Riga and replace two armies that Bagramian intended to employ in the Memel' operation. Bagramian planned his main attack west of Shiauliai with three armies and 5th Guards Tank Army and a secondary attack southwest of Shiauliai in cooperation with the 3d Belorussian Front. From 24 September to 4 October, Bagramian regrouped five armies from his right to his left flank. Bagramian's deception plan concealed the large-scale regrouping and the new main attack positions and incorporated active disinformation measures to simulate the intentions of attacking toward Riga. *Razvedka* ensured German regroupings would not interfere with the new assault.

On 5 October Bagramian's forces struck, and by 9 October 5th Guards Tank Army had overrun Third Panzer Army headquarters and reached the Baltic coast north and south of Memel', irrevocably severing contact between Army Groups North and Center. Within days Soviet forces commenced operations on the Gumbinnen approach into East Prussia, ending all German hopes of restoring the situation in the Memel' area and reestablishing contact with Army Group North.

Meanwhile, at the end of September, Tolbukhin's 3d Ukrainian Front completed its sweep of Bulgaria and neared the Yugoslavian border, and Malinovsky's 2d Ukrainian Front occupied the passes through the Carpathians and prepared to advance into Hungary. The *Stavka* ordered Malinovsky—in cooperation with the 4th Ukrainian Front, which had

deployed from the Crimea to the northern Carpathian region—"to destroy
the enemy group in Hungary and at the same time remove the country
from the war on the side of Germany."[57] 2d Ukrainian Front was to

> destroy the enemy in the Cluj, Oradea, Debrecen region and, while de-
> veloping the offensive to the north toward Nyiregyhaza and Chop, cooperate
> with the 4th Ukrainian Front in the destruction of the eastern Carpathian
> enemy group and secure the Uzhgorod-Mukachevo region.[58]

Since the 2d Ukrainian Front was deployed on an exceedingly broad front,
its operational force densities remained low throughout the operations;
logistical sustainment was tenuous at best. Temporary force regroupments
permitted periodic advances in individual sectors, but decisive deep operations such as those in other sectors were impossible. Consequently,
Malinovsky conducted a series of successive army or multiarmy operations, each preceded by a short operational pause and limited regrouping
of forces, in particular *front* mobile elements. The first of these operations
is known as the Debrecan Operation. Subsequent operations—which began on 29 October, 14 November, 29 November, 5 December, and 20
December—are known collectively as the Budapest Operation.

Malinovsky's operational concept for the Debrecan Operation required two rifle armies, 6th Guards Tank Army and Cavalry-Mechanized
Group Pliev, to attack toward Oradea and Debrecan in the center of the
front sector. On the right flank, four rifle armies and Cavalry-Mechanized
Group Gorshkov were to attack toward Cluj and Satu-Mare, and on the
left flank one army would clear northern Yugoslavia and seize bridgeheads
over the Tisza River.

The Debrecan Operation began on 6 October. While Cavalry-Mechanized Group Pliev advanced 100 kilometers northwest of the Tisza River,
6th Guards Tank Army failed to take Oradea. Malinovsky quickly shifted
Pliev's group eastward, and together the tank army and Pliev's group
took Oradea (12 October) and then Debrecan (20 October). Subsequently,
Cavalry-Mechanized Groups Pliev and Gorshkov sped north and seized
Nyiregyhaza on 22 October, only to be struck by a coordinated German
counterstroke, which severed the cavalry-mechanized groups' communications and forced them, by 27 October, to abandon much of their
equipment and withdraw south.

With German and Soviet forces tied down in heavy combat north of
Debrecan, the *Stavka* and Malinovsky now capitalized on German weak-

ness to the southwest by mounting a drive on Budapest from the 2d Ukrainian Front's left flank. The *Stavka* ordered Malinovsky to

> not later than 29 October go on the offensive between the Tisza and Danube Rivers with the forces of 46th Army and 2d Guards Mechanized Corps. . . . to break up enemy defenses on the west bank of the Tisza and secure the crossing there of 7th Guards Army; subsequently, 46th Army, reinforced by 4th Guards Mechanized Corps was to strike German forces defending Budapest.[59]

On 29 October Malinovsky's forces attacked, penetrated Hungarian defenses, and advanced to Kiskoros and Kecslemet. However, German resistance stiffened south of Budapest and brought the Soviet advance to a halt in the southern suburbs of the city on 3 November. With his attacks halted south of Budapest, Malinovsky now regrouped his forces to strike again on 10 November, this time with his right flank and center toward Budapest from the north and northeast. Farther south 4th Guards Army, under 3d Ukrainian Front control, deployed secretly to the banks of the Danube River near Sombor to attack across the river with 57th Army, which had already seized small bridgeheads on the river's west bank. Malinovsky's 10 November attack bogged down east of Budapest by 15 November, but Tolbukhin's assault farther south achieved greater success. On 28 November 57th and 4th Guards Armies commenced a general offensive west of the river, which by 3 December brought Soviet forces to the shores of Lake Balaton, southwest of Budapest.

In late November Malinovsky proposed a new plan to the *Stavka*— a plan that involved a large-scale regrouping and a two-pronged attack to envelop Budapest. On 5 December, Malinovsky's right flank would attack northwest of Hatvan, and 6th Guards Tank Army and Pliev's Cavalry-Mechanized Group would then exploit north and northwest of Budapest to envelop the city. Malinovsky's left flank would attack across the Danube River south of Budapest to seize Estergom and isolate the Hungarian capital in cooperation with Tolbukhin's forces. Malinovsky's new offensive also failed to achieve its ends. His left flank's attack stalled before strong German defenses between Lake Balaton and the southern outskirts of Budapest. 6th Guards Tank Army and Pliev's Cavalry-Mechanized Group smashed German defenses northeast of Budapest, penetrated into the hills north of the Danube, but failed to encircle the city.

Consequently, the *Stavka* directed the 2d and 3d Ukrainian Fronts to conduct another operation on 20 December to encircle Budapest. Malinovsky was to strike southward toward Estergom on the Danube River, while other *front* elements would strike Budapest from the east. Tolbukhin's forces were to attack northward toward Estergom to link up with 2d Ukrainian Front forces and encircle German forces in Budapest. The 20 December Soviet assault succeeded, and on 27 December, 2d and 3d Ukrainian Front forces united at Estergom, encircling large German and Hungarian forces in the Budapest region. Soon the larger purpose of the Budapest operation began bearing fruit. In late December IV SS Panzer Corps, consisting of SS Panzer Divisions "Totenkopf" and "Viking," began arriving in the region west of Budapest. This corps had been involved in defensive operations along the Vistula, but now the threat in Hungary had drawn it away from the central sector of the front. Within weeks, its presence along the Vistula would be sorely missed. At the strategic level, Soviet operations in Hungary had achieved their intended purpose—to draw German attention and forces from the central portion of the front.

In successive strategic operations during the summer phase of the campaign, the Soviets destroyed three German army groups deployed on the central and southern sectors of the Eastern Front. These operations required the strategic redeployment of massive forces between sectors. Strategic deception played a decisive role in the summer offensive, both to conceal attack locations and to maintain the secrecy of force redeployments. Faced with the growing Soviet strategic force superiority of over two to one, the Germans could ill afford to lose track of Soviet strategic reserves. Soviet freedom to move units with impunity, and without detection and German countermeasures, permitted the Soviets to create operational force superiority of up to five to one. German inability to detect redeploying Soviet operational and tactical reserves permitted the Soviets to convert, with impunity, these operational superiorities into tactical superiorities of more than eight to one. No defense could withstand such an onslaught, especially since each onslaught normally contained an armored nucleus which, after penetration of the tactical defenses, often went as far as its logistical umbilical permitted it to go. By the summer of 1944, this distance exceeded 250 kilometers.

Soviet strategic success and the implementation of effective deception plans were, in part, conditioned by more effective Soviet *razvedka,* which efficiently kept track of German redeployments and validated deception planning. The continuation of Soviet operations along the German flanks in the Baltic and in southeastern Europe also clearly achieved their intent.

While the Soviets made important gains, they also achieved their greater purpose—to deflect German attention and resources from the central sector of the front. Here, as well, *razvedka* contributed to Soviet success. In 1944 Soviet *razvedka* capitalized on 1943 experiences and improved. These improvements, most apparent in the Belorussian offensive of June 1944 and in subsequent operations in southern Poland and Rumania, related to each type of *razvedka* and to the integrated use of all means of intelligence collection.

Soviet intelligence activities during preparation of the Belorussian operation are illustrative of how *front razvedka* functioned in support of strategic operations during this stage of the war. As had been the case in earlier operations, intelligence performed two specific tasks. First, it sought to verify the impact of deception planning by determining the location of German forces—in particular, operational reserves—across the entire front. It was essential to ensure that these reserves remained concentrated where the Soviets postured offensively and were not transferred to sectors where the Soviets actually intended to attack. This required close monitoring of German tactical dispositions by troop, artillery, and engineer *razvedka* and surveillance of German operational reserves, primarily by agent, reconnaissance-diversionary, air, and radio *razvedka*. Second, Soviet intelligence had to determine the precise nature of German defenses in Belorussia to match operational and tactical planning to German dispositions. This task required the combined use of all *razvedka* assets. Intelligence collection and analysis had to be continuous if initial Soviet plans were to remain valid throughout the preparation period.

Shtemenko described the process and demonstrated the sensitivity of the General Staff to German troop movements.

> During the whole period of preparation for the Byelorussian operation our commanders and staffs at all levels kept a close watch on the enemy. Patrols went out day and night in search of information and information prisoners. All troops kept the enemy positions under constant observation. Operations officers tried to ferret out the enemy's secret intentions. We knew von Tippelskirch, commander of 4th German army, was a competent general. What was going on in his mind? What plans was he making?
>
> On June 10 Lieutenant Nigmatullin and partisans . . . of the 504th partisan detachment . . . captured a prisoner in the Mogilev area. He was a staff officer from the 60th Motorised Division. Under interrogation he stated that this division had arrived from Narva in a very battered condition and was badly in need of replacements. It had been deployed along the

Mogilev-Minsk Road. Was this a mere coincidence? Or had the enemy got wind of our offensive and started making systematic preparations to repel it?

It was becoming more and more difficult to keep the forthcoming operations secret. How could movements and exercises on such a huge scale be concealed? Still, we hoped to be able to do so.

Naturally, we were worried by the appearance of a new motorised division in the sector of the Second Byelorussian Front. We started paying more attention to the daily reports on the enemy's artillery-fire table and air operations and gradually deduced from numerous scraps of evidence that the 60th Motorised Division had been sent to the area merely as reinforcement.[60]

Throughout the planning period, German force dispositions did not materially change. The bulk of German panzer and panzer-grenadier divisions remained in southern Poland and Rumania, where the German High Command expected Soviet offensive action to materialize. Consequently, Soviet strategic plans of April and May remained valid in late June, July, and August. Zhukov described the success of Soviet strategic deception and supporting intelligence:

> For success in the upcoming operations this [secret transfer of forces] was very important since, according to the information of our intelligence organs, the High Command of German forces expected our first summer blow in the Ukraine and not in Belorussia. They clearly reached this conclusion because, due to the forested, swampy region, we could not transfer and properly use the four tank armies stationed in the Ukraine in Belorussia. However, the enemy was mistaken.[61]

As evidenced by Shtemenko, Soviet intelligence tracked German reserves effectively from May through June and thereafter, as well, as the summer offensive unfolded.

Much of this success was due to shorter-range operational-tactical *razvedka* conducted by Soviet *fronts* and subordinate formations in Belorussia and elsewhere along the front. Intelligence work in the four *fronts* preparing for the Belorussian operation demonstrated how intelligence organs operated. This frontal activity went on within the context of higher-level intelligence collection by the *Stavka* and GRU, relying primarily on long-range air *razvedka*, radio intercepts, and reconnaissance-diversionary groups. German studies of Soviet intelligence collection are replete with graphic illustrations of the scope of Soviet agent and reconnaissance-diversionary activities in their rear area (see maps 11 and 12). These examples bear mute testimony to German problems in concealing its force dispositions and movements.

In Belorussia itself, in addition to reconnaissance-diversionary activity, the Soviets relied heavily on air and radio *razvedka* to pinpoint German dispositions. Each of the four supporting air armies (1st, 3d, 4th, 16th) conducted air *razvedka,* primarily through visual observation and aerial photography by Iak-1, Po-2, and Il-2 aircraft of reconnaissance aviation squadrons and regiments of air armies. During the thirty days before the attack, over 40 percent of total air sorties engaged in intelligence collection. Using direct or oblique photography, the Soviets obtained detailed data on defenses in the main penetration sector, which they then translated into photo maps.[62] These maps provided a basis for detailed planning of the artillery preparation and initial penetration operation. At times, however, intelligence analysts placed too much faith in air *razvedka* and photography. Although 16th Air Army prepared superb maps from aerial photography, one critic noted

> Unfortunately, because of the poor tactical training of some photo interpreters when deciphering the aerial maps, false objects (mock-up tanks and artillery pieces) were interpreted as real. As a result, on the first day of operations, our artillery and aviation struck blows against the false targets.[63]

Despite the overzealousness of the interpreters, photography adequately revealed most German tactical defenses, and the sheer immensity of the Soviet artillery park compensated for the excess of identified targets.

Equal in importance to aerial *razvedka* was intelligence collection by radio intercept and radio location. The most important intercept means were separate radio battalions of special designation [*spetsial'nogo naznacheniia,* or *Spetsnaz*], serving *front* commands, which were dedicated to conducting radio *razvedka.* Two such battalions served the 1st and 3d Belorussian Fronts. The 3d Belorussian Front's 131st Separate Radio Battalion [*Spetsnaz*], which joined the *front* on 1 June 1944, concentrated on intercepting and jamming transmissions of German Third Panzer and Fourth Armies, while the 130th Radio Battalion of the 1st Belorussian Front concentrated on German Ninth Army at Bobruisk.[64] During the operation the 131st Radio Battalion was paired off with the 474th Separate

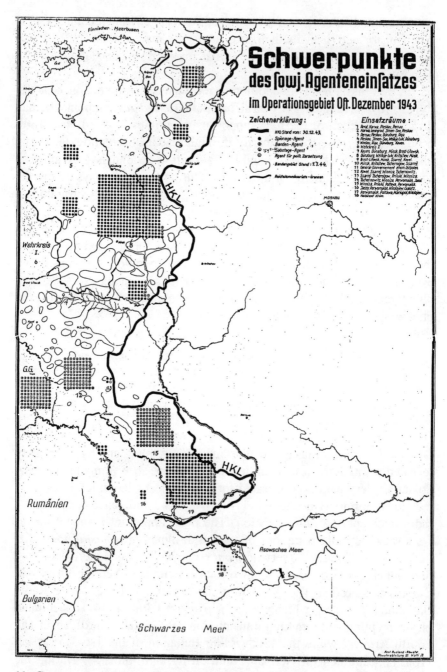

11. German assessment of "Banden" operating in their rear areas.

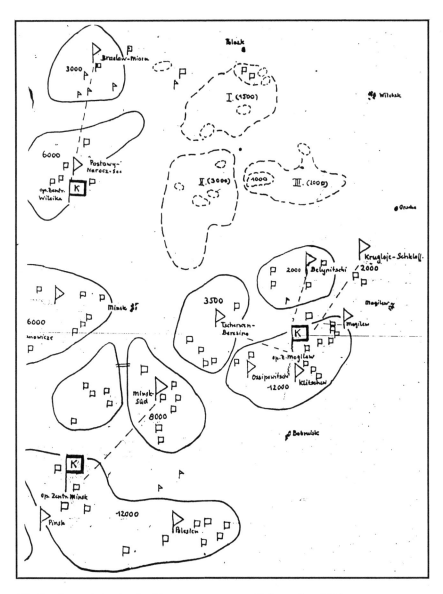

12. Soviet activity in the German rear area, Belorussia, 1944.

Radio Battalion Special Purpose [*osobogo naznacheniia,* or OSNAZ],
whose function was intercept only. Both played a significant role in
crushing German forces encircled at Bobruisk. Supplementing the work
of these *front*-level radio units were communications equipment close
reconnaissance teams (GBRSSs) formed within army signal regiments,
which also monitored enemy radio transmissions, a mission shared by all
communications stations and nets.[65] These teams contained two squads
for radio monitoring and two for wire communications monitoring. At
times *fronts* dispatched radio teams into the enemy rear area to cooperate
with partisans or to collect intelligence independently. One such group
operated deep in Belorussia from early May to late June, when it joined
advancing Soviet forces. While on its mission, it monitored German unit
locations and movements.[66]

Other specialized forces subordinate to *front* supplemented the work
of air and radio *razvedka*. Reconnaissance-diversionary teams and detachments from the Separate Motorized Rifle Brigade (Special Designation) operated in support of the 1st Belorussian Front, as did special
engineer *razvedka* companies subordinate to each *front*'s special designation engineer brigades and, in particular, guards battalions of miners
assigned from the reserves of the High Command (RVGK).[67] Independently, or in association with partisan intelligence detachments, these
forces formed an extensive web of intelligence collectors, which per-
meated the German rear, watching for every major force movement.

The extensive partisan structure in Belorussia performed a *razvedka*
function as well in direct subordination to *front* intelligence departments
and, on occasion, the GRU. These reconnaissance detachments also
sought to identify German units and report force movements. To do so,
they were equipped with radios air-dropped to them. By July 1944, 61
radio stations operated in the German rear in Belorussia, each with a
range of 200 to 300 kilometers. As described by one critic:

> The Belorussian underground conducted great intelligence work. A
> wide network of clandestine reconnaissance groups, created by the party
> underground, existed in the territory of the republic. The underground
> systematically conducted observation on moving troop trains, gathered
> helpful information about the strength and armament of garrisons, calcu-
> lated observed arriving staffs and units, noted their routes of movement
> and reconnoitered the location and nature of military objectives. The nu-

merous and varied information about the enemy rose from the underground and was transmitted across the front lines by partisan detachments.[68]

German intelligence maps testify to the immensity of the intelligence and security problem. The outcome of the strategic operation underscored the effectiveness of Soviet and partisan intelligence activities in the German rear.

Meanwhile, *front* commands organized troop, artillery, and engineer *razvedka* and personal reconnaissance [*recognostsirovka*] in their sectors to confirm or refute information received from higher headquarters. Troop *razvedka,* by definition, included observation, eavesdropping on enemy communications, reconnaissance sweeps and ambushes, and reconnaissance in force. 43d Army of Bagramian's 1st Baltic Front conducted *razvedka* for itself and for 6th Guards Army, which secretly deployed into its sector several days before the offensive. *Front* ordered the army to

Expose and precisely identify the grouping of enemy forces before the army, up to company and individual artillery and mortar batteries, and to determine their exact location

Verify and identify the firing system and engineer obstacles of the enemy defense

Determine the weak spots in the enemy defense, especially in the planned penetration sector of the army

Determine the degree of trafficability of the terrain in the "neutral" sector and in the depth of the dispositions of the enemy Vitebsk-Lepel' group and to reconnoiter the possibilities for forcing the Western Dvina River in the sector Terebeshevo, Pal'kovichi

Verify the enemy reserve concentration regions and approximately determine likely directions of their actions.[69]

To confuse the enemy regarding attack intentions, timing, and location, 43d Army intelligence employed *razvedka* assets in random fashion across the entire army front. During May it conducted ninety-six day and night reconnaissance sweeps, ambushes, and reconnaissances in force and during June another seventy-seven. Daytime sweeps by groups of twenty to thirty men, including sappers, supported by artillery and mortar fire, sought to obtain prisoners and identify minefields and gaps in enemy obstacles. Night sweeps by similar groups began operations at dusk. These activities were coordinated with systematic observation of enemy positions from a well-developed observation network of 2,340 observation posts, which employed visual observation devices and photography.[70] Groups of five to twenty-five men operated 30 to 100 kilometers in the German rear under *front* control, and other groups of five to seven men operated at tactical depths under army control.[71] Listening posts along the front and those established by reconnaissance groups within enemy lines monitored enemy positions, determined unit identifications, and disrupted German reconnaissance as well. By use of long-range reconnaissance patrols, cooperating partisan reconnaissance parties, and aerial photography, 43d Army intelligence thoroughly surveyed the Western Dvina River in the German rear to determine suitable crossing sites for advancing forces. Army intelligence analysts formed large-scale schematic maps of German defenses from this data and data received from aerial, radio, and troop *razvedka*.

43d Army conducted artillery instrumental *razvedka* by using sound and flash ranging and supplemented this with artillery aerial observation, all under control of the artillery reconnaissance battalion of the supporting artillery division. Sound battery stations operated round the clock to identify German artillery positions. The 206th Separate Reconnaissance-Correction Aviation Regiment (OKAP) and the 7th Aeronautic Battalion of Aerostatic Observation (VDAN) provided focused aerial observation of German defensive positions to complete the surveillance mosaic by firmly identifying twenty-five German artillery batteries in the main attack sector and a reserve infantry regiment and two separate heavy artillery battalions along the Western Dvina defensive line.[72] 43d Army intelligence correctly identified German reserve units from the 24th Infantry Division and 909th Assault Battalion deployed at and southeast of Polotsk. 6th Guards Army, which deployed into the region several days prior to the attack, shared intelligence data with 43d Army, which had covered its forward deployment and participated jointly with that army in the reconnaissance in force conducted just prior to the offensive.

1st Baltic Front conducted its reconnaissance in force one day before the offensive was to commence. The reconnaissance was designed to verify existing intelligence information, seize prisoners, and further reveal enemy defensive dispositions. 43d Army assigned the reconnaissance task to specially trained companies from advanced assault battalions assigned from second-echelon rifle corps. One company operated in each first-echelon rifle division sector, and each was supported by two artillery battalions, two 120mm mortar batteries, three or four 82mm mortar batteries, and direct fire from twelve regimental guns.[73] 6th Guards Army employed sixteen reinforced battalions to conduct its reconnaissance, with six additional battalions immediately available to reinforce their effort.[74] The reconnaissance forces, which advanced on 22 June at 0500 after a ten-minute artillery barrage and air strikes on enemy objectives, succeeded beyond the Soviets' expectations. Not only were German dispositions as projected, but the Germans were also surprised and lost many of their forward positions. Because of the reconnaissance success, both army commanders immediately decided to continue the attack, 6th Guards Army without an artillery preparation and 43d Army with one. Within two days, German defenses opposite the 1st Baltic Front had vanished.

Analogous *razvedka* activity in the 3d Belorussian Front sector produced similar results. Lieutenant General K. N. Galitsky, commander of 11th Guards Army, reported that by early June, "Troop, air and radio *razvedka,* as well as partisan reports, established that the enemy had created two defensive belts in the tactical zone of the defense" and provided the scale and dimensions of the defense.[75] Subsequent reconnaissance focused on the state and composition of enemy forces and relied primarily on the seizure and interrogation of prisoners. In Galitsky's judgment, this work was productive.

As a result of large scale and strenuous work in studying the enemy and processing all data received by the army staff, we established rather fully the disposition of enemy forces and their defensive system before the offensive.[76]

In the 2d Belorussian Front sector, intelligence efforts focused on supporting 49th Army, its main attack force. Air *razvedka* was particularly effective. For example, from 13 May to 22 June, the 164th Guards Separate Reconnaissance Aviation Regiment of 4th Air Army carried out visual observation of German positions and photographed enemy defenses along the entire front to a depth of from 8 to 12 kilometers and those in the main attack sector to a depth of 30 kilometers. The photographed area amounted to over 5,000 square kilometers, which were captured on more than 10,000 photos that were later worked into schematic maps. The 233d Assault Aviation Regiment assisted in the effort by employing Il-2 aircraft, manned by pilots and artillery or engineer scouts, to determine artillery positions and engineer obstacles in the tactical defense.[77]

Troop, engineer, and artillery *razvedka* in all 2d Belorussian Front armies mirrored practices used elsewhere and achieved similar results.

A detailed study of 49th Army operations gave high marks to troop *razvedka,* stating

> It is sufficient to state that only in the 20 days of June, that is during the preparatory period of the operation, army reconnaissance organs captured 11 prisoners belonging to the enemy 110th, 337th, and 12th Infantry Divisions and the 113th Combat Group. As a result of prisoner interrogation the grouping of the enemy in front of the army was verified.[78]

The same study praised engineer reconnaissance, which thoroughly reconnoitered the Pronia River in front of German defenses as well as the defenses themselves.

> As a result of engineer *razvedka,* filled out with information from other types of *razvedka,* the entire system of enemy engineer-defensive works in the forward area and in the tactical depth was revealed, the Pronia River was reconnoitered, and the places for bridge crossings and fords for the crossing of artillery and tanks were determined.[79]

Finally, the reconnaissance in force on the eve of the attack, "confirmed the existing data about enemy dispositions, verified the forward edge of his defense and his system of fire, and seized prisoners."[80]

The 1st Belorussian Front had the difficult task of advancing on Bobruisk along both sides of the Berezina River and of crossing the imposing Dnepr and Drut river barriers north and south of Rogachev. The latter sector combined well-developed German defenses with the river obstacles, and the left flank *front* sector west of the Berezina was punctuated with marshy and wooded terrain. Here, effective *razvedka* helped the Soviets overcome many of these terrain difficulties.

Rokossovsky, the *front* commander, praised his *front's razvedka* work.

> Special attention was given to air, ground and radio reconnaissance. The 16th Air Army carried out blanket aerial photography of the enemy's fortifications in the Bobruisk sector, and maps with the information obtained were circulated among the units. In the armies of the right wing alone some 400 trench raids were carried out, our scouts taking more than 80 tongues [*iazykov,* or prisoners] and many important documents.[81]

Lieutenant General P. I. Batov related how intelligence assisted his 65th Army in conducting its attack through the swampy and wooded area west of the Berezina River. Although the Germans had constructed "a strong and deeply echeloned field defense in the region . . . army *razvedka* discovered it."[82] Moreover, since the Germans assumed the difficult terrain was impassable for heavy forces and armor, they concentrated their defenses in drier open regions. Batov's subunits dispatched reconnaissance teams with engineers into the swamps and bogs. Besides taking prisoners, the teams marked out routes for the advance. According to Batov:

> The information of *razvedka* affirmed two of our assumptions: first, the enemy excluded the possibility of an offensive on that direction and therefore established a weak strong-point defense there; and second, the marshes were trafficable for troops and, if corduroy [log] tracks were laid, also for equipment. Thus, gradually preparations for our operation began, which were later called by a representative of the *Stavka* [Zhukov], "the engineer operation."[83]

The difficult nature of the terrain also assisted in the concealment of Soviet observation posts and the free passage of reconnaissance detachments to and from the German rear area. 28th Army, deployed on the left flank of 65th Army only days before the attack, also extensively employed sappers in its reconnaissance efforts to reveal German defenses and facilitate the offensive.

The three reconnaissance artillery battalions of gun artillery brigades and two corrective-reconnaissance aviation regiments provided artillery *razvedka* support for 65th and 28th Armies. After 5 June new artillery instrumental forces arrived in the sector, raising the total number of sound and flash-ranging battalions to seven, and the *front* received two aeronautic battalions of aerostatic observation equipped with observation balloons.[84] The artillery reconnaissance effort identified over 3,000 enemy targets, including 233 artillery batteries, 113 mortar batteries, 103 separate guns and mortars, 154 pillboxes, 237 blindage, 106 observation posts, and 1,750 machine gun nests. The 98th Separate Corrective-Reconnaissance Aviation Regiment flew 236 missions for aerial observation and photography and, as a result, photo interpreters twice prepared panoramas of the defense totaling over 3,000 square kilometers and containing a host of identified targets.[85] Visual air *razvedka* added over 2,000 targets to the *front* target list. Chief of *front* artillery, Major General V. I. Kazakov, claimed, "All this permitted rather full disclosure of the enemy defense. Artillery received necessary data in order to prepare accurate and effective fire."[86] 28th Army commander, Lieutenant General A. A. Luchinsky, summed up the impact of all *razvedka* efforts in his and Batov's sector:

> The Chief of the Intelligence Department [RO] of the army staff, Colonel V. N. Torokhov, reported to me that the enemy 36th, 35th, 129th and 292d Infantry Divisions were discovered in the first line of defense in the projected army offensive sector. In the depth of the defense one could suppose that the 102d Infantry Division could contest our advance from the Petrikov sector. . . .[87]

The *razvedka* chief estimated that an additional five divisions could oppose 28th Army later in the operation, presuming the German corps east of Bobruisk could regroup to the west.[88]

Not all assessments, however, were totally accurate. Intelligence analysts failed to detect the full strength of German defenses around Rogachev, where 3d Army was making one of the two main attacks of Rokossovsky's 1st Belorussian Front. Consequently, the initial Soviet attack in this sector developed too slowly and, subsequently, the axis of attack had to be shifted northward. Zhukov noted

> At the same time, however, the strength of the enemy defence on the Rogachev-Bobruisk sector had been under-estimated due to inadequate reconnaissance. As a consequence, the 3rd and 48th Armies were assigned excessively large penetration areas. Besides that, the two armies did not have sufficient means for a successful breakthrough. I failed in my duty as a representative of the Supreme Command to correct the Front commanders.[89]

This sampling of details concerning Soviet intelligence activities in Belorussia is but a pale reflection of the immensely complicated *razvedka* plan that unfolded under *Stavka* and *front* supervision. The results of those efforts were best summed up by a recent Soviet work on surprise:

> Intelligence and counterintelligence played an enormous role during preparations for the campaign in the Belorussian Operation. In general, Soviet intelligence correctly determined the disposition and the nature of the

enemy's defense, which made it possible to plan the most effective axes for the main strikes by the *fronts* and the breakthrough sectors.[90]

If there were flaws in *razvedka,* they pertained to deep observation and identification of German forces moving in the strategic and operational depths. Since in 1944 most German divisions either occupied forward positions or were in close tactical or operational reserve, the Soviets did not have to track many units. Large-scale movement between army groups was so unusual that, if missed by aerial observation, it was easily noticed by agent, reconnaissance-diversionary forces, or partisans. Moreover, the sudden absence of a unit from one sector of the *front* was a cue for the Soviets to concentrate on looking for it elsewhere. The Soviets knew the bulk of German reserves were initially located in southern Poland. Hence, they could concentrate their strategic and operational intelligence assets at key points to conduct surveillance over those few lateral communications routes leading northward.

Once the Belorussian operation had begun and the Germans began shifting reserves, the movement of these reserves was relatively unimportant, for they could, in no way, make up for the massive damage done to Army Group Center during the initial stages of the Soviet attack (see map 13). By 10 July Soviet intelligence in Belorussia had detected the arrival of German reserves from the south. Very shortly, other Soviet offensives commenced, first in the L'vov area and, days later, in the Kovel' sector. Faced with disaster in Poland, in late July the German High Command shifted the bulk of its reserve divisions in Rumania northward. It is evident that Soviet intelligence detected the bulk of these movements in timely fashion. As was the case in Belorussia, major damage had been done by the time German reserves regrouped. This pattern repeated itself in a brutally effective fashion through the end of August, when German Army Group South Ukraine, already stripped of reserves, succumbed to the last major Soviet summer offensive.

Subsequently, throughout the fall, the Soviets focused on holding their gains in the center of the front along the Vistula and Narev rivers, while they opened new offensives on the flanks. During the last phase of the summer-fall campaign, Soviet operations in the Baltic region, Carpathia, and the Balkans had the familiar effect of drawing dwindling German reserves from the critical central portion of the front. Again

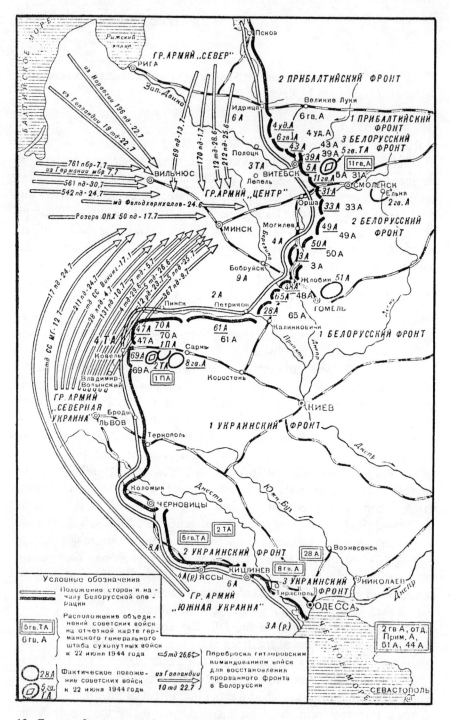

13. German force regrouping, June–July 1944.

Soviet intelligence effectively tracked their movements. In mid-August, when the Germans assembled reserves to halt the Soviet drive on Riga, intelligence detected the regrouping. *Stavka* representative Vasilevsky later wrote

> That day [13 August] I sent a report to the GHQ . . . in which I summed up our intelligence information and the results of recent fighting; at the same time I mentioned the line of defense that the enemy had formed along the River Memel. We knew that up to seven infantry divisions of the enemy had concentrated a troop grouping for an offensive from north on Mitava. At the same time, to the west of Siauliai the enemy had gathered another group of troops. It was quite possible that the adversary would try to break the wedge from both sides which we had driven in toward the Bay of Riga.[91]

Consequently, the Soviets shifted 4th Shock and 6th Guards Armies, plus other units, to block the attack.

In late September Soviet intelligence detected "there were over 8 enemy divisions in the sector of German Third Panzer Army in the Klaipeda region. The others had been sent on to Mitava to help Army Group 'North.'. . ."[92] Based on this information, the Soviets carried out a major secret regrouping and launched the Memel' attack, which drove through German positions to the Baltic Sea. In so doing they severed communications between German forces in the Baltic states and those in East Prussia.

Farther south, in the Carpathian region during September and October, the 1st Ukrainian Front's 38th Army and the 4th Ukrainian Front's 1st Guards and 18th Armies conducted the Eastern Carpathian (Dukla) operation to advance into Slovakia. While the operation failed, it did draw significant German forces (twenty divisions) from southern Poland to the newly threatened sector (see map 14).[93] Even if the Soviets failed to monitor the initial movement of these German divisions, during the course of the operation intelligence detected their presence. This information, combined with information about German troop regroupings in the Baltic region and in Hungary, facilitated Soviet planning for the decisive offensive along the main western strategic direction, which the *Stavka* planned to begin in January 1945.

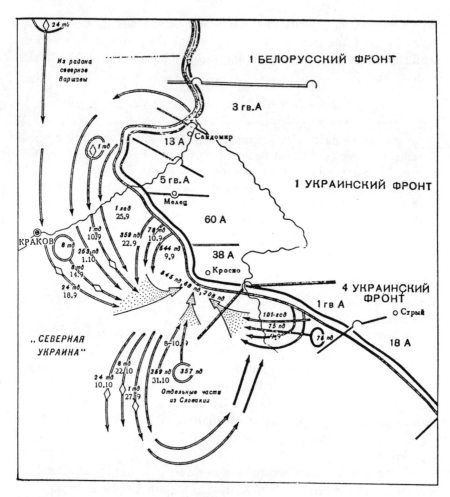

14. German force regrouping, September–November 1944.

The 1945 Campaign, January–May and August 1945

Soviet planning for the 1945 winter strategic offensive began in late October 1944, while Soviet forces on the main strategic direction were fighting to extend the offensive deeper into Poland (see map 15). Zhukov assessed the situation, concluded Soviet forces in the central sector needed a rest, and, on 3 November, ordered them on the defensive while operations continued on the flanks.

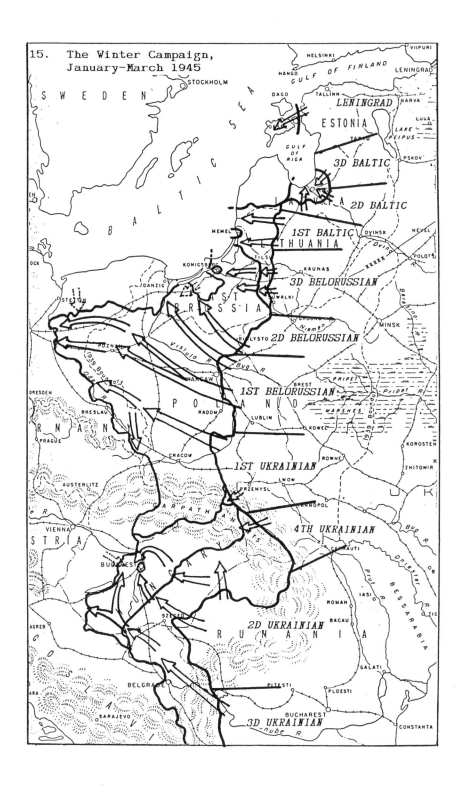

15. The Winter Campaign,
January–March 1945

By late October the *Stavka* and general staff had developed a concept for a two-stage campaign, commencing in November, that would end the war. The concept's aims were

—to rout the East Prussian grouping and occupy East Prussia;
—to defeat the enemy in Poland, Czechoslovakia, Hungary, and Austria;
—to move out to the line running through the Vistula mouth, Bromberg (Bydgoszcz), Poznan, Breslau (Wroclaw), Moravska Ostrava, and Vienna.
The Warsaw-Berlin line of advance—where the zone of the 1st Byelorussian Front was to be—was to be the direction of the main effort. The 2d and 1st Baltic Fronts and the Baltic Fleet were assigned to rout the Courland enemy grouping (the 16th and 18th armies). They were also to prevent the enemy forces pressed to the Baltic Sea from being transferred to other fronts.[94]

Shtemenko provided a rationale for the campaign:

It was assumed from the start that the last campaign of the war against Hitlerite Germany would be carried out in two stages. In the first stage, operations were to continue mainly on what might be described as the old line of advance—the southern flank of the Soviet-German front in the Budapest area. It was calculated that a break-through could be achieved here by inserting the main forces of the Third Ukrainian Front between the River Tisza and the Danube, south of Kecskemet. From there they would be able to assist the Second Ukrainian Front with thrusts to the north-west and west. . . . We had no doubt that the grave threat to their southern flank would force the German command to transfer some of their forces from the Berlin sector, and this in its turn would create favourable conditions for the advance of our main forces—the Fronts deployed north of the Carpathians. The General Staff firmly believed that by the beginning of 1945 the Soviet Army on the lower Vistula would reach Bromberg, capture Poznan and take over the line running through Breslau, Pardubice, Jihlava and Vienna, in other words, advance a distance of between 120 and 350 kilometers. After that would come the second stage of the campaign, which was to culminate in Germany's surrender.[95]

During November and December, Soviet offensives in the Baltic region and in Hungary confirmed the *Stavka*'s belief that the Germans would react to threats against their flanks by transferring reserves from their center. Meanwhile, the Soviets planned the January strategic offensive, which included two large-scale operations, both focused on the western strategic direction. The first, conducted by the 3d and 2d Belorussian Fronts, would strike the heavily entrenched German East Prussia group and protect the northern flank of the main strategic drive across Poland.

The 1st Belorussian and 1st Ukrainian Fronts would jointly launch the main strategic thrust. As described by Zhukov:

> The immediate operational objective for the 1st Byelorussian Front was to break the crust of the enemy defence in two different areas simultaneously, and having knocked out the Warsaw-Radom enemy grouping, to move out to the Lodz meridian. The subsequent plan of action was to advance towards Poznan up to the line running through Bromberg (Bydgoszcz)-Poznan and further south where tactical contact with the troops of the 1st Ukrainian Front was to be made.
>
> The subsequent advance was not planned, as the Supreme Command could not know beforehand what the situation would be by the time our forces reached the Bromberg-Poznan line.[96]

Rather than using a *Stavka* representative to plan and coordinate the operation, the *Stavka* coordinated directly through each *front* commander. On 15 November Zhukov and Konev took command of the 1st Belorussian and 1st Ukrainian Fronts. In mid- and late December the *Stavka* approved initial *front* plans, altered the concept slightly, and designated an attack date of 12 January, eight days earlier than planned, to assist the Allies, then struggling in the Ardennes.[97]

The *Stavka* ordered Zhukov's 1st Belorussian Front to launch three attacks. Its main attack from the Magnushev bridgehead would employ three rifle armies to penetrate German defenses and 1st and 2d Guards Tank Armies to exploit toward Poznan. Two armies, backed up by two tank corps, would conduct a secondary attack from the Pulavy bridgehead toward Lodz, while two other armies would envelop Warsaw. Konev's 1st Ukrainian Front would conduct one powerful assault from the Sandomierz bridgehead with six rifle armies supported by three tank corps. 3d Guards and 4th Tank Armies would then exploit toward Breslau. The two *front*s would attack in time-phased sequence on 12 and 14 January, respectively. Prior to the offensive, a large-scale regroupment was necessary to provide the two *front*s with sufficient forces to sustain an advance through Poland.[98]

The geographical configuration of the front made deception extremely difficult, for the Germans knew any attack would most likely emanate from the bridgeheads across the Vistula or from the area south of the Vistula. The Germans considered an attack inevitable and had predicted precise attack dates since late November. Since those attacks had not materialized, however, the credibility of subsequent predictions suffered. The primary offensive indicator would be a buildup of Soviet forces along the front, particularly in the bridgeheads. Therefore, to confuse the Germans regarding attack timing, the Soviets kept secret their buildup of forces and attempted to deceive the Germans regarding attack location. Soviet deception plans sought to, first, conceal the size of the regrouping effort and the timing and the scale of the offensive and, second, focus German attention on secondary sectors, in particular the region south of the Vistula River. Since the Soviets realized the Germans expected an attack in the near future, they intended to weaken German capacity to resist the attack, principally by concealing its scale. Given these objectives, Soviet deception planning achieved moderate success, primarily by masking the scope and scale of the attack. The Germans underestimated Soviet strength by between 30 and 40 percent, failed to reinforce the Vistula front, and were unable to cope with the massive assault from all three Vistula bridgeheads.

Early on 12 and 14 January, the Soviet *fronts* struck. Within hours each *front* had devastated German tactical defenses and begun an operational exploitation with its tank armies and separate tank corps. The ensuing operation tore apart German defenses across the breadth of Poland, and Soviet forces, spearheaded by armored units, raced toward Lodz and Breslau. By 26 January Soviet forces had reached Schneidemuhl in the north, bypassed and isolated German forces in Poznan, and reached the Oder River north and south of Breslau. Only in the south, around the industrial cities of Upper Silesia, was the Soviet advance slowed by German units hastily dispatched northward from Hungary. By 1 February, Zhukov's armored columns reached the Oder River near Kuestrin and Frankfurt, and Konev's forces breached the Oder River on a broad front from north of Breslau southward to Ratibor.

At this juncture, Zhukov made a controversial decision, which was supported by the *Stavka*. Fearing for his exposed flanks, where intelligence indicated fresh German forces were assembling, Zhukov ordered his forces to halt along the Oder while he prepared operations to clear his flanks. Zhukov later noted

Enemy resistance on the right flank of the front had become considerably stiffer by then. Air and ground reconnaissance detected the movement and concentration of considerable enemy forces in East Pomerania.

Swift and determined action was required to eliminate the threat from the north. On February 2, the Military Council of the Front had already ordered the 1st Guards Tank Army to leave its positions on the Oder to the neighbouring units to attend to, and to move out by forced march to the Arnswalde area. The 9th Tank and the 7th Guards Cavalry Corps were also redeployed there, and many artillery and engineer units and plentiful supplies streamed into the area.

The German counter-offensive from East Pomerania was becoming more imminent every day.[99]

The *Stavka* agreed with Zhukov's assessment and ordered his *front* and Rokossovsky's 2d Belorussian Front to plan and conduct what came to be known as the East Pomeranian operation, which commenced on 24 February.

While Zhukov's and Konev's *fronts* struck across central Poland, three Soviet *fronts* conducted a major operation against the German stronghold in East Prussia. Vasilevsky, *Stavka* representative for the 3d Belorussian Front, described Soviet perceptions on the strength of Germany's East Prussia bastion:

Throughout the years 1941–1945, Eastern Prussia had had important economic, political and strategic importance for the German high command. Here in the deep underground bunkers near Rastenberg Hitler's supreme command had had its headquarters right up to 1944; the Nazis themselves had given it the nickname Wolfsschanze (Wolf's Lair). If we could capture Eastern Prussia—the citadel of German militarism—it would mark an important step in the culminating stage of the war in Europe. The fascist command attributed great importance to Prussia. It was soundly to cover the approaches to the central regions of Germany. A number of fortifications, strongly-equipped frontal and blocking positions had been established on its territory and in the areas of northern Poland abutting it, as well as big defence centres bristling with permanent fortifications. The old fortresses had been considerably modernized; all the defences were reliably linked structurally with a concerted fire system established between them. The overall depth of the fortified area was as much as 150–200 km. The terrain of Eastern Prussia—its lakes, rivers, marshes and canals, the well-developed network of railways and highways, the solid stone structures—

was exceedingly suitable for defence. By 1945, the Eastern Prussian fortified areas and lines of defence including the fortresses which blended well with the natural obstacles were no less formidable than the West German Siegfried Line; in some places they were even superior to it. Defences were particularly strong from an engineering viewpoint on the main sector for us—Gumbinnen, Insterburg and Konigsberg.[100]

The Soviet concept for the East Prussian operation, developed in November 1944, called for the 3d and 2d Belorussian Fronts to launch coordinated assaults to cut off the German East Prussian group from German forces in Poland and pin them against the Baltic Sea. Then the 3d Belorussian and 1st Baltic Fronts would encircle German forces and destroy them piecemeal. After reaching the Vistula River south of Danzig, the 2d Belorussian Front, in coordination with the 1st Belorussian Front, would continue to operate on the main direction—across the Vistula River and through eastern Pomerania to Stettin on the Oder River. The operation was to begin in mid-January, as soon as the Vistula operation had begun. The Soviet *front* commanders, Rokossovsky (2d Belorussian) and Cherniakhovsky (3d Belorussian) worked directly with the *Stavka,* while Vasilevsky coordinated 1st and 2d Baltic Front operations. Cherniakhovsky planned his main attack toward Konigsberg, with three rifle armies supported by two tank corps and one army in second echelon. 1st Baltic Front forces would defend along the *front* right flank to the Neiman River and the Baltic Sea. Rokossovsky planned his main attack toward Mlava and Marienburg, with three rifle armies and 5th Guards Tank Army, while two armies would conduct a secondary attack on the *front*'s left flank toward Drobin and Grudziaga on the Vistula River.

Regrouping of forces for the East Prussian operation was less extensive than for the Vistula-Oder operation, and deception was only of limited value because the Germans knew in general where the bulk of Soviet forces were located.[101] This made it extremely important for the Soviets to mask successfully those limited regroupings, in particular the movement from the 1st Baltic Front sector of 5th Guards Tank Army, whose performance and impact on combat, in large measure, would determine Soviet success or failure in 2d Belorussian Front's sector. Hence, the Soviets took extraordinary measures to hide its presence, including the decision to move it into the forward area only after the offensive had begun.

The East Prussian operation began on 13 January, when the 3d Belorussian Front attacked westward toward Gumbinnen and Insterberg.

Heavy German resistance delayed the Soviet advance until 11th Guards Army, committed secretly from second echelon, struck a weak spot on the German left flank. Thereafter, German forces conducted a fighting withdrawal back to Konigsberg. To the south, along the Narev River, 2d Belorussian Front attacked on 14 January. Within three days 5th Guards Tank Army and three other mobile corps began an exploitation, which by 26 January reached the Baltic Sea, cutting off German forces in East Prussia from those in Pomerania. Reduction of the large surrounded German force lasted until April 1945. Meanwhile, the 2d Belorussian Front crossed the lower Vistula near Grudziaga and joined the neighboring 1st Belorussian Front in the task of destroying the German East Pomeranian grouping.

Throughout February and March, the *Stavka* ordered its forces to defend along the Oder River and clear its northern and southern flanks preparatory to the final drive on Berlin. In the north 1st and 2d Belorussian Fronts launched the East Pomeranian operation. Rokossovsky's *front* advanced from the Grudziaga region on 24 February, but with only limited success. When Zhukov's *front* joined the struggle on 1 March, German defenses collapsed, and Soviet forces pushed toward Coburg and Danzig, splitting up the German force and destroying it piecemeal. The mopping up of German forces in Pomerania took until late March to complete. To the south, on 8 February, Konev's 1st Ukrainian Front commenced the Lower Silesian operation by attacking out of bridgeheads across the Oder River north and south of Breslau. By 24 February Konev's troops had surrounded large German garrisons in Breslau and Glogau and had reached the Neisse River along a 100-kilometer front from Penzig to its intersection with the Oder River. On 15 March Konev's left wing began the Upper Silesian operation, which encircled German forces in Oppeln, cleared the west bank of the Oder, and pushed German forces to the Czechoslovak border. Shtemenko later emphasized the importance of these operations against the German flanks.

By April 4 the mopping up of the enemy's East Pomerania concentration was completed. Any danger of our offensive against Berlin being wrecked by flank or rear attacks from that part of Germany was now ruled out.

The enforced temporary postponement of the Berlin operation, which could not have been avoided, assured us of final victory. Thoroughly prepared and provided for in all respects, this operation became utterly overwhelming. Our final blows at the enemy in April–May 1945 were as inavertible as fate itself.

Such are the historical facts.[102]

An important, but often overlooked, aspect of this last strategic campaign was the role played in it by operations on the southern flank, in Hungary and Austria. Throughout January and February, before and after the Vistula operation, Hitler had transferred critical operational reserves to Hungary, where he thought the correlation of forces was such that he could win a victory with important political and economic consequences. In December 1944 he dispatched IV SS Panzer Corps to Hungary, where, for three months, it launched counterattacks to seize the Danube River line and relieve the German garrison encircled in Budapest. The limited and temporary success of these counterattacks convinced Hitler that a larger force could do even more. Therefore, after the front in Poland had stabilized along the Oder River, Hitler returned to his original plan. Shtemenko described Hitler's intent:

> Operations in western Hungary on the Vienna line of advance had extremely important consequences. Hitler had intended smashing the Soviet forces here, restoring the front along the Danube and transferring the forces thus disengaged, particularly panzer forces, to Berlin. Reserves from Italy and Western Europe, in particular, the Sixth SS Panzer Army, were concentrated in this area.[103]

In early March 1945 Hitler organized and conducted what would be the last major German offensive of the war, an attempt to defeat Soviet forces around Budapest and recapture the economically important Balaton oil fields. The Germans redeployed Sixth SS Panzer Army from the Western Front to Hungary to launch an assault in coordination with Sixth Army and Second Panzer Army to clear the Soviets from west of the Danube River and reoccupy Budapest. The German offensive was to commence on 6 March. Coincidentally, while the Germans were planning their offensive, the Soviet 2d and 3d Ukrainian Fronts planned an offensive of their own to begin on 15 March. The Soviet plan called for 3d Ukrainian Front forces to attack westward from Budapest to destroy defending German forces and advance on Vienna. Large reserves (9th Guards Army and 6th Guards Tank Army) were to spearhead the attack.

More than two weeks prior to the German offensive, Soviet intelligence learned of the Germans' intent and formed a dense and deep defense west of Budapest. The *Stavka* specifically prohibited use in the defense of those reserve forces designated to conduct the Soviet offensive and ordered offensive preparations to continue even during the impending defensive operation. Tolbukhin's defense concept required erection of defenses that would grind up attacking German forces. After German forces had been sufficiently worn down in defensive combat, Tolbukhin planned to launch his own offensive using *front* forces not involved in the defensive battle and *Stavka* reserves. Tolbukhin organized his defense without disrupting concurrent offensive preparations. Thus:

> The aim of the defensive battle was to retain occupied positions without the delivery of *front* and army counter-strokes. Counter-attacks would be conducted only in exceptional cases, based on their success.[104]

The *front* was prepared for the defense on 3 March, and its extensive regrouping was complete by late on 5 March.

The German offensive commenced on 6 March and by 15 March had penetrated only to a depth of 25 kilometers. Judiciously using its reserves, the 3d Ukrainian Front absorbed the shock of the German offensive; its defenses bent but did not break. While the German offensive slowly developed, the Soviets implemented their plans for the Vienna operation. On 9 March, the *Stavka* revised 2d and 3d Ukrainian Fronts' missions and ordered 3d Ukrainian Front to launch its main attack on 15 and 16 March from west of Budapest, spearheaded by secretly regrouped 9th Guards Army. 2d Ukrainian Front's forces, led by 6th Guards Tank Army, were to attack on 17 or 18 March westward along the south bank of the Danube River. Later, 2d Ukrainian Front forces north of the Danube River and 3d Ukrainian Front forces south of Lake Balaton were to join the offensive. Although the ensuing Soviet offensive achieved surprise, it developed slowly because of weather problems and heavy German resistance. Ultimately, however, the 2d and 3d Ukrainian Fronts drove German forces from Hungary to the gates of Vienna, which fell by 15 April after only desultory resistance.

During the latter stages of the Vienna operation, the Soviets prepared for what they perceived to be the final race for Berlin. It is clear that there was more at stake than just preparations for one final operation. Since early February Soviet political concerns over the actions of its Western allies affected strategic planning. It is likely that the decision to clear their flanks before proceeding to Berlin was, in part, conditioned by Soviet concern over the fate of Berlin—and Prague as well. Should the Allies have struck for Berlin and Prague, in violation of the Yalta Agreement, the Soviet High Command wanted the bulk of its forces available to deal with that eventuality.

Most high-level Soviet commanders, and Soviet actions themselves, speak to that concern. Zhukov noted

> As the end of the war drew near, several political issues in our relations with the Allies become exacerbated. This should have come as no surprise.
>
> The former sluggishness in the actions of the Anglo-American Command was replaced by utmost haste. The governments of Great Britain and the USA were prodding the command of the expeditionary forces in Europe to demand that the Allied troops advance faster into the central parts of Germany so as to occupy them before the Soviet Army moved in.[105]

After quoting an extensive 1 April communication from Churchill to Roosevelt, which ended with the admonition "I therefore consider that, from a political standpoint, we should march as far east into Germany as possible, and that, should Berlin be in our grasp, we should certainly take it." Zhukov added, "I later learned that the British Command and several American generals had done everything to ensure that the Allied forces would capture Berlin and areas to the north and south."[106] Shtemenko evidenced similar suspicions as he wrote

> Vienna was liberated on April 13th and our troops pushed on westwards. This turn of events not only operated in our favour at Berlin; it also had a noticeable effect in activating the Allies, who now began advancing at a much faster rate. The considerable enemy grouping which they had surrounded in the Ruhr was split up and soon abandoned all resistance. The main American and British forces, overcoming weak opposition, swept forward towards the Elbe and the Baltic coast in the area of Lubeck.
>
> There could be no doubt that the Allies intended capturing Berlin before us, although according to the agreements reached at Yalta the capital of Germany had been assigned to the Soviet zone of occupation.[107]

He added

> But we did not intend to be caught napping either. By this time the General Staff had all the basic ideas for the Berlin operation worked out.

In the course of this work we kept in very close contact with the Front chiefs of staff A. M. Bogolyubov, M. S. Malinin, and V. D. Sokolovsky (later with I. Y. Petrov) and, as soon as the first symptoms appeared that the Allies had designs on Berlin, Zhukov and Konev were summoned to Moscow.[108]

Planning for the Berlin operation commenced on 1 April, the day after the completion of 1st Ukrainian Front's Upper Silesian operation and three days before the 1st and 2d Belorussian Fronts concluded operations to clear German forces from eastern Pomerania. That day Zhukov and Konev met in Moscow with Stalin, the *Stavka,* and the General Staff to formulate plans for the Berlin operation. Two days later, the *Stavka* approved the concept of the operation and the plans of the two *front* commanders. The attack date was set for 16 April, leaving just two weeks for preparations. The *Stavka* ordered Soviet forces to destroy German forces defending on the Berlin direction, capture Berlin, and advance to the Elbe to link up with Allied armies. This was to be done within 12 to 15 days by ''the delivery of several powerful blows on a wide front to encircle and dismember the Berlin group and destroy each segment individually.''[109]

In the center sector, Zhukov's 1st Belorussian Front was to launch its main attack from the Kuestrin bridgehead, where four rifle armies and one tank corps would penetrate German defenses. Thereafter, 1st Guards and 2d Guards Tank Armies would lead the advance directly on Berlin. On Zhukov's left flank, Konev's 1st Ukrainian Front was to launch its main attack with three rifle armies supported by two tank corps across the Neisse River toward Cottbus. 3d and 4th Guards Tank Armies would then exploit toward Brandenburg, Dessau, and the southern limits of Berlin. To the north, on Zhukov's right flank, Rokossovsky's 2d Belorussian Front was to attack in the Stettin-Schwedt sector with three rifle armies supported by five mobile corps, to destroy German forces around Stettin and advance to occupy Anklin, Demmin, Waren, and Wittenburg.

Creation of these shock groups required extensive regrouping by all three *fronts.* A total of twenty-eight armies regrouped, fifteen of them a distance of up to 385 kilometers and three between 530 and 800 kilometers. With only a few exceptions, these movements were accomplished within fifteen days (compared with twenty-two to forty-eight days available to move forces prior to the Belorussian, East Prussian, and Vistula-Oder operations). By the night of 15 April, the Soviets had built a formidable force along the banks of the Oder and Neisse rivers. In addition to these forces, the three fronts disposed of at least three reserve armies (3d, 28th, and 31st), which could be used to meet any eventuality, including Allied interference in the Berlin operation.[110]

The final Soviet offensive in the European war began on 16 April. Although Zhukov's force experienced considerable difficulty on the direct route to Berlin, Konev's forces were markedly more successful, earning for Konev the right to participate in the seizure of the German capital. To the relief of the Soviets, the last strategic operation unfolded successfully, as Allied forces adhered to their agreements, peacefully linking up with the Red Army and ultimately withdrawing to their respective sectors.

As a postscript to European operations, in August 1945 the Soviets conducted their most geographically challenging and extensive strategic operation of the war.[111] In response to Allied requests for Soviet assistance in the war against Japan, the Soviets planned operations against Japanese forces in Manchuria and on the northern island possessions of Japan (the Kuriles and Sakhalin). On the basis of opposing force strength, the Manchurian operation was somewhat larger than the Belorussian operation. Using the Belorussian experience as a guide, to guarantee success in the operation the Soviets had to double their strength in the Far East to more than 1.5 million men.

Several conditions delayed Soviet preparations for the Manchurian operation, increased the importance of the operation, and magnified the significance of surprise and deception. Shtemenko noted

> Our efforts to achieve surprise were much hindered by the fact that the Japanese had for long been convinced of the inevitability of war with the Soviet Union. Strategic surprise seemed altogether impossible. Nevertheless, in considering this problem, we reflected more than once on the first days of the war we were still fighting. Our country had also expected war and prepared for it, but the German attack had come as a surprise. So there was no need to abandon the idea prematurely.[112]

First, the immense size of the theater of operations and its distance from European Russia required the Soviets to move almost 700,000 men and massive amounts of equipment and supplies over 9,000 kilometers along the limited umbilical of the Trans-Siberian Railroad from the European theater to the Far East. To maintain strategic surprise, this movement had to be as secret as possible. Second, the Soviets were confronted with severe time constraints. Japanese reinforcement of Manchuria, American use of the atomic bomb, and possible ensuing Japanese collapse made it imperative that the offensive achieve its goals in a matter of days, rather than weeks or months. Manchuria had to be secured within thirty days and the main entrances into central Manchuria within one week, as much for political as for military considerations. From virtually every perspective, deception could make the difference between success and failure. Moreover, the Soviets would have to employ deception to achieve surprise in an initial period of war. This required political finesse to dull Japanese apprehensions over possible Soviet war intentions and the creation and orchestration of a deception plan without the context of ongoing combat. The Soviets could not rely on the "noise" of war to conceal their deception. Ultimately, the Soviets did conceal their intention to attack, as well as the locations, scale, and form of the attack.

The Soviets planned a three-front offensive to conquer Manchuria. The Trans-Baikal Front, attacking from eastern Mongolia and spearheaded by 6th Guards Tank Army, was to penetrate the forbidding terrain of western Manchuria, while the 1st Far Eastern Front struck westward from the Vladivostok area against heavier Japanese troop concentrations in eastern Manchuria. These two *fronts* were to link up and entrap all Japanese forces in the region, while the 2d Far Eastern Front, in the north, pressured the Japanese along a wide front. Deception to conceal the deployment of the Trans-Baikal Front was particularly important. The most challenging aspect of *razvedka,* in support of deception and the operation as a whole, was that it could not rely on the full range of collection assets. Extensive air *razvedka* could not be used because it could compromise the surprise the Soviets sought to achieve.

Ultimately, the operation developed successfully. The Soviet attack achieved surprise and paralyzed Japanese defenders. By 15 August the Soviets had achieved most of their objectives in a strategic operation whose success has since made it a model of how the Soviets would like to operate in the initial period of any future war.

During 1945, in increasingly challenging circumstances, Soviet intelligence played a critical role in strategic planning and the formulation of deception plans. Intelligence collection and analysis during the Vistula-Oder operation typified that role. From the standpoint of conducting strategic and operational *razvedka* and deception, the Soviet High Command and *fronts* faced a different set of circumstances and problems in 1945 than they had faced earlier in the war. The Eastern Front's length had shrunken considerably, resulting in increased concentrations of Soviet and German forces. The Germans knew the Soviets were going to attack, probably in many sectors, and the geographical configuration of the front posed definite problems. Soviet forces faced heavy defenses on the East Prussian–Konigsberg direction and heavy German concentrations on the western outskirts of Budapest. Soviet forces were mired in mountain fighting across the width of the Carpathian Mountains, and on the Western Direction they occupied restrictive bridgeheads across the Narev and Vistula rivers, from which they would have to launch their new offensive. Thus, the Soviets would have difficulty masking their intent to attack and the attack's location, strategically and operationally. Continued operations in Hungary could distract the Germans but only regarding the scale of offensives elsewhere.

To solve these problems, strategically, the Soviets sought primarily to conceal the scale of their offensives rather than their location or timing, while using operational and tactical deception to blur German perceptions regarding attack timing and location. This necessitated strenuous *Stavka* efforts to conceal regrouping and concentration of forces on the critical Western Direction. All the while the Soviets continued operations in Hungary to fix German reserves in that region and postured forces on the Western Direction to distract German attention from the key Konigsberg approach and the Narev and Vistula bridgeheads. *Razvedka* plans fulfilled the important functions of validating the effectiveness of deception plans, monitoring the movement of German reserves (in particular from East Prussia and Hungary), and facilitating a rapid and complete penetration of German defenses along the Vistula River. Although the Soviets were certain they could penetrate German defenses, intervention of fresh German reserves could significantly limit the depth of the Soviet advance, given the existence of extensive preplanned, but unmanned, German defense lines constructed at varying depths across Poland. Within an atmosphere of strict secrecy, Zhukov and Konev prepared deception plans that incorporated active measures to disinform the Germans about the location of the attack and passive measures to conceal the arrival of reserves and concentration of attack forces in their respective bridgeheads.

Throughout late fall 1944, continuous GRU *razvedka* enabled *Stavka* and *front* planners to adjust their concept for the Vistula-Oder operation and formulate a thorough *razvedka* plan. In late October the *Stavka* estimated that, given German strength in Poland, the 1st Belorussian and 1st Ukrainian Fronts would be able to penetrate to a depth of up to 150 kilometers. A subsequent assessment in early November indicated German strength was still too formidable for a large-scale Soviet attack to succeed in the near future. At that point the decision was made to mount a two-phase campaign with the Polish phase commencing in January. This would accord well with the planned final Allied drive into Germany expected early in 1945.

In November and December, Soviet *razvedka* focused on German troop transfers to East Prussia and Hungary in response to the first phase of the Soviet offensive against German positions in East Prussia and Hungary. Shtemenko noted

> Our expectations were confirmed. Soviet attacks in November–December 1944 caused the enemy, according to our calculations, to concentrate 26 divisions (including seven Panzer divisions) in East Prussia and 55 divisions (including nine Panzer divisions) near the capital of Hungary. . . . The German command was once again compelled to obey our will and left only 49 divisions, including a mere five Panzer divisions, on what was for us the main sector of the front.[113]

If this was not enough information upon which to base a decision to attack, news received in late December and early January confirmed the Soviet decision. In early January Soviet intelligence detected the movement of German IV SS Panzer Corps, a critical operational reserve, from the Warsaw area to Hungary. Specifically:

> On 30 December 1944, our radio *razvedka* established that radio stations of the enemy's 3d and 5th Tank Divisions and 4th Tank Corps had ceased to operate. On 1 January 1945, *razvedka* agents reported that soldiers wearing the insignia of 5th Tank Division had been spotted in Czestochowa and on 3 January, radio *razvedka* detected movement of radio stations of the 3d and 5th Tank Divisions in the direction of Kryukov. Finally, the seizure of a prisoner from the 3d Tank Division in the area of Komarno definitely confirmed the transfer of the 4th Tank Corps to the new area.[114]

Fresh intelligence assessments of enemy force dispositions and Polish terrain in late November prompted *Stavka* adjustments in the offensive scheme. Initially, the 1st Belorussian Front was to have attacked due west from the Pulavy and Magnushev bridgeheads while 1st Ukrainian Front did likewise from the Sandomierz bridgehead toward Kalisz on 1st Belorussian Front's left flank to avoid the heavily built-up Silesian industrial region. New data, however, altered this plan.

On November 27, Zhukov arrived in Moscow in answer to a summons from GHQ. On the basis of Front reconnaissance data he had reached the conclusion that it would be very difficult for the First Byelorussian Front to attack due west because of the numerous well-manned defense lines in that area. He thought that success was more likely to be achieved by aiming the main forces at Lodz with a follow-up toward Poznan. The Supreme Commander agreed with the amendment and the operational aspects of the plan for the First Byelorussian Front's initial operation were slightly modified.

This altered the position of the Front's left-hand neighbor. There was no longer any point in the First Ukrainian Front's striking at Kalisz, so Marshal Konev was given Breslau as his main objective.[115]

While the *Stavka* modified its strategic plans, the two *fronts* developed *razvedka* plans to reveal enemy defenses along the Vistula River and determine enemy dispositions across Poland to the Oder River. The first mission involved

> determining the exact disposition of the enemy combat formation and of elements of the enemy defense down to company strong points and the location of artillery and mortar batteries to a preciseness of 100 meters; revealing the location of staffs and command and observation posts down to battalion; and discovering the weakest places in the enemy defense along the Vistula.[116]

The second mission required determining the strength and composition of enemy defensive positions in the depths and detecting, identifying, and tracking operational reserves and potential reinforcements for German forces defending along the Vistula. These were difficult tasks, for unlike earlier operations, the Soviets were now operating on non-Soviet soil. As Zhukov explained, this posed new problems for intelligence.

> Preparations for the Vistula-Oder operation were very different from those of similar scale on Soviet territory. Before, we were fed with intelligence by guerrilla [partisan] detachments operating behind enemy lines. Now, there was none of this any more.
>
> We could only gather intelligence through secret service agents and through aerial and ground reconnaissance. . . . Our supply routes along railroads and motor roads now lay in Poland where, besides true friends and the people loyal to the Soviet Union, there were enemy intelligence agents. The new conditions required special vigilance and secrecy of manoeuvres and deployments.[117]

Front razvedka plans covered the entire duration of the offensive rather than only 15 to 20 days, as had been the case in earlier operations. Planning periods for army-level *razvedka* varied according to *front* missions, conditions, and policies. For example, 60th Army of 1st Ukrainian Front planned for fifteen-day periods, its corps for periods of five to ten days, and rifle divisions usually for two- to three-day periods. *Fronts* coordinated *razvedka* work of all their units, which included reconnaissance aviation regiments, reconnaissance-corrective aviation regiments, separate special designation radio battalions, and organs of agent *razvedka* and reconnaissance subunits of thirty-five first-echelon divisions and fortified regions of armies, as well as eleven artillery instrumental *razvedka* battalions (AIR).[118]

Comparison of German defensive dispositions and force transfers during the two months prior to the offensive with Soviet accounts of *razvedka* and examination of the course of the operation indicates that Soviet *razvedka* organs did their job well. The Soviet deception plan was generally successful, the Soviets were able to pinpoint the location of German reserves, and the penetration operation developed more rapidly than planned. The effectiveness of Soviet forces in the early phases of the operation did such damage to defending German forces that ultimately the offensive plunged westward well beyond the planned objective of Poznan to the Oder River, only 60 kilometers from Berlin. Certainly, some of this success was attributable to the weakness of German defenses and the absence of large German operational reserves. This absence was due to the large German transfer of forces southward from September to December 1944 in response to Soviet activity in the Carpathian Mountain region and in Hungary. Soviet intelligence was able to monitor movement of these reserves and was aware of their location in early January.

Soviet strategic and operational intelligence collection organs, responsible for monitoring German troop movements and for determining the nature of German defenses across the expanse of Poland, accomplished both tasks successfully. During the nine favorable flying days between mid-November and 12 January, Soviet 1st Belorussian Front air *razvedka* operated successfully. 16th Air Army commander, General S. I. Rudenko, gave high marks to air *razvedka,* stating

> The air *razvedka* plan, drawn up by the staff of the air army under the supervision of General P. I. Braiko was fulfilled. Our RO led by Colonel G. K. Prussekovy applied much creative effort and organizational skill in order to employ all types of aviation effectively and purposefully.[119]

During the period, the army conducted 1,700 reconnaissance aircraft sorties, with these results:

> The total area of aerial photography comprised 109,000 square kilometers. Of this total enemy defensive positions to a depth of 8 kilometers were photographed three times over, and the enemy defense sectors in front of the Magnushev and Pulavy bridgeheads to a depth of 25–40 kilometers [were photographed] four times every 10–12 days. Perspective [oblique] photography of the forward edge and the entire tactical defense zone in front of the bridgehead occurred repeatedly. All of this provided the capability of discovering the nature and system of the defense and the grouping of enemy field and antiaircraft artillery throughout the entire tactical depth.

> In the operational depth army rear positions and cut off positions along the Pilitsa River were photographed twice and the Warta and Poznan defensive positions once. As a result of the survey a series of intermediate positions between the Vistula and rear belt were revealed, six antitank positions from 20 to 60 kilometers long were uncovered, as well as an entire aerodrome net with aviation forces based on them.[120]

Chuikov, commander of 8th Guards Army, seconded Rudenko's judgment by stating, "With satisfaction I mention that our army air *razvedka* coped with its missions. Information gathered by it received high marks from the *front* staff and staffs of neighboring armies."[121] The 1st Ukrainian Front achieved similar results as its air *razvedka* photographed over 103,000 square kilometers of territory and monitored movement of German reserves in the key sector south of the Vistula River.[122] A general critique of air *razvedka*'s role added

> Reconnaissance aviation uncovered beyond the Vistula River enemy prepared defensive belts, six antitank positions . . . and determined concentration areas of enemy reserves and enemy artillery groupings. All crossings over the Vistula and Pilitsa Rivers were photographed, and airfield nets with aviation units were uncovered. The information from air *razvedka* permitted the High Command and *front* commands to plan correctly the offensive operations.[123]

Radio *razvedka* by *front*s and armies helped reveal German tactical defensive dispositions and movement of reserves. A critique of 1st Belorussian Front radio *razvedka* declared

> Radio *razvedka* of the *front* ascertained the dispositions of 9th Army, and the staffs of all corps and five (of seven) enemy divisions, operating

in the first line. It had undoubted merit in revealing the operational regrouping occurring in this period in the sector of this army. Thus radio *razvedka* was the first to notice the withdrawal by the German-Fascist command of 4th SS Tank Corps to Hungary where a counterattack was being prepared. According to its data, the *front* staff succeeded in establishing the transfer of the left flank 56th Tank Corps from 4th Panzer Army to 9th Army, as well as the change in the defensive sector of 8th Army Corps.

The successful activity of radio *razvedka* organs was caused first of all by the presence in the *front* composition of radio equipment which was powerful for its times (four radio battalions OSNAZ and the forces themselves had six army groups for close communications *razvedka*).[124]

Soviet sources are less exact regarding the impact and effectiveness of agent and reconnaissance-diversionary *razvedka*. Scattered accounts of agent actions provide fragmentary information, such as this report: "On 1 January, *razvedka* agents reported that soldiers wearing the insignia of 5th Tank Division [SS] had been spotted in Czestochowa."[125] One Soviet critique, referring to agent *razvedka* as *"spetsial'naia"* [special], stated

> For example, in the Vistula-Oder operation special *razvedka* of the 1st Ukrainian Front revealed the basing of aviation and the capacity of the aerodrome net in the *front* sector, and also established the concentration regions of three divisions, the 17th and 4th Tank Army staffs, the 48th Tank and 42d Army Corps staffs, and added other information concerning the grouping of enemy forces, and his operations and intentions.[126]

Once again, extensive German reports illustrated the extent of Soviet agent and reconnaissance-diversionary *razvedka*. German periodic intelligence studies assessed significant numbers of agents, bands, and reconnaissance units in their rear area, labeled under the categories of bands, agents, scouting groups, detachments, and so forth (see map 16). German documents also illustrated how the Soviets used these agents or groups for deceptive purposes. For example, a study of German intelligence procedures employed in the east contained a section on how intelligence dealt with enemy agents. In addition to cataloguing all agent activities, German intelligence concluded

> The places at which the agents were detected or apprehended, as these entries increased in density in certain sectors of the front, were found

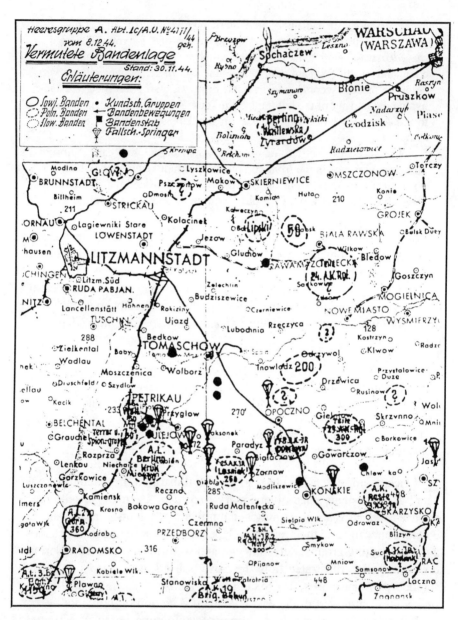

16. German Army Group As assessment of Soviet reconnaissance-diversionary activity, December 1944.

through experience to indicate very closely where the Russians were planning to engage in large scale operations.[127]

A report on agent activity prepared on 5 January 1945 revealed agent activity to be concentrated west of Warsaw and south of Krakow (see map 17).[128] In fact, these were the regions where Soviet deception plans were attempting to simulate attack preparations to distract German attention from the real main attack sectors adjacent to the Vistula River bridgeheads. These and other German documents vividly attest to the effective Soviet use of agents and reconnaissance-diversionary teams in deception operations. At the same time, they tacitly underscore the growing role of these *razvedka* organs in the more common role of intelligence gathering.

Soviet troop, artillery, and engineer *razvedka* were particularly effective and contributed to rapid Soviet success in the penetration operation. The Soviets gathered detailed information on enemy troop and artillery dispositions throughout the tactical depths of the German defense and determined the positions of German operational reserves. Extensive sweeps, ambushes, and raid activity produced a steady stream of prisoners and documents to confirm data obtained from ground and aerial observation.

> As a result, troop *razvedka* studied in detail all groupings of enemy forces within the limits of the main defensive belt. By the beginning of the operation, *front,* army, and division staffs had sufficiently complete information about the composition of the combat formation of fascist formations, defending in first echelon.
> In cooperation with engineer [*razvedka*] troop *razvedka* found out the true outline of the forward edge of the defense, the engineer obstacle system in the forward region and particularly in the depths of the defense, as well as the junction [boundary] of divisions, regiments and battalions; and on the Pulavy bridgehead even the junction between companies. Together with artillery [*razvedka*] it revealed the enemy firing system.[129]

Moskalenko, commander of 38th Army, reinforced this judgment, stating, "As a result, by the beginning of the operation the system of enemy trenches, fortifications, obstacles, and observation posts was uncovered and studied by all officers down to company and battery commanders, inclusively."[130] An account of 47th Army offensive preparations echoed Moskalenko's view.

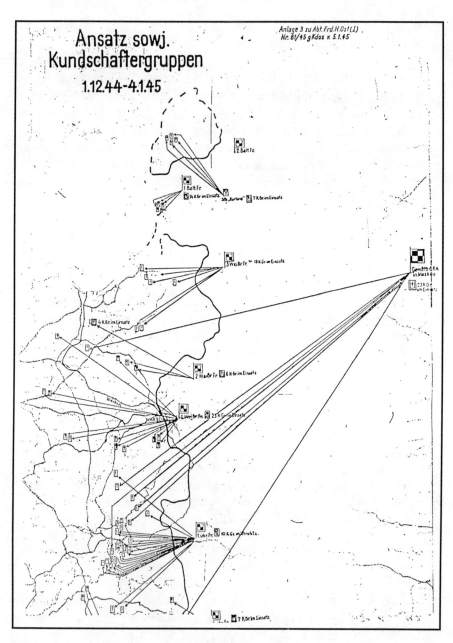

17. Assessment of Soviet reconnaissance-diversionary activity, 5 January 1945, by German *Fremde Heere Ost*.

As a result, by the start of the offensive the configuration of the forward edge had been determined, the fire plan and weapons of the enemy defenses had been discovered down to the individual submachine gun, the coordinates had been determined for 18 artillery and mortar batteries, 12 assault guns, 17 machine guns, 11 covered trenches and 2 pillboxes. This comprised around 70 percent of the basic enemy weapons in the corps' sector of advance.[131]

Reconnaissance in force conducted during the preparatory period and just prior to the offensive deceived the Germans regarding attack timing and location and verified the results of earlier *razvedka*. In 47th Army's sector north of Warsaw, where the Soviets planned diversionary operations, the reconnaissance fulfilled both functions.

The plan of operations foresaw the conduct in our sector of a reconnaissance in force which was timed to correspond with the beginning of the shock group's offensive from the Magnushev bridgehead. The mission—to disorient the enemy and at the same time feel out his force and secure prisoners. The *razvedka* was successful. The so-called Modlin junction, on which the Hitlerites placed great hopes, judging by all, was not as strong as it had been in October of the previous year. Our advanced battalions succeeded in penetrating the depth of the enemy defense almost a kilometer and seized several tens of prisoners.[132]

In the 1st Ukrainian Front sector, reconnaissance in force confused the Germans and permitted refinements in artillery fire plans. "Information obtained by reconnaissance in force allowed the *front* commander to make several changes in the artillery support of the offensive. In particular, the artillery preparation was planned with a pause for platoons to conduct demonstrative attacks."[133] This demonstrative action forced the Germans to "show their hands," and the subsequent artillery preparation pulverized German defenses.

Thorough artillery *razvedka* added to the detailed picture composed by Soviet intelligence staffs, particularly in main attack sectors where 90 percent of artillery intelligence-gathering assets were concentrated. Artillery instrumental *razvedka*, reconnaissance-corrective aviation, and the dense network of artillery observation posts within rifle and artillery units provided an accurate picture of enemy defenses.

As a result of these measures, in the penetration sector [of 1st Belorussian Front] artillery *razvedka* uncovered and determined the coordinates of 468 artillery and mortar and 57 antiaircraft batteries, 1,480 open firing points, 245 firing points with covers (pillboxes), 406 blindages and 154 observation posts.[134]

Artillery *razvedka* also assisted in analysis of forward enemy defenses by identifying antitank and antipersonnel obstacles and other defensive structures.

Engineer *razvedka* contributed to success both in the preparatory period and during the reconnaissance in force. Joint artillery and engineer observation in 5th Guards Army's sector "illuminated" the enemy defensive system, located thirty-six 105mm artillery batteries, fifteen 75mm batteries, thirty-three antiaircraft batteries, twelve 81mm mortar batteries, and seventeen 119.8mm mortar batteries. In addition, *razvedka* revealed that German forces manned only the first and second positions of the main defensive belt. "All of this permitted the army command to have complete information about the enemy and make correct decisions."[135] A 60th Army critique of engineer *razvedka* noted the work of engineer observation posts and engineer reconnaissance parties dispatched deep into the enemy rear and concluded

> Such organized [engineer] *razvedka* permitted us to determine the overall grouping of enemy force operations on our army's sector and ascertain the nature of his defensive structures which, in turn, provided the possibility of more exactly determining the missions of army formations.[136]

Engineer *razvedka* forces also played an important role in the reconnaissance phase just prior to the main attack. According to a senior engineer:

> By the start of the Vistula-Oder Operation of the 1st Belorussian and 1st Ukrainian fronts (January 1945), it had been possible to remove all our own minefields in the jump-off areas and make passages in the enemy minefields in front of the forward edge of its defenses. Here, just on the bridgeheads in front of the breakthrough of the defenses on the 1st Belorussian Front, the combat engineers removed 80,000 antipersonnel and about 42,000 antitank mines. As a total in this operation, in the zone of the 1st Belorussian Front, the engineer troops made 872 passages in the enemy minefields. Here 19,483 antitank and 14,201 antipersonnel mines were removed.[137]

Extensive Soviet *razvedka* prior to the offensive accurately assessed German strength across Poland. By the end of December 1944, the General

Staff assessed that there were forty-nine German divisions, including five panzer divisions, in the main sector of the *front*. Assessments of German forces defending in individual Soviet army sectors were even more accurate, in part because of efficient *razvedka* and in part because of the fewer number of German formations.

A 1st Belorussian Front order issued in early December to 5th Shock Army revealed the intelligence picture at that time:

To the Commander of 5th Shock Army
Copy: To chief of the Red Army General Staff

> 1. Units of the enemy 251st and 6th Infantry Divisions, reinforced by six RGK [reserve of High Command] artillery battalions, two RGK antitank battalions, an RGK assault gun brigade, and one RGK mortar regiment, defend strongly fortified positions on the line: Varka, Grabuv, Zales'ny, Vyboruv, Grabuv Pilitsa, Bzhozuvka, Stzhizhina, Gelenuvek, Gelenuv, Lipa, Lezhenitse. The enemy has fortified these positions for more than four months and has developed them to a depth of from 10 to 15 kilometers. The most developed defense system and the densest enemy combat formation is in the sector Tsetsyliuvka-Lezhenitse.
>
> The main artillery groupings are in the regions:
>   a) Up to four battalions—Zbyshkuv (5 kilometers south of Varka), Budy Boskovol'ske, Boska Volia;
>   b) Up to three battalions—Stanislavuv, Dutska, Volia, Male Bozhe.
>
> Enemy reserves are in the regions: presumed 383d Infantry Division— M. Brone; tank division of an unknown number—Bialobzhegi, Charnotsin (22 kilometers west M. Edlinsk) (17 kilometers southwest of Varka); infantry division of unknown number—Nove Miasto, Tomashuv; presumed 25th Tank Division—Stanislavitse (4 kilometers southwest of Kozenitse), Pionki; grenadier division of unknown number and presumed 174th Reserve Division—Radom. . . .

Commander of
1st Belorussian Front Forces
Marshal of the Soviet Union
G. Zhukov
Chief of staff of 1st Belorussian Front
Colonel-General Malinin[138]

Member of the
Military Council
Lieutenant-General
Telegin

This assessment accurately plotted the tactical defenses of German 251st and 6th Infantry Divisions and the strength of their fire support. It correctly assessed the location of 25th Panzer Division, and the second panzer division identified corresponded to 19th Panzer Division, which was also located in this sector. The grenadier division referred to was either 10th or 20th Panzer Grenadier Division, operating between the Magnushev and Sandomierz bridgeheads. The reserve division identified replicated the German security division operating to the rear of German tactical defenses.[139]

In late December intensified *razvedka* activity by 47th Army north of Warsaw accurately determined German tactical dispositions.

On 29 and 30 December 1944, the Nazi Command regrouped its troops, having positioned two infantry regiments of the 73d Infantry Division in the first echelon and one regiment in the second. In the reserve was around 1.5 infantry battalions and up to 15 tanks. The basic portion of the enemy artillery was positioned in the forests to the west of Hotomow (around 16 batteries).[140]

Farther south, in the Sandomierz bridgehead, 5th Guards Army also formed an accurate picture of the dispositions and strength of defending German units.

Before the army front, in the sector of the penetration defended units of the 168th, 304th, and 68th Infantry Divisions reinforced by tanks, artillery, and mortars. The strength of enemy divisions reached 6000 men, and companies were 60–80 men strong, predominantly German but with small quantities of Austrians. The average density of artillery reached 10–12, and in some sectors up to 20–25 guns per kilometer of front, and up to 10 machine guns, 3 tanks, and 150–170 rifles per kilometer. In the Buska-Zdrui areas, the corps tank reserve was located—the 501st Separate Tank Battalion with 50 machines. Enemy operational reserves were located in the depth of the defense. In the army offensive sector we expected two infantry and one tank division to appear.[141]

A critique of 1st Belorussian Front *razvedka* summarized its overall achievement regarding German order of battle:

As a result of the complex and purposeful use of forces and means of all types of *razvedka,* missions assigned by commanders to *front razvedka* during the preparatory period, were fully carried out: by the beginning of the offensive the 1st Belorussian Front staff possessed accurate information about the compositions, grouping, and the combat capabilities of formations and units of German-fascist forces operating in the sector of the forthcoming offensive. The enemy tactical defense zone on the direction of the *front* main attack was especially revealed in detail.[142]

Once in possession of this data, the *front* ensured it was put to good use.

> The *front* staff carried out great efforts to provide generalized data to the forces. In particular, they were sent detailed characteristics of enemy divisions defending the Vistula defensive line, schemes of defensive positions throughout the entire depth of the defense, maps of aviation unit basing and his aerodrome network and reconnaissance sketches of the main defense belt on a scale of 1:25,000 and 1:50,000, which during the ten days before the offensive were passed down to company and battery commanders.[143]

Soviet *razvedka* deprived German defenders of what little chance they had to defend successfully along the Vistula. The devastating nature of the ensuing assaults ensured that Soviet forces would penetrate far beyond their ultimate objective of Poznan, in this case all the way to the Oder River.

Once the operation had begun, the Soviets grappled with the difficult task of conducting *razvedka* on the march. How deep the operation would penetrate depended, in large measure, on how effectively they fulfilled this task. In 1945 the Red Army relied primarily on air, radio, and mobile ground *razvedka* to determine enemy dispositions and intentions during the course of an operation. Soviet performance during the Vistula-Oder operation illustrated the progress Soviet commanders had made in this regard.

All Soviet rifle and mobile forces employed multiple patrols, groups, and detachments to conduct ground *razvedka*. Groups and patrols served divisions and regiments during the tactical penetration, while detachments of mobile corps and brigades led the exploitation and pursuit phase of the operation. By 1945 most reconnaissance detachments were fully motorized and had their own armor and antitank support.

Once the penetration phase had been completed, Soviet mobile forces commenced the exploitation led by forward detachments and reconnaissance detachments. Combined-arms armies formed their own reconnaissance detachments to operate well forward in the gaps between the exploiting mobile forces and less mobile main force infantry. These reconnaissance detachments of reinforced tank or rifle battalion size ranged from 20 to 40 kilometers in advance of their parent forces and cooperated closely with aviation units to reconnoiter enemy rear or intermediate defense lines and monitor German withdrawal or the arrival of reserves. For example:

> Reconnaissance detachments of 2d Guards Tank Army, arriving in the Sokhachev area (50 kilometers west of Warsaw), determined that part of the rear [defensive] positions were occupied by the 391st Security Division and that enemy 46th Tank Corps formations were withdrawing westward from Warsaw. By decisive action of 2d Guards Tank Army forces, the 391st Security Division was crushed, and with the arrival of 2d Guards Tank Army at Sokhachev withdrawal routes of the Warsaw group westward were cut. As a result it [the Warsaw group] was forced to turn northwest where it crossed the Vistula under constant joint action of our aviation and ground forces and suffered great losses.[144]

Numerous similar examples exist of actions by reconnaissance groups and detachments late in the operation, as Soviet mobile forces raced across central Poland.

Ground *razvedka* also provided the initial intelligence of a German buildup in Pomerania, which ultimately led to Zhukov's recommendation that the offensive be halted on the Oder River. Accordingly:

> On 22 January in the Torun region, a prisoner was captured from the German 31st Infantry Division which had been located earlier in the Baltic. From *razvedka* organs, operating in the enemy rear, came information about the beginning of force transfers from Danzig to the southwest, that is to the front right flank. Simultaneously enemy opposition near Bromberg, Nakel and Schneidemuhl stiffened considerably.[145]

Subsequent identification by a reconnaissance detachment of 2d Guards Tank Army of the 15th SS Infantry Division near Nakel raised initial concerns for security on the right flank. As a consequence:

> That *razvedka* information predetermined the decision of the *front* commander to employ 3d Shock Army (the *front* second echelon) to cover the *front* right flank. Simultaneously, armies operating on the Kustrin and Frankfurt directions were ordered to increase the tempo of their offensive in order to rapidly overcome enemy fortifications and reach the Oder.[146]

Radio *razvedka* organs at *front* and army level concentrated on detecting changes in German dispositions and the arrival of new German formations once the operation began.

> *Radiorazvedka* on the first day of the offensive revealed the dislocation of staffs of not only formations [corps and divisions], but also many units [regiments] of the enemy first echelon, and in the course of the operation constantly tracked their movements. They discovered, in timely fashion, the location of operational reserves and determined the direction of withdrawal of German-fascist forces.[147]

Soviet critiques reserved special praise for army close communication *razvedka* groups, which

> assisted the commanders of divisions and corps to recognize the immediate plans of the enemy to counter the advance of our forces and to undertake necessary measures. Thanks to these, in the 61st Army sector in the course of the first two weeks of the offensive we disrupted five counterattacks by companies and battalions and detected the withdrawal of the enemy to the third [defensive] position in front of our army's left flank corps.[148]

Once the penetration phase had ended and weather improved, air *razvedka* began playing a key role in determining enemy intentions and dispositions. In fact, the deeper Soviet forces advanced, the more important was air *razvedka*. *Front* air forces began flying *razvedka* missions on 16 January after bad weather improved, although earlier bomber and fighter flights had conducted minimal aerial observation. The priority missions of both 16th and 2d Air Armies were to monitor the movement of enemy reserves and continuously observe conditions on the field of battle. Soviet control of the skies facilitated accomplishment of both missions. Subsequently:

> Special attention was paid to the assault aircraft and ground forward detachment which cleared the path for all formations. Cooperation with this detachment in the operational depth meant that pilots had to conduct *razvedka* in its interest, discover enemy units, especially artillery and tank, and crush them from the air.[149]

Improved air-ground radio communications procedures and equipment prompted smoother operation of the system. According to Rudenko:

If air and ground crews were to communicate with one another through their staffs, this required considerable time. Therefore we decided to employ such a communications system which included the following aspects. Our aviation commanders had to be collocated with commanders of tank sub-units and direct assault aircraft strikes on those targets, which were of the highest priority to destroy.[150]

Almost immediately after the offensive commenced, *razvedka* data began to flow in from fighter and assault aircraft. On the morning of 13 January in 1st Ukrainian Front's sector, pilots of 2d Air Army reported movement and concentration of enemy forces on the flank of 4th Tank Army south of Kielce and north of Chmel'nik. Subsequent air strikes by 8th Bomber and 2d Assault Aviation Corps disorganized the planned German counterattack; by evening of 13 January, German forces began withdrawing to their third defense belt. "Air *razvedka* reported the movement of withdrawing enemy columns toward Czestochowa, Sosnovets and Krakow," and again air units struck at German columns.[151] This scattered air activity on the first few days of the offensive helped rout German forces defending at Sandomierz.

On 16 January, after weather had cleared, air *razvedka* expanded to encompass the entire front. Opposite the Magnushev and Pulavy bridge-heads, reconnaissance aircraft "determined the direction of withdrawal of German forces and the location of friendly forward detachments and main force formations."[152] Most important, on 17 January 16th Air Army detected the arrival in sector of significant German reserves.

Air *razvedka* determined that tanks were unloading in the Lodz region. This was tank corps "Grossdeutschland" transferred from Prussia. The commander of 16th Air Army assigned the 241st Bomber Division the mission of launching air strikes. Operating in eight groups, the crews in three passes destroyed the railroad railbed at the arrival and departure switches and almost fully knocked out the rail center. Bombing from various directions and various heights disorganized the German air defense. Tankers soon secured Lodz, seized 400 rail cars with military equipment and cargo and 28 repaired engines. Because of the blows of aviation and *front* mobile forces, tank corps "Grossdeutschland" suffered considerable losses and was forced to withdraw, having failed to advance into battle.[153]

Shortly thereafter, 16th Air Army *razvedka* detected German occupation of the "Warta defensive line with up to five infantry divisions."[154]

Air *razvedka* also contributed to detection and identification of German forces concentrated in the Silesian industrial region on 1st Ukrainian Front's left flank. By 19 and 20 January resistance had stiffened in the area, forcing Konev to shift the axis of 3d Guards Tank Army's advance from Breslau southward toward Oppeln and Ratibor. By 23 January air, radio, and troop *razvedka* had identified elements of the German force.

> In the evening of January 23 we worked out from our reconnaissance data the composition of the enemy group defending the Silesian industrial area. It consisted of nine infantry divisions, two panzer divisions, several so-called combat groups, two separate brigades, six separate regiments and 22 separate battalions, including several machine-gun training battalions and an officers' penal battalion. Judging by appearance we could have expected the arrival of 2–3 more infantry divisions and one panzer division in the nearest future.[155]

Late in the operation, *razvedka* data convinced the Soviets to halt their forces along the Oder River and, instead of driving on Berlin, to mount operations to clear their flanks. Between 30 January and 2 February, Zhukov received ominous *razvedka* reports that reinforced earlier suspicions of a growing threat from Pomerania. His air army commander Rudenko recalled

> At the time it became well known; the Germans were urgently forming 11th Army under the command of Himmler. . . . For air *razvedka* over Pomerania we selected our best pilots and navigators. They were required to inspect in detail the vast region daily and not miss one column which could be moving east—the more so since the forested area and bad weather also assisted the hidden movements of the enemy.
>
> *Razvedchiki* flew in PE-2 aircraft and photographed the territory. By the pictures we could exactly determine where the forces were going and how they were organized.[156]

Despite bad weather and German security measures, which prevented continuous observation and detection of significant movements, Rudenko's airmen persisted in their efforts.

> We continued intensively to conduct *razvedka* from the skies reporting in timely fashion to the *front* staff about all that the enemy did in the so-called "tent" hanging over us from the north. Finally all types of *razvedka* succeeded in determining that by the beginning of February between the Oder and the Vistula two fascist armies had concentrated: the 2d and the

11th possessing over twenty divisions. Our air searches discovered that the flow of forces to Eastern Pomerania was continuing. Actually the quantity of enemy divisions there, as was later revealed, rose to forty.[157]

These reports plus others received from ground *razvedka* units reporting a German buildup along the Oder River prompted the Soviets to terminate the Vistula-Oder operation in early February.

Air *razvedka* during the course of the operation assisted the development of deep ground operations. It "discovered enemy reserves moving toward the field of battle, ascertained the location and movement of enemy columns withdrawing to rear defensive lines, detected the weakest defensive sectors" and assisted combat aircraft in fulfilling their missions.[158] It functioned in close cooperation with other equally mature means of *razvedka,* in particular radio and mobile ground reconnaissance, and played a significant role in the successful Soviet sustainment of continuous operations to depths of from 500 to 700 kilometers.

Throughout all phases of the Vistula-Oder operation, *razvedka* played a major role in the formulation and execution of Soviet deception plans. Throughout September and October Soviet intelligence kept track of German troop movements into the Carpathian region, and it did the same when subsequent Soviet operations in Hungary drew some of these forces farther south to the Debrecan region. Later, in December, it detected the movement of IV SS Panzer Corps from the Warsaw area to Budapest. These strategic movements set the stage for the Soviet Vistula-Oder deception plan. By posturing for assaults north of Warsaw and between the Vistula River and the Carpathian Mountains, the Soviets capitalized on previous attack patterns and German expectations. Thereafter, up to 12 January, German operational reserves in central Poland remained relatively static. The fact that the Germans never reinforced their forces on the Vistula front confirmed Soviet judgments regarding the success of their deception plans, as did German movement of tactical infantry reinforcements south of the Vistula River just before the offensive (in particular, the 344th and 359th Infantry Divisions).[159]

In one of the clearest cases to date, the Soviets used their intelligence collection techniques to deceive the Germans. Fully understanding that German intelligence viewed Soviet agent and reconnaissance-diversionary operations as indicators as to where the main attack would occur, the Soviets concentrated those activities during December and January in the regions west of Warsaw and south of the Vistula River city of Krakow. There is strong evidence that *front* RUs employed planted line crossers, and deserters as well, to provide German intelligence with false information.[160]

The Soviet deception plan succeeded to a considerable extent, in part, because of efficient intelligence work. German intelligence documents clearly indicated they expected an attack somewhere in the central sector of the Eastern Front, but repeated reassessments decreased the urgency of the warnings. In the end, the German High Command, based on its intelligence assessments, chose not to reinforce the Vistula front. Soviet *razvedka* compounded this German failure by successfully tracking German movements while the Germans failed to detect major Soviet regroupings and underestimated Soviet strength along key sectors of the Vistula by up to 40 percent. The German Vistula-Oder disaster was a Soviet deception success, and this success was conditioned in large measure by effective Soviet *razvedka*. While Soviet numerical superiority remained the biggest factor in their achievement of victory, effective intelligence work contributed to the Soviet ability to generate that superiority without German knowledge. *Razvedka* contributed to the rapid development of the penetration operation by forming an accurate picture of German tactical dispositions. Once the operation had begun, sound intelligence ensured the initiative would remain in Soviet hands until time and distance had taken its toll on advancing Soviet forces. This, in part, explained the extraordinary depth of the Soviet advance.

Soviet *razvedka* in the Vistula-Oder operation typified similar Soviet efforts elsewhere in 1945, when the Soviets had sufficient time to plan their operations. On those occasions when *razvedka* failed, it was often because of the fluid nature of combat and rapidly changing situations. This occurred on those few occasions when German forces delivered counterattacks (such as in January and February 1945, when IV SS Panzer Corps unexpectedly struck Soviet defenses west of Budapest), and during the waning stages of operations, when the Soviets were operating deep in the German rear (such as in early February, when the Germans rapidly moved reinforcements to the Oder River line).[161] These instances when intelligence weakened in no way subverted Soviet achievement of planned strategic aims.

Summary

Soviet strategy in the third period of war grew in scope and ambition and took on a more subtle political flavor. With the strategic initiative firmly in Soviet hands, strategic operations became totally offensive, more grandiose, and incessant. While earlier operations occurred on separate strategic directions, by 1944 they took place along the entire strategic front, successively in 1944 and simultaneously in 1945. Each operation was conducted within the context of a deception plan coordinated by the *Stavka*—a plan that encompassed the entire campaign. These plans successfully concealed both the location and scale of the strategic offensives and, to some extent, the timing as well.

By war's end operations by groups of *fronts* involved from 100 to 200 divisions, up to 2.5 million men, 20,000 to 40,000 guns or mortars, 3,000 to 6,000 tanks or self-propelled guns, and 2,000 to 7,500 aircraft. These operations had decisive objectives (usually the encirclement and destruction of large enemy groups), huge scope, high maneuverability, and significant military-political or economic results. They spanned frontages from 450 to 1,400 kilometers (4,400 kilometers in Manchuria) and thrust to a depth of up to 600 kilometers while destroying as many as 50 to 100 enemy divisions. Often the political and economic goal of the operation was as important as the military goal, and these goals affected the nature of military operations (for example, the operations against Finland, the drive into the Balkans, and the Manchurian offensive).

Strategic offensive operations, conducted under a cloak of deception, sought to achieve multiple penetrations of the enemy front and subsequent rapid encirclement of enemy forces. The Korsun'-Shevchenkovskii operation and subsequent operations on the right bank of the Ukraine encircled large German groups. A series of successive encirclement operations in Belorussia in June through July 1944 destroyed German Army Group Center and the Iassy-Kishinev operation encircled and destroyed Rumanian forces and German Sixth Army in Rumania. The East Prussian and East Pomeranian operations pinned large German forces against the Baltic Sea. The pace of Soviet offensive operations increased in accordance with their increased depth to produce rates of advance of 15 to 20 kilometers per day for rifle units. Armored and mechanized units advanced at even higher rates (up to 100 kilometers per day).

During 1944 the Soviet capacity for conducting strategic deception and *razvedka* matured and became a motive force for achieving strategic success. In 1943 the Soviets had been able to conceal their operational intent on numerous occasions, but the Germans were able to discover where Soviet strategic priorities lay. Consequently, Soviet strategic offensives were more difficult and more costly in terms of Soviet losses.

In 1944, however, the Soviets were able to conceal their strategic priorities and to capitalize on strategic patterns formed in 1943, as well as on German preconceptions and political notions (mostly Hitler's).

In the winter campaign, the Soviets conditioned the Germans to expect a year-long drive through the Ukraine into Poland and Rumania by constantly conducting operations in that direction. Then, in the spring, the Soviets implemented an elaborate strategic deception plan to conceal a strategic redeployment of forces and prepare a secret strategic strike against German forces in Belorussia. As had been the case before Kursk, the Soviets planned in advance for all stages of the summer offensive, and all of those stages were based on the premise that the initial strategic deception would accomplish its aims. The deception succeeded, and Soviet *razvedka* kept track of the movement of German operational and tactical reserves.

The success of the June strategic offensive against Army Group Center exceeded Soviet expectations. As German reserves moved north to stabilize the situation, the 1st Ukrainian Front struck Army Group Northern Ukraine in coordination with a 1st Belorussian Front attack toward Lublin. As both forces reached the Vistula River, Soviet forces struck in the Baltic and in Rumania, driving back Army Group North and shattering Army Group South Ukraine. By late fall continued Soviet operations on both flanks had drawn German reserves from the center and created new German vulnerabilities in Poland and southern East Prussia, thus paving the way for future Soviet successes in the forthcoming 1945 winter offensive.

These successes were made possible by improved Soviet capabilities for shifting large strategic reserves secretly across the front and moving them into the forward area without the Germans detecting their presence and by effective Soviet monitoring of German troop movements and defensive dispositions. The Soviets timed and concealed these regroupings so well that the Germans were unable to counter them, even if portions of the strategic deception plan and *razvedka* failed.

Much of Soviet *razvedka* success in the third period of war was a product of new procedures established by more comprehensive regulations published in 1944 and by more effective implementation of those procedures. The 1944 *Red Army Field Regulations* evidenced the growing sophistication of *razvedka*. It reiterated the importance of *razvedka* but insisted that raw intelligence information be treated skeptically, stating, ''The operations of reconnaissance units or subunits must be bold and active. The enemy can be forced to show his strength only by combat.''[162]

In the main, the regulation repeated the contents of the 1942 and 1943 regulations but placed even greater emphasis on operational and strategic *razvedka* means, noting, "Aerial photo *razvedka,* which permits studying reconnoitered objectives with great reliability and completeness, is of greatest value."[163] Its indices of aerial *razvedka* depth increased to 100 kilometers for army and 500 kilometers for *front* (strategic) reconnaissance aviation. Communications had improved to such an extent that aircraft were expected to "pass observation data by radio in the clear, encoding only the designation of points."[164] Aerial *razvedka* reports were "received from the aircraft simultaneously by the radio of combined-arms and air staffs which had sent the aircraft on reconnaissance."[165]

According to the regulation, operational *razvedka* by *front*s and armies relied primarily on aircraft, mobile forces, and radio intercept supplemented by tactical *razvedka* data and information from partisans. Tactical *razvedka* by corps, divisions, and regiments relied on aircraft and ground force actions of a variety of detachments, groups, and patrols. Special *razvedka* was the task of the chiefs of combat arms and services (artillery and engineers). The regulation highlighted the importance of radio intelligence, stating, it "provides an opportunity for determining the location of headquarters and probable enemy groupings; intercepting radio messages; and monitoring individual conversations, instructions, and reports being passed over wire facilities."[166] Finally, it specified in detail the contents of *razvedka* plans, but for security's sake enjoined divisions and corps to assign *razvedka* missions to subunits "only verbally" and only to the extent necessary for performing the *razvedka* mission. In addition, it "categorically prohibited" reconnaissance units from carrying combat documents or maps with notes about friendly force dispositions along on reconnaissance.[167]

Organizationally, the 1944 regulation created new officer positions at *front* and army headquarters to facilitate smoother processing of information. "Agent" officers were required to know "constantly and in detail, the situation and state of large units assigned to them, to report on their large units to the commander and chief of staff, immediately on demand, and to acquaint the large units with the combat missions assigned by the commander and oversee their execution." Their use reduced the number of stages in information gathering and eliminated staff "parallelism."[168] Designated "information" officers manned information control points within armies to centralize control over all data from senior or subordinate headquarters. These officers worked closely with agent officers "to considerably improve the gathering and study of information on the combat situation at all control levels." While information gathering was streamlined, the Soviets refined reporting procedures, created new reporting schedules, and created new report formats. Of particular importance was a new summary of information covering twenty-four hours of combat activity.[169]

In the summer of 1944, while new regulations were being published and circulated, a Soviet staff reorganization upgraded the *razvedka* department [*otdel'*] of each *front* into a *razvedka* directorate [*upravlenie*] with its own expanded subordinate functional departments. The efficiency of these new organizations and procedures became apparent in the Vistula-Oder operation.

Confronted in 1945 with the task of organizing strategic operations in the circumstances of a truncated, more concentrated front, Soviet planners drew on the experiences of three years of war and shifted the focus of their deception. Concealing offensive intent in the climactic stages of war was clearly impossible. Geographical considerations, principally the more restricted length of the front and the growing number of natural barriers to a broad front advance along many directions, inhibited Soviet concealment of main strategic and operational attack directions. Faced with these altered circumstances, Soviet planners still attempted to use deception to conceal offensive intent and location but now placed primary emphasis on concealing the timing and scale of the offensive.

The Soviets increased the scale and improved the secrecy of strategic regrouping and concentration of forces by shifting multiple armies between *front*s and from *Stavka* reserve into projected attack positions. Prior to the summer campaign of 1944, the Soviets had strategically regrouped two tank armies and five combined-arms armies. In the late fall of 1944, they had done so with three tank and ten combined-arms armies. Then, prior to the April Berlin offensive, the Soviets regrouped twenty-eight armies, of which eighteen conducted moves of strategic proportion. Between June and August 1945, the Soviets transported one *front*, one tank army, three combined-arms armies, and almost 700,000 men the breadth of the continent into the Far East.

The secrecy with which this movement was accomplished was even more important than the scale of the strategic regrouping. In virtually all cases the Soviets were able to conceal between 50 and 100 percent of the forces regrouped. That resulted in a proportionate German and Japanese underestimation of the force opposing them. In every case it turned prospective operational defeat on the part of the deceived into a strategic disaster. Conversely, the diminished number of German reserves of any type eased the job of Soviet *razvedka,* which by virtue of its greater efficiency, kept track of German movements. Soviet sensitivity to German troop movements and the ability of *razvedka* to decipher in detail the nature of German tactical defenses combined to hasten German and, ultimately, Japanese defeat.

5 Conclusions

Throughout the course of the Second World War, there was a close and understandable correlation between the skill with which the Soviets planned and conducted strategic operations and the degree of success those operations achieved. Soviet military skill steadily improved, and success reflected that improvement. The growth of Soviet military skill resulted from the harsh and unforgiving wartime education of commanders, staffs, and soldiers. In addition to skill, other factors—such as the immense natural manpower pool of the Soviet nation, the inevitable attrition of German forces, and Allied assistance and cooperation with the Soviets—admittedly contributed to and provided a context for growing Soviet strategic success. Improved skills, however, remained the single most important factor in the ultimate Soviet achievement of strategic victory. Skill encompassed a host of realms, including operational acumen, staff efficiency, force tactical proficiency, and logistical competence. Among those many realms was that of intelligence collection and analysis.

Obviously, intelligence performance affected the course and outcome of operations. The effect was most pronounced and noticeable at the tactical and operational levels, but since strategic outcome depended on the resolution of tactical and operational questions, the strategic impact of intelligence work was inevitably present, albeit in a manner often indirect and difficult to measure. It is equally obvious that intelligence seldom played the most vital role in the success or failure of strategic operations. For example, one can argue that in the most successful Soviet strategic operations of the war, those in the summer of 1944, the most significant factors contributing to Soviet strategic success was the ability to deceive the Germans, the ability to concentrate large forces secretly, and the ability of Soviet forces to operate more effectively than in earlier operations. Although *razvedka* played a considerable role in these operations, it is likely Soviet deception would have succeeded, even if the Soviets had not been able to verify the effects, and Soviet forces would have prevailed even if *razvedka* had done a less effective job of deciphering the nature of German defenses. On a few notable occasions, however, effective intelligence played an even more vital role in achieving strategic aims. For example, in the Manchurian operation of August 1945, timely Soviet strategic victory directly depended on the knowledge that Japanese forces had left major sectors of the Grand Khingan Mountains undefended. In this case, the presence of even weak Japanese forces in key mountain passes could have thwarted Soviet plans.

Since intelligence was but one factor contributing to strategic success or failure, its importance can be judged only by analyzing each strategic campaign and operation to avoid incorrect generalizations. It is also important to realize that there were two distinct aspects of intelligence—collection and analysis—and that these aspects were not always equally effective. The two aspects often had differing impacts on the outcome of specific operations. For example, in the period preceding Operation Barbarossa, though intelligence collection was clearly adequate, proper analysis failed, in part because political authorities inhibited it. On other occasions, adequate collection and analysis was rendered superfluous by faulty political judgments or military misperception, as in southern Russia in early 1943. Seldom, however, could quality intelligence analysis occur in the absence of effective intelligence collection.

Soviet intelligence experiences indicated that success depended upon mastery of three distinct but phased and related steps: intelligence collecting, intelligence analysis, and political-military decision making. Each step depended directly on the preceding, and, if one step failed, that failure negated positive work done at lower steps. Only when all three steps were congruent and political-military authorities fully appreciated and took part in the process, did the entire intelligence continuum work as an effective unity. War experience clearly underscored this fact.

On the eve of war, Soviet intelligence organs at all levels possessed ample warning of the German Barbarossa buildup. Agent reports and official notifications by foreign governments succinctly highlighted German offensive intentions. At the lowest command level, tactical indicators of impending hostilities were numerous and credible. The responsibility for Soviet failure to react in time rested primarily with Stalin, who mistrusted the data and refused to accept reality, since it did not accord with his strategic outlook. The consequence was the initial Barbarossa disaster and the failure of prewar Soviet military strategy to cope with combat in the initial period of war.

Subsequently, throughout the summer and fall of 1941, the Soviets were cast into a reactive stance. Throughout this period the Soviets experimented with various means of controlling strategic operations, but settled on the use of three headquarters to control operations on strategic directions. The strategic imperative was to forestall Soviet military collapse and stabilize the front. In time, the Soviets measured the success of this strategy by their ability to maintain possession of Moscow and other symbolic, but strategically important, points. Intelligence collection and analysis, which still suffered from initial wartime disruption, did not materially contribute to achievement of those ends. Conversely, it contributed to the September and October catastrophies at Kiev, Viaz'ma, and Briansk. Once the German offensive had run its natural course and lost momentum on the outskirts of Moscow, Soviet strategists seized the initiative and began the winter campaign of 1941 and 1942. Soviet strategy in the Moscow operation, and the campaign as a whole, was immature and crude. The Soviets failed to establish strategic objectives commensurate with their actual capabilities, and this gap between theoretical strategic plans and combat realities thwarted full Soviet success. During the winter, intelligence contributed in only a minor way to Soviet offensive efforts, and, in fact, intelligence failures inhibited Soviet accomplishment of their strategic goals. These mixed experiences, however, indicated what could be accomplished in the future if *razvedka* means and procedures were improved and integrated.

In the spring of 1942, the Soviets confidently formulated a new coherent military strategy to govern operations throughout the summer. They retained strategic direction headquarters to coordinate *front* operations and adopted a strategy that incorporated a strategic defense on the Moscow direction with local offensives elsewhere along the front. Again, an overly ambitious strategic plan combined with successful German deception and Soviet intelligence failures to produce a second spring and summer of recurring disasters. As had been the case in 1941, the ill effects of poor intelligence collection were compounded by poor strategic leadership (Stalin's), which misinterpreted intelligence data and allowed preconception to rule supreme. The Khar'kov, Kerch, and Voronezh debacles resulted—although, thereafter, the Soviets avoided the disastrous force losses they had experienced in 1941.

By the fall of 1942, as German forces approached Stalingrad and the

Caucasus, Stalin abandoned the unwieldy strategic direction command structure and instead adopted a system using *Stavka* representatives to coordinate the planning and conduct of strategic operations. More important, he gave greater voice to key military figures in charting the course of campaigns and strategic operations. Hence, planning for the winter campaign of 1942 and 1943 was more focused and thorough than in earlier periods. The winter campaign was the first series of operations that took place within the context of a coherent campaign plan, even though the plan turned out to be unrealistic and fell short of achieving its objectives. The efficiency of Soviet intelligence collection and analysis markedly improved in late 1942, in part because the Soviets implemented a comprehensive system for analyzing and exploiting war experience. These improvements contributed to the success of Soviet strategic operations in November and December 1942 and in the first months of 1943. Intelligence continued to perform well, even after the coherence of the strategic campaign plan eroded in February. During the latter stages of the winter campaign, Stalin and other *Stavka* elements again allowed hope, optimism, and subjectivity to blur objective judgment. Misjudgment of accurate intelligence data, overoptimism, and misperception combined to produce Soviet operational failures in February and March 1943 and bring the Soviet winter offensive to a halt.

Razvedka modestly contributed to Soviet victory at Stalingrad by verifying the effects of Soviet deception and determining most Axis force dispositions. It accurately assessed weak sectors in the Axis defense and kept track of large-scale German force movements. Although intelligence sometimes failed to detect specific German units, it performed the detection task well enough to permit the Soviets to counter major German Stalingrad relief attempts. Even as late as February, intelligence collection was fairly accurate, although inaccurate agent reports (particularly from abroad) contributed to *Stavka* failure to properly interpret enemy intentions.

The period of combat lull between March and July 1943 provided time for the Soviet strategic leadership to develop mature future strategic plans and to refine *razvedka* collection means and intelligence-processing procedures. These improvements and more accurate intelligence information from abroad contributed to Soviet successes in the summer-fall campaign of 1943. The Soviet strategic plan for the summer-fall campaign was the most comprehensive to date, and it incorporated the realistic initial defensive stance, which, in large measure, conditioned subsequent victory.

The summer-fall strategic campaign plan encompassed a series of operations extending well into the fall and incorporated the first truly strategic-scale deception plan. Soviet intelligence verified German reaction to the Soviet strategic deception plan, and that plan became a critical ingredient in Soviet attainment of strategic success. The *razvedka* plan, despite occasional weaknesses and local failures, essentially performed its dual mission of tracking German operational reserves and revealing the nature of German defenses. At this stage of the war, it accomplished the latter more efficiently than the former but did both well enough to enhance the scale of ensuing Soviet victory. As a result, the summer-fall campaign was the first Soviet strategic venture that achieved virtually all of its goals. In addition, in summer 1943 a clearer relationship began to emerge between Soviet military strategy and that of her allies. This relationship matured in 1944 and 1945 to become a distinct factor in Soviet strategic success (see Appendix B).

During the winter campaign of 1944, which followed fall operations in virtually uninterrupted fashion, the Soviets replicated their strategic plan for the winter of 1942 and 1943, only this time successfully. While conducting diversionary operations elsewhere, the Soviets focused their efforts on clearing German forces from the Ukraine. In the two-phase, multioperation campaign, the Soviets relied on operational and tactical *razvedka* in support of operational deception to preempt German force regroupment and timely reaction of German operational reserves. Intelligence accorded Soviet commanders at least initial local advantage in each operation. Intelligence failures, when they occurred, resulted from the depth and complexity of combat and commanders' misperceptions of German actions during exceptionally fluid combat situations. For the first time, during the winter campaign of 1944, the Soviets continued the strategic offensive despite the spring thaw, which in earlier years had brought operations to a grinding halt. This strategic decision to continue the offensive into March made German withdrawal from the Ukraine inevitable.

The summer-fall campaign of 1944 was by far the ultimate Soviet strategic venture in the war, in terms of planning effectiveness, deception efficiency, *razvedka*, and results. At the outset, German operational reserves were sufficient, if properly employed, to have forestalled the debacle that ensued. Soviet success in the initial operations of the campaign (Belorussia, L'vov, and Kovel') condemned the Germans to a series of inescapable and crippling disasters, the net effect of which was to strip from the Germans virtually any capability for staving off ultimate defeat. Prior to the Belorussian operation, Soviet deception, verified effectively by *razvedka,* ensured that the destruction of German Army Group Center would be virtually complete. As subsequent operations unfolded in July and August, the Germans never regained their balance. Throughout the summer, three German army groups were smashed, German operational reserves withered, and Soviet forces advanced into East Prussia, to the Vistula River in Poland, and through Rumania into the heart of the Balkans. Subsequent operations on the flanks exploited German weakness and conditioned the Germans for ever more devastating defeats on the critical central direction in the winter of 1945. As a result of the German defeats in 1944, although still effective, *razvedka*'s role diminished in 1945, for German defeat was a foregone conclusion.

In the initial phase of winter campaign operations and the Berlin operation, intelligence efficiently performed its normal task of "illuminating" German defenses. During the ensuing exploitation phases of these operations, intelligence collecting organs demonstrated increased efficiency "on the march," although Soviet analytical agencies demonstrated detectable wariness over the potential impact of last-minute defeats and projected Allied actions. That wariness was reflected by the air of caution in Soviet strategic planning. In these last wartime operations, the *Stavka* eschewed using representatives to coordinate major operations and, instead, appointed its most experienced *Stavka* representatives to command specific key *fronts*. This permitted Stalin even more direct control over operations and enabled him to react faster to whatever developments arose. Throughout both the summer-fall and the winter campaign, the Soviets closely coordinated their strategic actions with those of the Allies, and the Soviets reacted more carefully to military developments in the West.

In the August 1945 Manchurian operation, the Soviets formulated and implemented a military strategy for use in the initial stages of a war. Here political realities played as significant a role as military considerations, as the Soviets contributed to the final defeat of Japan by seizing her most valuable continental stronghold. Here also, intelligence played a slightly different role in that it worked within distinct restrictions to divine Japanese dispositions and intentions while it kept one eye focused on the U.S.-Japanese conflict. *Razvedka* provided the essential basis for success in ensuing military operations and permitted the last-minute Soviet decision to commit initially heavy tank forces through the forbidding but undefended Grand Khingan Mountains into the vital central plains of Manchuria. Intelligence information concerning Japanese reinforcement of Manchuria and U.S. use of atomic weapons against Japan also prompted the last-minute Soviet decision to accelerate the timing of the operation.

During wartime, *razvedka* played both a positive and a negative role in the formulation of military strategy, depending on the type of collection means, the information obtained, and the period of war. High-level international agent *razvedka* had potential importance in the prewar period but was essentially ignored. During the first two years of war, the information foreign agents provided proved tentative and often unreliable. At the same time, official information from Allied governments assisted the Soviets, particularly in early 1943. Thereafter, Soviet skepticism regarding agent information, which in any case was seldom timely enough to use in planning, and conscious Allied decisions to stem the flow of intelligence seems to have minimized its effect on Soviet military strategy. Nevertheless, Soviet knowledge of Allied plans and operations, obtained either officially or unofficially, helped shape Soviet strategic planning.

Longer-range operational and strategic collection means, including air, agent, and reconnaissance-diversionary *razvedka,* increased in importance throughout the war, but particularly after the summer of 1943. In conjunction with partisan *razvedka,* it played a considerable role in validating Soviet strategic planning and deception in 1944 and, to a lesser extent, in 1945. Shorter-range operational *razvedka* —involving reconnaissance-diversionary, air, and radio means—functioned effectively by late 1942 and helped improve Soviet capabilities for developing tactical battlefield successes into ever deeper operational exploitations.

Tactical troop, artillery, and engineer *razvedka,* whose importance is often denigrated because of its mundane low-level nature, functioned successfully after mid-1942. By the time of the Stalingrad operation, the Soviets normally had a fair understanding of the nature of enemy tactical defenses, particularly in main attack sectors. This improved to such a degree that from the summer of 1943, the Soviets could precisely determine the nature of tactical defenses and adjust attack preparations accordingly. More important, the Soviets realized that this good coverage of German tactical defenses across the breadth of the front, to an increasing extent, permitted them to detect operational regroupings as well, since German panzer and panzer-grenadier forces were forced by circumstances to occupy positions in the immediate rear of the front, where tactical *razvedka* could detect their presence. In 1944, as the quantity of German forces further diminished, this tendency increased, making German mobile units subject to even more timely detection by Soviet intelligence. In this sense, Soviet tactical *razvedka* began to exert a greater impact than its tactical nature indicated. In essence, it became operational, and even strategic, in its importance.

Throughout the war, *razvedka* performed a supporting role in the formulation of strategy and in the planning and conduct of strategic operations. Depending on the operation, the role was either positive or negative. Seldom, if ever, was it decisive. Even when it contributed to strategic disaster for the Soviets, as it did early in the war, the Soviets were able to restore the situation. In the last analysis, in 1941 and 1942, even if the Soviets had acted correctly on the basis of intelligence or had possessed better intelligence overall, the proficiency of the German Army would have produced Soviet defeat. Only the scale of those defeats might have been diminished. And later in the war, when Soviet strategic successes multiplied, intelligence was not the decisive factor in these successes. Other factors—like force size, more competent leadership, and effective deception—would have produced victory despite the availability of good intelligence. Again, however, that victory would have occurred more slowly. The performance of intelligence organs, however, also reflected the improved size and competence of the Red Army.

Among the many unanswered questions regarding wartime Soviet intelligence is the role that high-level message intercept and decryption had on Soviet strategy. Obviously, available archival materials are not sufficient to judge whether or not the Soviets possessed that capability, and the materials may never be. It is entirely possible that they did possess means similar to Ultra. If so, the same strictures apply to this intelligence that applied to other strategic sources. The capability, if present before November 1942, did not make an appreciable difference in the outcome of operations, nor did it make a difference in the winter of 1943. If the Soviets possessed the capability in the summer of 1943 or later in the war, it, like other intelligence sources, provided only marginal advantage, given its nature and timeliness and the relative effectiveness of other collection means.

Another unanswered question relates to Soviet knowledge of the plans of her allies and the degree to which this knowledge affected Soviet strategy. It is clear that, to an increasing extent, from 1943 to the end of the war, the Soviets attempted to assist or, conversely, benefit from Allied operations. The two questions that emerge are To what extent did the Allies share their strategic plans and aims? and What was the Soviet reaction in terms of strategic planning? What is clear is that the Soviets fully appreciated the potential value of a "second" front from 1941 and that, once a second front or lesser equivalents developed, the Soviets took advantage of them.

Wartime *razvedka* experiences helped shape Soviet military strategy during the war; wartime *razvedka* experiences also sharpened Soviet appreciation for the subject in the postwar years, especially as it applies in a prewar period and the initial period of a war. Today the Soviets realize that a keen awareness of their potential enemies' political and military condition is a necessary prerequisite for planning and carrying out strategic operations in the initial period of war and during war as a whole.

Appendix A: Army Intelligence Collection and Analysis

The documented case of the Briansk Front's 61st Army illustrates how the *razvedka* process worked. The army commander determined intelligence objectives, specific targets, information required, time constraints, and often personally assigned missions to the intelligence-gathering unit. The army chief of staff analyzed missions from *front* and army commanders, established the sequence of their execution, determined concentration of efforts, resources to be committed to collection, and units and reserves that would conduct reconnaissances in force. The intelligence chief and his staff officers executed these missions. They drew up draft intelligence plans and orders; verified execution of tasks; collected, processed, and synthesized intelligence data; prepared reports and summaries for army and *front* headquarters; passed intelligence to neighboring units; and worked with translators to interrogate prisoners and process captured enemy documents. Prewar exercises had indicated that army commanders required intelligence reports two to three times a day and division commanders the same reports every three to four hours. The first two years of experience, however, showed this system was inadequate. Instead, the army commander received reports every two to three hours and division commanders every one to two hours, particularly during fluid operations.

The intelligence chief personally prepared the combat intelligence plan, which was then approved by the chief of staff. Planning for defensive operations covered 10- to 15-day periods; offensive plans encompassed the entire operation. Plans corresponded to the stages of the operation and were more detailed for the preparatory stage and for execution of the first day's intermediate mission. Thereafter, less detailed plans focused on the principal concentration areas and army offensive or defensive axes.

They also included intelligence coverage of main partisan activities in support of the offensive. The plan specified *razvedka* objectives, missions, areas of concentration of intelligence efforts, assignment of specific tasks and equipment, timetables for mission execution, and sequencing and timing of intelligence reporting. A map on a scale of 1:100,000 or 1:200,000 with graphic representation of intelligence measures was appended to the plan.

Combat intelligence orders required by the plan were drafted for rifle corps, separate divisions, and chiefs of arms and services (such as artillery and engineers). Requests for air *razvedka* assistance went to *front* headquarters, and instructions were drafted designating tasks for partisan detachments to perform. The intelligence section cooperated with the operations section to arrange for reconnaissance in force by combat units. Orders described opposing forces, intelligence missions, timetables for execution, and reporting procedures. Missions to arms and services were assigned orally. Requests for *front* air *razvedka* support specified areas and axes for the conduct of visual reconnaissance, zones, scale, timetable for photographic reconnaissance, and the quantity of and timetable for preparing photographic terrain mosaics (if it was feasible to prepare them).

The army relied for its own intelligence collection on reconnaissance units of subordinate headquarters (division reconnaissance companies and regimental reconnaissance platoons). By early 1943 combat subunits routinely assisted by conducting reconnaissance in force in support of the *razvedka* effort. Since the army and subordinate corps had no organic intelligence-gathering personnel or facilities, it relied on the *front* for specialized support from air, agent, and reconnaissance-diversionary organs. Links with partisan units provided the army with its deepest intelligence-gathering asset. Otherwise, the army collection effort generally ranged to a depth of up to 15 kilometers and relied primarily on observation; night and day raids; ambushes; radio and telephone eavesdropping; and, by late 1942, reconnaissance in force. After 1942 the army began employing long-range intelligence-reconnaissance detachments, often parachuted into the operational depths of the enemy rear.

The experiences of 61st Army were fairly typical for 1943, although certain armies developed particular talents for specific types of *razvedka*.

Appendix B: The Relationship Between Soviet Strategic Operations and Strategic Operations in Other Theaters During the Second World War

One of the most intriguing questions regarding Soviet military strategy in the Second World War is the degree to which that strategy related to military operations elsewhere in Europe and the world (see Table B-1). Though not a direct aspect of intelligence, Soviet knowledge of military conditions elsewhere, the plans of the Soviets' allies, and Germany's actions against the Allies certainly affected Soviet strategy.

Events in Europe—such as the German-Polish War, the German defeat of Western European powers in 1940 prior to Operation Barbarossa, and the outbreak of war between the U.S. and Japan after Barbarossa—had a significant impact on Soviet military strategy. The German-Polish War and subsequent German-Soviet dismemberment of Poland eliminated the buffer between Germany and the Soviet Union and prompted heightened Soviet concern for the security of her western borders. Soviet occupation of Latvia, Lithuania, Estonia, and Bessarabia and Soviet aggression against Finland were all manifestations of a more militant Soviet political and military stance conditioned, in part, by Soviet concerns over future German eastward expansion. The fall of the Low Countries and France in May and June 1940 and German failure in the ensuing Battle of Britain accentuated Soviet fears of war with Germany and prompted Soviet adoption of an extremely pacific political stance vis-à-vis Germany; simultaneously, in the military realm, the Soviets prepared for future war by

Table B-1   Correlation of Soviet and Allied Operations

Allied Operations	Soviet Operations
23 Oct. 1942: El Alamein	
8 Nov. 1942: Torch (North Africa)	19 Nov. 1942: Stalingrad
Feb.–Mar. 1943: Tunesia	Feb. 1943: Donbas-Khar'kov
10 July 1943: Sicily	12 July 1943: Orel'
July–Aug. 1943: Sicily	3 Aug. 1943: Belgorod-Khar'kov
9 Sept. 1943: Salerno	Sept.–Oct. 1943: To the Dnepr
Sept.–Oct. 1943: To Naples	Nov.–Dec. 1943: Kiev-across the Dnepr
22 Jan. 1944: Anzio	Jan.–Feb. 1944: Right Bank of Ukraine I
Mar.–May 1944: Casino	Mar.–Apr. 1944: Right Bank of Ukraine II
June 1944: Drive to Rome	
6 June 1944: Normandy	23 June 1944: Belorussia
	13 July 1944: L'vov-Sandomierz
25 July 1944: Breakout	
15 Aug. 1944: Anvil-Dragoon	20 Aug. 1944: Iassy-Kishinev
24 Aug. 1944: Fall of Paris	
16 Dec. 1944: Ardennes (to 25 Dec.)	
	12 Jan. 1945: Vistula-Oder
7 Mar. 1945: Remagen	15 Mar. 1945: Vienna
11 Apr. 1945: Elbe	16 Apr. 1945: Berlin

developing a strategic defensive plan that could protect the Soviet Union and military reform programs to create a military that could meet both defensive and offensive requirements of Soviet military doctrine.

Once the Russo-German War had begun, the outbreak of the U.S.-Japanese War in December 1941 eased Soviet concerns over her eastern borders and permitted wholesale shifting of reserves from the Far East, Trans-Baikal, and Siberia to help relieve the military crisis at Moscow and enable the Soviets to conduct their first major strategic counter-offensive. From December 1941 to November 1942, the absence of major operations elsewhere in Europe or in peripheral theaters forced the Soviets to go it alone in the development and implementation of military strategy.

Periodic and ever louder Soviet appeals for creation of a second front in the West reflected Soviet desires for overall assistance and, more subtly, Soviet wishes to coordinate their strategic operations with those in other theaters.

It is not yet possible to define precisely the subsequent relationship between Soviet strategic operations and those of her allies—that is, whether the Soviets consciously planned so as to take advantage of conditions elsewhere or, conversely, planned operations to assist Allied strategic efforts. In reality, Soviet military strategy probably did both. What is certain is that from a purely chronological standpoint, coincidentally or otherwise, there existed a relationship between Soviet strategic operations and strategic developments elsewhere. The relationship certainly went well beyond happenstance, and the Soviets themselves speak of the interdependence of operations in separate theaters. In the broadest sense, whatever relationship existed reflected Soviet knowledge of—thus intelligence about—the strategic situation in other theaters.

A clearer and more direct relationship between strategic operations on the Eastern Front and those in other theaters began to emerge in the fall of 1942. In late October British forces in North Africa struck Rommel's Afrika Korps at El Alamein and began an inexorable drive westward toward Tunisia. In early November the United States conducted Operation Torch, which threatened the German position in North Africa and prompted transfer of German forces from Europe to Tunisia. On the Eastern Front, Soviet forces commenced their winter campaign on 19 November by attacking and encircling German and Rumanian forces at Stalingrad. During the ensuing three months, while Allied forces pressed German forces in Tunisia, the Soviets conducted a series of offensives across southern Russia into the Donbas with apparent abandon. While German forces in Africa were weak in comparison to German forces on the Eastern Front, it is likely the Soviets counted, in part, on the deteriorating German situation in North Africa to lessen the likelihood of additional German forces being sent east to deal with the deteriorating situation in southern Russia. In fact, German reinforcements did move east (II SS Panzer Corps and several infantry divisions), and these forces helped the Germans stabilize the front by March 1943. Conversely, the African operation diverted from Russia a sizeable number of German aircraft, which could have been employed during and after the Stalingrad operation.

In July 1943, shortly after the Germans began their Kursk offensive,

Allied forces landed in Sicily. The landing occurred on 10 July, two days before the German Kursk assault was brought to a halt at Prokhorovka and two days before the Soviets delivered their first Kursk counterstroke against the Orel' salient. While Allied forces completed their defeat of German and Italian forces on Sicily in July and August, the Soviets delivered their main Kursk counterstroke in the Belgorod-Khar'kov operation (3 August). Meanwhile, the Allied Sicilian venture forced the Germans to withdraw the headquarters and one division of II SS Panzer Corps from Russia (the Germans had intended to withdraw all three divisions of the corps, but the crisis around Khar'kov prevented it).

The Allied invasion of the Italian peninsula in September 1943 (Salerno) coincided with the expansion of the Soviet post-Kursk offensive to encompass the entire front from Smolensk to the Black Sea, which culminated in November, when the Soviets breached the Dnepr River line. Later, from January to May 1944, the Allied landing at Anzio and battles around Casino took place while Soviet forces were conducting operations to clear the Ukraine of German forces. Expanded operations in Italy and increased Allied air activity over Germany further diluted German air strength in the East and granted the Soviets air superiority.

From late 1942 through early 1944, there is no concrete data upon which to base precise judgments regarding how Soviet military strategy reacted to strategic conditions in other theaters. While the timing of offensive activity in the East and West matched nicely (as did lulls in the two regions), only conjecture can provide tentative answers. Beginning in the summer of 1944, however, clearer ties between strategic operations in the East and in the West do emerge. From this time on, the motivation underlying these linkages becomes the central question.

On 6 June 1944, the Allies began the Normandy operation, which certainly increased Germany's concern over her western front. In July and August, Allied forces broke out of the Normandy beachhead in Operation Cobra and collapsed Axis defenses in southern France with Operation Anvil-Dragoon. By late August the German western front had collapsed, and Allied forces liberated Paris. During this period the Soviets commenced their summer-fall campaign by striking on 23 June at German Army Group Center in Belorussia. Although the Soviets claim the timing of this operation was, in part, intended to assist the Allied breakout from Normandy, the Soviet strategic operation also benefited in the broadest sense from the opening of the real second front. Subsequent Soviet offensives, in July into southern Poland and in August into Rumania and

Bulgaria, likewise capitalized on the collapse of German defenses in the West. Soviet operations into the Balkans were also prompted by strategic political considerations, such as the growing likelihood of British and American operations in Greece or Yugoslavia. As the front stabilized in the West during October and November 1944, it did likewise on main attack directions in the East.

In mid-December 1944 German forces launched the Ardennes counteroffensive, which produced temporary crisis among the Soviet allies. In late December the German Ardennes thrust was halted, and by early January 1945 the Allies had eliminated the "bulge" and were preparing for operations into Germany proper. Soon after, from 12 to 15 January, the Soviets commenced two massive strategic thrusts into Poland and East Prussia, which collapsed German defenses and, by the end of January, propelled Soviet forces to the Oder River and Konigsberg. The Soviets claim these operations were timed to assist the Allies in the Ardennes, but the Soviets themselves clearly profited from the concentration of German forces and materiel required to conduct the Ardennes counteroffensive. Allied operations from mid-January to early March 1945 concentrated on penetrating the "Westwall" defenses and advancing to the Rhine, a process that turned out to be slow and painstaking. Soviet activity in the east likewise focused on meticulous operations to clear Pomerania and Silesia and maintain Soviet positions in Hungary. On 7 March 1945 Allied forces seized a bridge over the Rhine at Remagen. Just over one week later, the Soviets thrust from the Budapest area toward Vienna. Soon, other Allied forces seized other Rhine River crossings, and, in thirty days of rapid advance, Allied armies penetrated into central Germany, encircled German forces in the Ruhr, and reached the Elbe (on 11 April). Four days after the vanguard of U.S. forces reached the Elbe, the Soviets began the Berlin operation.

Four months later, in August 1945, Soviet forces, at the request of their Western allies, began operations in Manchuria. Although the Soviets had planned this operation for months, they launched the operation earlier than planned, in part because of U.S. use of atomic weapons against Japan.

For whatever motives, from June 1944 to August 1945, Soviet forces and those of her allies operated in interdependent fashion. The degree to which this was planned has still to be proven. Yet, in June major Soviet offensive activity in Belorussia followed the Allied Normandy landings by seventeen days. The second major Soviet offensive against German forces in Poland, which began on 12 July, preceded the Allied breakout from Normandy (Operation Cobra of 25 July) by thirteen days. The landing of Allied forces in southern France on 15 August and the threatened (but failed) encirclement of German forces at Falaise preceded the Soviet offensive into Rumania by five days. In January 1945, the two major Soviet offenses occurred about four weeks after German commencement of their Ardennes counteroffensive and two weeks after the German counteroffensive had been terminated. Subsequently, the Soviet Vienna offensive began eight days after Allied forces first breached the Rhine. Finally, the Berlin offensive commenced just short of two weeks after Allied forces had encircled German forces in the Ruhr and five days after lead U.S. elements first reached the Elbe River at Magdeburg.

From the dates of the major Soviet strategic offensives in 1944 and 1945, it is clear that they were timed to correspond with major periods of combat in the West or the Far East, for they occurred shortly (about two weeks) after the initiation of major U.S.-British or German activity in the West. Though these strategic operations, in some instances, clearly assisted U.S. and British efforts, the Soviets profited as well from the strategic situation in the West. Thus, all three major phases of the Soviet summer offensive of 1944 capitalized on U.S. or British operations in the West and clearly assisted the Western allies. The Soviet winter offensive, while easing the Allied situation in the Ardennes, capitalized even more on the German counteroffensive and Allied counterstrokes. Subsequently, the Soviet Vienna and Berlin operations were facilitated, and probably hastened, by U.S.-British successes in central Germany during March and early April 1945. Finally, in August 1945 Soviet strategic operations in Manchuria were assisted by U.S. use of atomic weapons against Japan, which figured heavily in Japan's decision to surrender on 15 August.

In many cases, Allied sharing of strategic plans and intentions facilitated and affected Soviet strategic planning. In other cases (Ardennes and Berlin), the developing situation and concern over Allied intentions shaped Soviet strategic aims and conditioned Soviet planning. It is clear that whatever relationship existed between Soviet operations and operations elsewhere, the relationship was restricted to the strategic level.

Notes: Chapter 1

1. N. V. Ogarkov, "Strategiia voennaia" [Military strategy], *Sovetskaia voennaia entsiklopediia* [Soviet military encyclopedia], 8 vols. (Moscow: Voenizdat, 1976–1980), Vol. 7, 555–556. Hereafter cited as *SVE* with appropriate volume.

2. *Ibid.*, 556.

3. *Ibid.*

4. R. G. Simonian, "Razvedka" [Intelligence and reconnaissance], *SVE*, 7:32.

5. V. S. Prokhorov, I. V. Shcherbakov, "Obespechenie boevykh deistvii" [Protecting combat actions], *SVE*, 5:651.

6. Simonian, "Razvedka," 32.

7. R. G. Simonian, "Strategicheskaia razvedka" [Strategic *razvedka*], *SVE*, 7:552.

8. R. G. Simonian, "Operativnaia razvedka" [Operational *razvedka*], *SVE*, 6:52.

9. R. G. Simonian, "Takticheskaia razvedka" [Tactical *razvedka*], *SVE*, 7:640.

10. Simonian, "Razvedka," 32.

11. *Ibid.*

Notes: Chapter 2

1. *Polevoi ustav krasnoi armii (PU-1936)*, (*vremennyi*) [Field service regulations of the Red Army (PU-1936) (tentative)] (Moscow: Voenizdat, 1936), 9. Translated by Translation Section, The Army War College, Washington, D.C., 1987. For an explanation of Soviet prewar military theory, see David M. Glantz, *Soviet military operational art: In pursuit of deep operations* (London: Frank Cass, 1989).

2. Among other articles, see A. I. Starunin, "Operatovnaia vnezapnost' " [Operational surprise], *Voennaia mysl'* [Military thought], No. 3 (March 1941), 27–35 and A. Kononenko, "Boi v flandrii (Mai 1940 gg)" [The battle in Flanders (May 1940)], *Voenno-istoricheskii zhurnal* [Military-historical journal], No. 3 (March 1941), 3–20. (Hereafter, the two sources mentioned in this note will be referred to as *VM* and *VIZh*, respectively.) Starunin's superb analysis of German use of surprise in Poland and France ended with the enjoinder "One required high vigilance and constant combat readiness so that the enemy can not take forces by surprise." Three months later, Starunin's warning went unheeded, and his lessons were not learned.

3. V. D. Danilov, "Sovetskoe glavnoe komandovanie v predverii otechest-vennoi voiny" [The Soviet main command on the threshold of the patriotic war], *Novaia i noveishaia istoriia* [New and newest history], No. 6 (November–December 1988), 4.

4. P. I. D'iachenko, "Razvedka v okruzhenii" [Reconnaissance in an encirclement], *VM*, No. 9 (September 1940); A. I. Shtromberg, "Operativnoe ispol'zovanie tankov v oborone" [Operational use of tanks on the defense], *VM*, No. 11–12 (November–December 1940); P. I. Vedenichev, "Protivovozdushnaia oborona v sovremennoi voine" [Antiaircraft defense in contemporary war], *VM*, No. 11–12 (November–December 1940).

5. V. N. Lobov, "Strategiia pobedy" [Strategy of victory], *VIZh*, No. 5 (May 1988), 6.

6. N. Pavlenko, "Na pervom etape voiny" [During the first phase of war], *Kommunist* [Communist], No. 9 (June 1988), 90.

7. Iu. G. Perechnev, "O nekotorykh problemakh podgotovki strany i Vooruzhennykh Sil k otrazheniiu fashistskoi agressii" [Concerning some problems in the preparation of the nation and armed forces to repel fascist aggression], *VIZh*, No. 4 (April 1988), 46.

8. S. Alferov, "Strategicheskoe razvertyvanie sovetskykh voisk na Zapadnom TVD v 1941 godu" [Strategic deployment of Soviet forces in the Western TVD in 1941], *VIZh*, No. 6 (June 1981), 26–33; V. A. Anfilov, *Proval blitskriga* [The failure of blitzkrieg] (Moscow: "Nauka," 1974).

9. See *Lage der Roten Armee im europaischen Russland abgeschlossen am 20.*

VI. 41, Abteilung Fremde Heere Ost, H3/1346, NAM T-78, 677, which shows all assessed Soviet unit locations in the border military districts. Records of German army groups and armies participating in Operation Barbarossa confirm this intelligence picture. Later intelligence documents of the same commands confirm the actual Soviet order of battle as described in a multitude of Soviet sources.

10. For contemporary Soviet views on deception [*maskirovka*], see David M. Glantz, *Soviet military deception in the Second World War* (London: Frank Cass, 1989).

11. A. M. Vasilevsky, *A lifelong cause* (Moscow: Progress Publishers, 1978), 82. A translation of *Delo vsei zhizni* (Moscow: Izdatel'stvo politicheskoi literatury, 1973).

12. Perechnev, 49.

13. V. I. Bel'iaev, "Usilenie okhrany zapadnoi granitsy SSSR nakanune Velikoi Otechestvennoi voiny" [Strengthening security of the USSR's western frontier on the eve of the Great Patriotic War], *VIZh*, No. 5 (May 1988).

14. A. G. Khor'kov, "Nakanune groznykh sobytii" [On the eve of menacing events], *VIZh*, No. 5 (May 1988), 47.

15. Danilov, 17–19.

16. Khor'kov, 49.

17. Danilov, 15.

18. Vasilevsky, 84.

19. G. K. Zhukov, *Reminiscences and reflections,* 2 vols. (Moscow: Progress Publishers, 1985), 1:273. Translation of *Vospominaniia i razmyshleniia* (Moscow: Izdatel'stvo Agentstva Pechati Novosti, 1974). Hereafter cited as *Reminiscences,* with appropriate volume.

20. Vasilevsky, 84–85.

21. P. T. Kunitsky, "Vosstanovlenie prorvannogo strategicheskogo fronta oborony v 1941 godu" [The restoration of the penetrated strategic defensive front in 1941], *VIZh*, No. 7 (July 1988), 53–54; G. P. Pastukhovskii, "Razvertyvanie operativnogo tyla v nachal'nyi period voiny" [Deployment of the operational rear in the initial period of war], *VIZh*, No. 6 (June 1988).

22. Vasilevsky, 88.

23. Kunitsky, 58.

24. Vasilevsky, 92.

25. *Ibid.,* 92–93.

26. Zhukov, 1:336.

27. Vasilevsky, 100–101.

28. S. M. Shtemenko, *The Soviet General Staff at war, 1941–1945,* Book 1 (Moscow: Progress Publishers, 1985), 41. A translation of *Sovetskii general'nyi shtab v gody voiny* (Moscow: Voenizdat, 1981); Zhukov, 1:371–380.

29. Vasilevsky, 113.

30. *Ibid.*, 119.
31. *Ibid.*, 120.
32. Pavlenko, 91.
33. Zhukov, 1:283.
34. *Ibid.*, 385.
35. *Ibid.*, 297.
36. *Ibid.*, 312.
37. Anfilov, 244.
38. I. Kh. Bagramian, *Tak nachinalas' voina* [How war began] (Kiev: Izdatel'stvo khudozhestvennoi literatury "Dnipro," 1975), 89.
39. Zhukov, 1:387.
40. *Ibid.*
41. Vasilevsky, 108.
42. A. I. Eremenko, *V nachale voiny* [In the beginning of war] (Moscow: "Nauka," 1965), 300–306.
43. *Ibid.*, 308–309.
44. K. S. Moskalenko, *Na iugo-zapadnom napravlenii 1941–1943* [On the Southwestern direction 1941–1943], 2 vols. (Moscow: "Nauka," 1973), 1:82.
45. *Ibid.*, 82–83.
46. Anfilov, 551.
47. L. M. Sandalov, *Na moskovskom napravlenii* [On the Moscow direction] (Moscow: "Nauka," 1970), 201.
48. *Ibid.*
49. Zhukov, 2:33. Zhukov cites archival materials, which provided the following estimate of German strength:

To continue the thrust towards Moscow the German Command brought up more forces; by November 15 it had in the Western Front zone 51 divisions, including 31 infantry, 13 tank and 7 motorized divisions, which were fully manned, and well equipped with tanks, artillery and combat material.

On the Volokolamsk-Klin and Istra sectors the enemy had, against Rokossovsky's army, concentrated the 3rd and 4th Panzer groups, consisting of seven tank, three motorized, and four infantry divisions, supported by about 2,000 artillery pieces and a powerful air group.

The enemy striking force against the 50th Army on the Tula-Kashira sector comprised the 24th and 47th Motorized corps, 53rd and 43rd Army corps totalling twelve divisions, including four tank and three motorized divisions, and also having powerful air support.

The German 4th Field Army comprising six army corps had been deployed on the Zvenigorod, Kubinka, Naro-Fominsk, Podolsk and Serpukhov sectors. Through frontal attacks, this Army was to pin down the troops of the Western Front, sap them of their strength, and then strike a blow in the central sector towards Moscow.

The archival citation appears in the 1971 English translation of Zhukov's memoirs but is specifically omitted in the 1985 version.

50. Zhukov, 1:323.

51. David M. Glantz, *The Soviet airborne experience,* Research Survey No. 4 (Ft. Leavenworth, Kansas: Combat Studies Institute, 1984), 132.

52. Vasilevsky, 121.

53. *Ibid.,* 122–123.

54. Pavlenko, 92.

55. P. A. Kurochkin, *Obshchevoiskovaia armiia v nastuplenii* [The combined-arms army on the offensive] (Moscow: Voenizdat, 1966), 68.

56. Eremenko, 404.

57. Moskalenko, 1:107.

58. I. Kh. Bagramian, *Tak shli my k pobede* [Thus we marched to victory] (Moscow: Voenizdat, 1977), 6. Hereafter cited as *Tak shli.*

59. "Kharakter oborony nemtsev na demianskom platsdarme" [The nature of German defenses on the Demiansk bridgehead], *Sbornik materialov po izucheniiu opyta voiny No. 9 noiabr'–dekabr' 1943 g* [Collection of materials for the study of war experience No. 9 November–December 1943] (Moscow: Voenizdat, 1944), 150–165. Hereafter cited as *Sbornik materialov No. 9,* with appropriate pages.

60. "Nekotorye vyvody po desantnym operatsiiam za 1941 god" [Some conclusions regarding amphibious (*desant*) operations in 1941], *Sbornik materialov po izucheniiu opyta voiny No. 1 iiul'–avgust 1942 g* [Collections of materials for the study of war experience No. 1 July–August 1942] (Moscow: Voenizdat, 1942), 13. Hereafter cited as *Sbornik materialov No. 1,* with appropriate pages.

61. Earl F. Ziemke, "Operation Kreml: Deception, strategy, and the fortunes of war," *Parameters,* Vol. 9, No. 1 (March 1979), 72–83.

62. Zhukov, 2:71.

63. Pavlenko, 92.

64. Vasilevsky, 156.

65. *Ibid.,* 162.

66. Bagramian, *Tak shli,* 67.

67. Pavlenko, 92.

68. Bagramian, *Tak shli,* 51.

69. *Ibid.,* 52.

70. *Ibid.,* 69.

71. *Ibid.,* 67.

72. *Ibid.,* 90.

73. *Ibid.,* 103–105.

74. *Ibid.,* 107.

75. Zhukov, 2:77.

76. A. M. Vasilevsky, "Nezabyvaemye dni" [Unforgettable days], *VIZh,* No. 9 (August 1965), 9.

77. Ziemke, 82–83.

78. Moskalenko, 1:214.

79. *Ibid.*, 1:215.

80. *Ibid.*

81. *Ibid.*, 1:244–245.

82. *Ibid.*

83. Shtemenko, 76–77.

84. *Ibid.*, 77.

85. Vasilevsky, *A lifelong cause,* 165.

86. Shtemenko, 81–82.

87. *Ibid.*, 85.

88. *Ibid.*, 88.

89. *Ibid.*, 98.

90. Pavlenko, 92.

91. V. P. Krikunov, "Iz opyta raboty komanduiushchikh i shtabov armii na mestnosti" [From the experience of the work of commanders and staff on the terrain), *VIZh,* No. 7 (July 1987), 22.

92. These critiques appear in the Soviet General Staff war experience studies volumes 1–3, published by the Ministry of Defense under the collective title *Sbornik materialov po izucheniu opyta voiny* [Collection of materials for the study of war experience].

93. *Red army field service regulations 1942* (Moscow: Voenizdat, 1942). Translation by chief of the General Staff, Canada, July 1944, 43.

94. *Ibid.*, 46.

95. *Ibid.*

Notes: Chapter 3

1. K. K. Rokossovsky, ed., *Velikaia pobeda na Volge* [Great victory on the Volga] (Moscow: Voenizdat, 1965), 219.

2. Zhukov, *Reminiscences*, 2:95.

3. *Ibid.*, 2:95–96.

4. Vasilevsky, *A lifelong cause*, 188.

5. Rokossovsky, *Velikaia pobeda*, 219.

6. Zhukov, *Reminiscences*, 2:121.

7. A. M. Samsonov, ed., *Stalingradskaia epopeia* [Stalingrad epic] (Moscow: "Nauka," 1968), 50.

8. A. M. Vasilevsky, "Nezabyvaemye dni" [Unforgettable days], *VIZh*, No. 10 (October 1965), 8.

9. For critiques of Red Army performance in the Stalingrad, Middle Don, and Kotel'nikovo operations, see *Sbornik materialov*, Volumes 4–8. See also forthcoming book, David M. Glantz, *From the Don to the Dnepr; Soviet offensive operations, December 1942–August 1943* (London: Frank Cass, 1990).

10. Vasilevsky, *A lifelong cause*, 233–234.

11. A. G. Ershov, *Osvobozhdenie Donbassa* [The liberation of the Donbas] (Moscow: Voenizdat, 1973), 32.

12. *Ibid.*, 25.

13. Shtemenko, 105.

14. *Ibid.*, 115.

15. Zhukov, *Reminiscences*, 2:119–120.

16. Vasilevsky, *A lifelong cause*, 193.

17. N. N. Voronov, *Na sluzhbe voennoi* [In military service] (Moscow: Voenizdat, 1963), 270.

18. I. M. Chistiakov, *Sluzhim otchizne* [In service to the fatherland] (Moscow: Voenizdat, 1975), 96.

19. P. I. Batov, *V pokhodakh i boiakh* [On marches and in battles] (Moscow: Izdatel'stvo DOSAAF SSSR, 1984), 181.

20. See *Sbornik materialov*, volumes 6–8.

21. V. Morozov, "Pochemu ne zavershilos' nastuplenie v Donbasse vesnoi 1943 goda"? [Why was the offensive in the Donbas not completed in the spring of 1943?], *VIZh*, No. 3 (March 1963), 16. Reportedly, the Dora spy ring operating in Switzerland passed to GRU "Centre" the following reports based on Swiss intelligence materials:

11 February

"German troops in the Donetz area were in full retreat."

16 February

"All German counter-attacks have failed. . . . The Germans are being

234   David M. Glantz

overtaken by a new disaster. Losses to be expected on the German side will greatly exceed their losses at Stalingrad.''

17 February

"The object of German resistance . . . is now confined to covering the German withdrawal from the Donetz bend.''

See Anthony Read and David Fisher, *Operation Lucy* (London: Sphere, 1982), 152. The authors claim virtually no Ultra material was passed through the Lucy ring during this period.

22. *Ibid.*, 16–17.
23. *Ibid.*, 18.
24. *Ibid.*, 23.
25. N. M. Skomorokhov, ed., *17-ia vozdushnaia armiia v boiakh ot Stalingrada do Veny* [17th Air Army in battles from Stalingrad to Vienna] (Moscow: Voenizdat, 1977), 39.
26. Morozov, 17.
27. *Ibid.* Another Dora ring report dated 21 February read "The consequence of the fall of Khar'kov and the collapse of the improvised German Donetz front are assessed as disasters at German high command. More than forty German divisions are in danger of being cut off." See Read and Fisher, 153.
28. For details in German planning, see E. Ziemke, *Stalingrad to Berlin* (Washington, D.C.: Center for Military History, 1968), 124–125.
29. G. Zhukov, "Na Kurskoi duge" [In the Kursk Bulge], *VIZh*, No. 8 (August 1967), 73. Hereafter cited as Zhukov, "Na Kurskoi duge."
30. Shtemenko, 218–219.
31. Zhukov, "Na Kurskoi duge," 76.
32. *Ibid.*, 81.
33. Glantz, *Soviet military deception*, 146–179.
34. "Podgotovka k Kurskoi bitve" [Preparations for the battle of Kursk], *VIZh*, No. 6 (June 1983), 71.
35. Vasilevsky, *A lifelong cause*, 277–278.
36. *Ibid.*, 278.
37. Zhukov, *Reminiscences*, 2:212–215.
38. Vasilevsky, *A lifelong cause*, 278.
39. A. A. Grechko, ed., *Istoriia vtoroi mirovoi voiny 1939–1945 T-7* [A history of World War II], Vol. 7 (Moscow: Voenizdat, 1976), 253. Hereafter cited as *IVMV* with appropriate volume and date.
40. *Ibid.*
41. *Ibid.*, 373 and N. A. Svetlishin, "Nevel'skaia operatsiia," *SVE*, 5:1978, 560–561.
42. Vasilevsky, *A lifelong cause*, 303–304.
43. Zhukov, *Reminiscences*, 2:150–152.
44. Shtemenko, 216.

45. "Podgotovka k Kurskoi bitve," 67.

46. Timothy P. Mulligan, "Spies, ciphers and 'Zitadelle': Intelligence and the Battle of Kursk, 1943," *Journal of Contemporary History*, Vol. 22 (1987), 237.

47. Zhukov, *Reminiscences*, 2:166.

48. F. H. Hinsley, *British intelligence in the Second World War*, Vol. 2, (New York: Cambridge University Press, 1981), 624.

49. "Podgotovka k Kurskoi bitve," 67.

50. Vasilevsky, *A Lifelong Cause*, 270–271.

51. *Ibid.*, 271.

52. Zhukov, *Reminiscences*, 2:170–172.

53. Vasilevsky, *A lifelong cause*, 271.

54. K. Moskalenko, "The Voronezh Front in the battle of Kursk," *The battle of Kursk* (Moscow: Progress Publishers, 1974), 99.

55. Zhukov, "Na Kurskoi duge," 76.

56. V. Matsulenko, *Operativnaia maskirovka voisk* [Operational *maskirovka* of forces] (Moscow: Voenizdat, 1975), 50–51.

57. Vasilevsky, *A lifelong cause*, 271–272.

58. Mulligan, 239.

59. Shtemenko, 233.

60. Mulligan, 239.

61. *Ibid.*

62. Zhukov, *Reminiscences*, 2:176.

63. *Ibid.*, 2:180.

64. Vasilevsky, *A lifelong cause*, 273.

65. German movements and dispositions from 29 June through 1 July taken from AOK 9, Ia, *Anlage zum KTB*, Lage vom 17.6–4.7.43 fruh, NAM T-312/295/304; PzAOK 4, Ia, *Lagenkarte 4 Pz. Armee*, Stand 29.6.43–1.7.43 2200, NAM T-313/369; PzAOK 1, Ia, *Lagenkarten*, Lage 29.6.43–1.7.43, NAM T-313/60.

66. Moskalenko, 2:51–52.

67. A. Konenenko, "Voprosy voennovo iskusstva v bitve pod Kurskom" [Questions of military art in the battle of Kursk], *VIZh*, No. 4 (April 1964), 116.

68. M. F. Katukov, *Na ostrie glavnogo udara* [At the point of the main effort] (Moscow: Voenizdat, 1976), 211.

69. Vasilevsky, *A lifelong cause*, 273.

70. *Razvedka v boevykh primerakh* (*Velikaia Otechestvennaia voina 1941–1945 gg i poslevoennyi period*) [*Razvedka* in combat examples (The Great Patriotic War 1941–1945 and the postwar period)] (Moscow: Voenizdat, 1972), 198–199. Hereafter cited as *Razvedka*.

71. *Ibid.*, 190.

72. *Ibid.*

73. *Ibid.*, 191.

74. M. M. Kir'ian, ed., *Fronty nastupali: po opytu Velikoi Otechestvennoi voiny*

[The *fronts* have attacked: Based on the experience of the Great Patriotic War] (Moscow: "Nauka," 1987), 77–78.

75. "Organisation Des Sovjet Nachrichtendienstes in Kriege" [The organization of Soviet intelligence services in the war], *Abteilung Fremde Heere Ost*, October 1943, NAM T-78/677. Hereafter cited as "Die Organisation." In summer 1944, the *front razvedka* department (RO) became a *razvedka* directorate (RU). This expanded organization, which itself now contained subordinate departments, reflected the growing complexity of intelligence gathering, analyzing, and assessment. See Kir'ian, *Fronty*, 178–179.

76. S. Ostriakov, *Voennye chekisty* [Military *chekists*] (Moscow: Voenizdat, 1979), 179.

Notes: Chapter 4

1. Vasilevsky, *A lifelong cause,* 306–307.
2. Shtemenko, 267.
3. *Ibid.*
4. Zhukov, *Reminiscences,* 2:231.
5. Shtemenko, 268.
6. *Ibid.*
7. A. Rakitsky, "Udar pod Leningradom" [Blow at Leningrad], *VIZh*, No. 1 (January 1974), 26.
8. A. S. Zhadov, *Chetyre goda voiny* [Four years of war] (Moscow: Voenizdat, 1978), 157. Zhadov was 5th Guards Army commander.
9. I. S. Konev, *Zapiski komanduiushchego frontom 1943–1945* [Notes of a *front* commander 1943–1945] (Moscow: "Nauka," 1972), 98. Hereafter cited as *Zapiski.*
10. Details on the operation in I. M. Belkin, *13 armiia v Lutsko-Rovenskoi operatsii 1944g* [13th Army in the Lutsk-Rovno operation 1944] (Moscow: Voenizdat, 1960).
11. A. N. Grylev, *Dnepr-Karpaty-Krym: Osvobozhdenie pravoberezhoi Ukrainy i Kryma v 1944 gody* [Dnepr-Carpathians-Crimea: The liberation of the right bank of the Ukraine and Crimea in 1944] (Moscow: "Nauka," 1970), 104–105.
12. *Ibid;* V. M. Ivanov, "Nikopol'-krivorozhskaia operatsiia 1944" [The Nikopol'–Krivoi Rog operation 1944], *SVE*, 5:1978, 599–601.
13. Vasilevsky, *A lifelong cause,* 325.
14. Grylev, 130.
15. A description of the circumstances of Vatutin's death is in Zhukov, *Reminiscences,* 2:251–253.
16. Grylev, 135; Erich von Manstein, *Lost victories* (Chicago: Henry Regnery, 1958), 527, states, "Although the weather prevented our air reconnaissance from telling what movement or troop concentrations were taking place on the other side, the Army Group was able to assess the enemy's intentions . . . by the end of February." Manstein does not elaborate on how the army group made the assessment.
17. Grylev, 137.
18. *Ibid.*, 160; for some details, see V. M. Ivanov, "Umansko botoshanskaia operatsiia 1944" [The Uman-Botoshany operation 1944], *SVE*, 8:1980, 195–196.
19. Grylev, 179; for some details, see F. D. Vorob'ev, "Bereznegovato-snigirevskaia operatsiia 1944" [The Bereznegovatoe-Snigirevka operation 1944], *SVE*, 1:1976, 450–451.

20. V. M. Ivanov, "Rogachevsko-zhlobinskaia operatsiia 1944" [The Rogachev-Zhlobin operation 1944], *SVE*, 7:1979, 135–136; Grylev, 205–217.

21. Grylev, 200–205.

22. K. V. Krainiukov, *Oruzhie osobogo roda* [Weapons of a special sort] (Moscow: Voenizdat, 1977), 91.

23. Moskalenko, 2:206.

24. *Ibid.*, 207.

25. *Ibid.*, 210.

26. *Ibid.*, 215.

27. M. I. Povaly, *Vosemnadtsataia v srazheniiakh za rodinu: Boevoi put' 18-i armii* [The Eighteenth in battles for the homeland: The combat path of Eighteenth Army] (Moscow: Voenizdat, 1982), 344.

28. Moskalenko, 2:215.

29. *Ibid.*, 226; Povaly, 351, cited the same report and attributed the information to "prisoner reports and as a result of the study of documents."

30. Moskalenko, 2:228; Povaly, 346, notes Soviet radio intercepts, stating

Radio transmission of fascist commanders, intercepted by our army radio stations, bear witness to the strength of our fire:

"Bring the assault guns forward for direct fire and bring them to full readiness!"

"A hurricane of fire is falling on me. I cannot raise my head. Communications are completely intercepted. I cannot leave the blindage."

"Prepare yourselves! The Russians will attack. What region are they firing on? Why do you not answer? I absolutely cannot hear you. What are you doing? How are the soldiers?"

"The radio is completely overwhelmed. Now we are bringing order to things. Among the soldiers there is a massive phenomenon—bleeding from the ears and mouth and strong contusions. They are attacking me. . . ."

31. Moskalenko, 2:233.

32. *Ibid.*, 235.

33. *Ibid.*, 238.

34. *Ibid.*, 241.

35. *Ibid.*, 242.

36. Grylev, 135.

37. Moskalenko, 2:275.

38. Zhukov, *Reminiscences,* 2:255.

39. Grylev, 150.

40. *Ibid.*

41. Moskalenko, 2:321.

42. Zhukov, *Reminiscences,* 2:255.

43. *Ibid.*, 256.

44. Grylev, 159.

45. Shtemenko, 299.

46. The Western Front—operating on the Vitebsk, Orsha, and Mogilev directions—was subdivided into the 2d and 3d Belorussian Fronts. The Belorussian Front, operating on the Rogachev and Mozyr directions, became the 1st Belorussian Front and, in so doing, absorbed the three Soviet armies of the former 2d Belorussian Front in the Kovel' area. This reorganization created three *fronts*, which would cooperate with a fourth (1st Baltic) in the critical Belorussian operation. Subsequently, elements of two *fronts* (1st Belorussian left wing and 2d Ukrainian) would conduct the operations through central and southern Poland, and two *fronts* (2d and 3d Ukrainian) would advance into Rumania.

47. The strategic plan required the movement of 5th Guards Tank Army from the southern Ukraine to Belorussia, movement of 2d Guards and 51st Armies from the Crimea to Belorussia, transfer of 28th Army from the southern Ukraine to Belorussia, shifting of 8th Guards Army and 2d Tank Army from Moldavia to the northern Ukraine, and the lateral transfer of 6th Guards Army from the 2d to the 1st Baltic Front.

48. Vasilevsky, *A lifelong cause*, 358.

49. *Istoriia Velikoi Otechestvennoi voiny Sovetskogo Soiuza 1941–1945* [A history of the Great Patriotic War of the Soviet Union 1941–1945] (Moscow: Voenizdat, 1962), 4:206–207; Konev, *Zapiski*, 231–232. *Zapiski* contains full planning details.

50. S. Petrov, "Dostizhenie vnezapnost' v L'vovsko-sandomirskoi operatsii" [The achievement of surprise in the L'vov-Sandomierz operation], *VIZh*, No. 7 (July 1974), 33–36.

51. B. Petrov, "O sozdanii udarnoi gruppirovki voisk v Liublinsko-brestskoi nastupatel'noi operatsii" [Concerning the creation of the shock group of forces in the Lublin-Brest offensive operation], *VIZh*, No. 3 (March 1978), 83.

52. Zhukov, *Reminiscences*, 2:309–310.

53. Shtemenko, 378–379.

54. *Ibid.*, 381.

55. *Ibid.*, 368.

56. K. L. Orlov, *et al.*, ed., *Bor'ba za sovetskuiu pribaltiku v Velikoi Otechestvennoi voine, T.2,: K. Baltiskomu moriu* [Struggle for the Soviet Baltic in the Great Patriotic War, Vol. 2: To the Baltic Sea] (Riga: Izdatel'stvo "Liesma," 1967), 175.

57. P. Ia. Malinovsky, *Budapesht-Vena-Praga* [Budapest-Vienna-Prague] (Moscow: "Nauka," 1965), 42. Hereafter cited as Malinovsky, *Budapesht*.

58. M. M. Malakhov, "Debretsenskaia operatsiia 1944" [Debrecan operation 1944], *SVE*, 3:1977, 119.

59. Malinovsky, *Budapesht*, 79. For details on this and subsequent operations, see D. Glantz, ed., "Operations in Hungary, 26 October–31 December 1944,"

A Transcript of Proceedings 1986 Art of War Symposium, From the Vistula to the Oder: Soviet Offensive Operations—October 1944–March 1945 (Carlisle Barracks, PA: Center for Land Warfare, 1986), 99–279.

60. Shtemenko, 328–329.

61. G. K. Zhukov, "Razgrom fashistskikh voisk v belorussii" [The destruction of Fascist forces in Belorussia], *Osvobozhdenie belorussii 1944* [The liberation of Belorussia 1944] (Moscow: "Nauka," 1974), 24. Hereafter cited as *Osvobozhdenie belorussii.*

62. S. Rudenko, "Osobennosti boevykh deistvii aviatsii v Belorusskoi operatsii" [Characteristics of combat actions of aviation in the Belorussian operation], *VIZh,* No. 2 (February 1971), 2.

63. A. Tsikin, "Aviatsiia 16-i vozdushnoi armii pri razgrome gruppirovki protivnika pod Bobruiskom" [The aviators of 16th Army during the destruction of the enemy Bobruisk group], *VIZh,* No. 7 (July 1962), 19.

64. A. Paly, "Radioelektronnaia bor'ba v khode-voiny" [Radio-electronic struggle during war], *VIZh,* No. 5 (May 1977), 12.

65. V. Chikin, "Razvedka v operatsiiakh 61-i armii [*Razvedka* in 61st Army operations], *VIZh,* No. 10 (October 1979), 56.

66. I. P. Grishin, *et. al.,* ed., *Voennye sviazisty v dni voiny i mira* [Military signalmen in war and peace] (Moscow: Voenizdat, 1968), 224.

67. S. Kh. Aganov, *Inzhenernve voiska Sovetskoi armii 1918–1945* [Engineer forces of the Soviet Army 1918–1945] (Moscow: Voenizdat, 1985), 261.

68. E. F. Ivanovsky, *et al.,* ed., *Krasnoznamennyi belorusskii voennyi okrug* [Red Banner Belorussian Military District] (Moscow: Voenizdat, 1983), 207–208.

69. S. P. Kiriukhin, *43-ia armiia v vitebskoi operatsii* [43d Army in the Vitebsk operation] (Moscow: Voenizdat, 1961), 33.

70. *Ibid.;* A. Sinitsky, "Sposoby vedeniia voiskovoi razvedki" [Means of conducting troop *razvedka*], *VIZh,* No. 4 (April 1976), 89. The 3340 observation posts were broken down as follows:

Combined arms 1,246
Artillery   954
Others   140

Density of these posts was 30 per kilometer of front.

71. Sinitsky, 94.

72. A. P. Beloborodov, *Vsegda v boiu* [Always in battle] (Moscow: Voenizdat, 1978), 283; N. M. Khlebnikov, *Pod grokhot soten batarei* [Under the rumble of hundreds of batteries] (Moscow: Voenizdat, 1979), 279.

73. Beloborodov, 285; Kiriukhin, 77.

74. Chistiakov, 221; G. N. Kovtunov, *Vsei moshchiu ognia* [By all the power of fire] (Moscow: Voenizdat, 1982), 167.

75. K. N. Galitsky, *Gody surovykh ispytanii 1941–1944* [Years of harsh education 1941–1944] (Moscow: "Nauka," 1973), 452.

76. *Ibid.,* 457.

77. K. A. Vershinin, "4-ia vozdushnaia armiia v boiakh za osvobozhdenie belorussii" [4th Air Army in battles for the liberation of Belorussia], *Osvobozhdenie belorussii,* 226. Vershinin reported that 4th Air Army's air *razvedka* was effective.

> From 13 May to the beginning of the operation, the crews of the 164th Guards Separate Reconnaissance Aviation Regiment photographed along the entire enemy front to a depth of 8 to 12 kilometers and up to 30 kilometers in the main attack sectors. The total area photographed exceeded 5000 square kilometers. More than 10,000 photo prints were prepared.

At the same time, 233d Assault Aviation Division JP-2 aircraft, with artillerymen or sappers onboard, studied the engineer and artillery features in the German defenses.

78. A. A. Sidorenko, *Na mogilevskam napravlenii* [On the Mogilev direction] (Moscow: Voenizdat, 1959), 65.

79. *Ibid.,* 67.

80. *Ibid.,* 68.

81. K. Rokossovsky, *A Soldier's Duty* (Moscow: Progress Publishers, 1985), 237.

82. Batov, 407.

83. *Ibid.,* 409.

84. V. I. Kazakov, "Vospominaniia komanduiushchego artilleriei fronta" [Memoirs of a *front* artillery commander], *Osvobozhdenie belorussii,* 500.

85. *Ibid.*

86. *Ibid.,* 501.

87. A. Luchinsky, "28-ia armiia v Bobruiskoi operatsii" [28th Army in the Bobruisk operation], *VIZh,* No. 2 (February 1969), 68.

88. *Ibid.*

89. Zhukov, *Reminiscences,* 2:276.

90. M. M. Kir'ian, *Vnezapnost' v nastupatel'nykh operatsiiakh Velikoi Otechestvennoi voiny* [Surprise in offensive operations of the Great Patriotic War] (Moscow: "Nauka," 1986), 28–29.

91. Vasilevsky, *A lifelong cause,* 394.

92. *Ibid.,* 398.

93. Moskalenko, 2:487.

94. Zhukov, *Reminiscences,* 2:308.

95. Shtemenko, 379.

96. Zhukov, *Reminiscences,* 2:313.

97. Shtemenko, 381.

98. The *Stavka* reinforced the 1st Belorussian Front with 33d, 61st, and 3d Shock Armies, 1st Guards Tank Army, and numerous supporting units. The 1st Ukrainian Front received 6th, 21st, 52d, 59th Armies, 3d Guards Tank Army, and 7th Guards Tank Corps.

99. Zhukov, *Reminiscences*, 2:325.

100. Vasilevsky, *A lifelong cause*, 399–400.

101. Internal movements involved the concentration of three armies in the north and three armies in the south, 2d Shock Army, moved into the area from the Baltic region, and 70th Army regrouped from east of Warsaw. The most important move involved the 2d Belorussian Front's exploitation force, 5th Guards Tank Army. On 30 November 1st Baltic Front released the tank army to *Stavka* reserve. After extensive movement, on 15 January it assembled in concentration areas northwest of Wyszkow.

102. Shtemenko, 398.

103. *Ibid.*, 399.

104. M. M. Malakhov, *Osvobozhdenie vengrii i vostochnoi avstrii (oktiabr' 1944g-aprel' 1945g)* [The liberation of Hungary and eastern Austria (October 1944–April 1945) (Moscow: Voenizdat, 1965), 176.

105. Zhukov, *Reminiscences*, 2:338.

106. *Ibid.*, 339.

107. Shtemenko, 399–400.

108. *Ibid.*, 400–401.

109. G. K. Zhukov, "Berlinskaia operatsiia 1945" [The Berlin operation 1945], *SVE* 1:1976, 457.

110. German *Fremde Heere Ost* intelligence reports mention other units as well, which the Soviets do not mention the existence of before war's end. In late 1944 a fragmentary intelligence report mentioned Soviet creation of a 7th and an 8th Tank Army in the Kiev Military District. Although these armies did not appear publicly by war's end, immediately after the war, a 7th Mechanized Army was identified in Poland and, later, an 8th Mechanized Army in the Carpathian Military District. It would have been in character for Stalin to retain a tank army or two in his hip pocket as insurance against unforeseen Allied actions.

111. For details, see D. M. Glantz, *August storm: The Soviet 1945 strategic offensive in Manchuria*, Leavenworth Papers No. 7 (Fort Leavenworth, KS: Combat Studies Institute, 1983); D. M. Glantz, *August storm: Soviet tactical and operational combat in Manchuria, 1945*, Leavenworth Papers No. 8 (Fort Leavenworth, KS: Combat Studies Institute, 1983).

112. Shtemenko, 419.

113. *Ibid.*, 381–382.

114. N. N. Popel', V. P. Savel'ev, P. V. Shemansky, *Upravlenie voiskami v gody Velikoi Otechestvennoi voiny* [Troop control in the Great Patriotic War] (Moscow: Voenizdat, 1974), 81.

115. Shtemenko, 386.

116. R. Simonian, "Razvedka v interesakh podgotovki i vedeniia frontovoi nastupatel'noi operatsii" [*Razvedka* in the interests of preparing and conducting a *front* offensive operation], *VIZh*, No. 12 (December 1977), 11.

117. Zhukov, *Reminiscences*, 2:311.

118. Simonian, "Razvedka v interesakh," 11–12.

119. S. I. Rudenko, *Kryl'ia pobedy* [Wings of victory] (Moscow: "Mezhdurnarodnye otnosheniia," 1985), 257.

120. Simonian, "Razvedka v interesakh," 12–13.

121. V. I. Chuikov, *Ot Stalingrada do Berlina* [From Stalingrad to Berlin], (Moscow: Voenizdat, 1980), 505.

122. A. Efimov, "Primenenie aviatsii pri vedenii operatsii v vysokikh tempakh i na bol'shuiu glubinu" [The use of aviation in conducting an operation at high tempos and at great depths], *VIZh,* No. 1 (January 1985), 24.

123. M. N. Kozhevnikov, *Komandovanie i shtab VVS Sovetskoi Armii v Velikoi Otechestvennoi voine 1941–1945 gg* [The command and staff of the Soviet Army Air Force in the Great Patriotic War 1941–1945] (Moscow: "Nauka," 1977), 195.

124. Simonian, "Razvedka v interesakh," 13.

125. Popel', *et al.,* 81.

126. I. Korotchenko, *Razvedka* [Intelligence], *VIZh,* No. 3 (March 1982), 31.

127. *The German G-2 Service in the Russian campaign (Ic Dienst Ost),* (Washington, D.C.: Military Intelligence Division, War Department, 22 July 1945), 38.

128. *Ansatz sowj kundschaftergruppen 1.12.44–4.1.45,* Anlage 3 zu Abt. Fremd. H. Ost (I) Nr. 81/45 gKdos v 5.1.45.

129. Simonian, "Razvedka v interesakh," 13.

130. Moskalenko, 2:512.

131. S. Alferov, "Iz opyta proryva oborony strelkovym korpusom" [From the experience of penetrating defenses by a rifle corps], *VIZh,* No. 3 (March 1983), 51.

132. M. Kh. Kalashik, *Ispytanie ognem* [Ordeal by fire] (Moscow: "Mysl," 1985), 327.

133. I. Viazankin, "Sovershenstvovanie organizatsii i vedeniia razvedki boem" [Improvement in the organization and conduct of reconnaissance in force], *VIZh,* No. 11 (November 1969), 33.

134. Simonian, "Razvedka v interesakh," 14.

135. M. M. Kir'ian, *S sandomirskogo platsdarma* [From the Sandomierz bridgehead] (Moscow: Voenizdat, 1960), 73.

136. S. I. Blinov, *Ot Visly do Odera* [From the Vistula to the Oder] (Moscow: Voenizdat, 1962), 38.

137. E. Kolibernov, "Inzhenernoe obespechenie proryva oborony protivnika po opytu voiny" [Engineer support in the penetration of an enemy defense based on war experience], *VIZh,* No. 8 (August 1980), 45–46.

138. V. S. Antonov, *Put' k Berlinu* [The path to Berlin] (Moscow: "Nauka," 1975), 182–183. Confirmed by copy of original order provided by the Soviets to the author.

139. OKH *Lage Ost,* Stand. 11-12.1.45 abds. (original).

140. Alferov, 51–52.
141. Zhadov, 227; I. A. Samchuk, P. G. Skachko, Iu. N. Babikov, I. L. Gnedoi, *Ot Volgi do El'by i Pragi* [From the Volga to the Elbe and Prague] (Moscow: Voenizdat, 1970), 217.
142. Simonian, "Razvedka v interesakh," 14.
143. *Ibid.*
144. *Ibid.*, 15.
145. *Ibid.*, 17.
146. *Ibid.*
147. *Ibid.*, 15–16.
148. *Ibid.*, 16.
149. Rudenko, *Kryl'ia pobedy,* 258.
150. *Ibid.*, 259.
151. *Sovetskye voenno-vozdushnye sily v Velikoi Otechestvennoi voine 1941–1945 gg* [The Soviet Air Force in the Great Patriotic War 1941–1945] (Moscow: Voenizdat, 1968), 369–370. Hereafter cited as *Sovetskye voenno-vozdushnye.*
152. *Ibid.*, 374.
153. A. Fedorov, "16-ia vozdushnaia armiia v vislo-oderskoi operatsii" [16th Air Army in the Vistula-Oder operation], *VIZh,* No. 10 (October 1971), 92.
154. *Sovetskye voenno-vozdushnye,* 378.
155. I. Konev, *Year of victory* (Moscow: Progress Publishers, 1984), 34. A good translation of *God pobedy* [Year of victory] (Moscow: Voenizdat, 1966).
156. Rudenko, *Kryl'ia pobedy,* 300.
157. *Ibid.*, 301.
158. *Sovetskye voenno-vozdushnye,* 382.
159. OKH *Lage Ost,* stand 10-12.1.45 abds (original).
160. "*Fremde Heere Ost* (I) No. 81/45, Estimate of the Overall Enemy Situation: 5 Jan. 1945," *The German G-2 Service in the Russian Campaign* (Ic-Dienst Ost), United States Army, 22 July 1945). See appendix on deserter and line-crosser reports.
161. Although the Soviets knew from intelligence sources that IV SS Panzer Corps had deployed from the Warsaw region to Hungary, once in Hungary Soviet intelligence lost track of its location. Curiously enough, the Soviets reacted promptly to movement of all other German army units, suggesting that, while the Soviets could intercept regular radio communications, they could not do so for SS units.
162. *Polevoi ustav krasnoi armii* [Field regulations of the Red Army], (Moscow: Voenizdat, 1944). Translated by JPRS (JPRS-UMA-PS-006), 17 January 1985, 34.
163. *Ibid.*, 35.
164. *Ibid.*
165. *Ibid.;* information confirmed in *Auszug aus der Uebersetzung de Dienst-*

vorschrift ueber das Zusammenwirken der Fliegertruppe mit den Erdtruppen [Extract from translation of Soviet Service regulation concerning cooperation between air and ground forces] from Detailed Report No. 34, 5 September 44, of German *Fremde Heere Ost*. Translated by the Directorate of Military Intelligence, AHQ, Ottawa, Canada, 1952. See also, translation of captured German document "Breakthrough and Pursuit," prepared in 1944 and translated in 1951, which critiqued Soviet air reconnaissance, stating

Flawless air-photo-reconnaissance (1:5,000–1:10,000), supplemented by engineer and artillery reconnaissance, was required to permit map distribution 5 days before the attack. Observation was carried out according to a detailed army plan. Its mission was to detect last-minute changes in enemy positions in order to correct or supplement maps of the enemy defense system.

166. *Ibid.*, 37.
167. *Ibid.*, 38.
168. Popel', *et al.*, 84.
169. Chikin, 58.

Index